FOR THE FAMILY?

For the Family?

HOW CLASS AND GENDER SHAPE WOMEN'S WORK

Sarah Damaske

OXFORD
UNIVERSITY PRESS

OXFORD
UNIVERSITY PRESS

Oxford University Press, Inc., publishes works that further
Oxford University's objective of excellence
in research, scholarship, and education.

Oxford   New York
Auckland   Cape Town   Dar es Salaam   Hong Kong   Karachi
Kuala Lumpur   Madrid   Melbourne   Mexico City   Nairobi
New Delhi   Shanghai   Taipei   Toronto

With offices in
Argentina   Austria   Brazil   Chile   Czech Republic   France   Greece
Guatemala   Hungary   Italy   Japan   Poland   Portugal   Singapore
South Korea   Switzerland   Thailand   Turkey   Ukraine   Vietnam

Published by Oxford University Press, Inc.
198 Madison Avenue, New York, New York 10016

www.oup.com

Oxford is a registered trademark of Oxford University Press

Library of Congress Cataloging-in-Publication Data
Damaske, Sarah.
For the family? : how class and gender shape women's work / Sarah Damaske.
    p.   cm.
Includes bibliographical references and index.
ISBN 978-0-19-979150-7 (hardback : acid-free paper) — ISBN 978-0-19-979149-1 (paperback : acid-free paper)
1. Women—Employment—United States—Economic aspects. 2. Social classes—United States—Economic aspects.
3. Women—United States—Economic conditions. 4. Women—United States—Social conditions.
5. Work and family—United States. I. Title.
HD6095.D36   2011
331.40973—dc22   2011010834

1 3 5 7 9 8 6 4 2

Printed in the United States of America
on acid-free paper

To my mother, Frances D. Knapp, and my grandmother, E. Lucille Nichols.
Their work, inside and outside the home, inspired my own.

Contents

List of Tables/Figures

Tables

Figures

Acknowledgments

This book would not have been possible without the women whose stories are shared on its pages. The names of the eighty participants cannot be listed, but I thank them for their time, their energy, and their willingness to share their lives. Social science research depends on the kindness of strangers, and I often found myself overwhelmed by the women's spirit of generosity. I can only hope that this book does justice to their lives and that the policy suggestions contained in it might benefit others.

Writing this book would have been much more difficult if not for the following people. I am deeply grateful for their intellectual encouragement, critical insights, moral support, and friendships. This book stems from my doctoral dissertation at New York University, where Kathleen Gerson served as my dissertation chair. Kathleen is a generous mentor and wonderful friend and she always provides deeply incisive and critical feedback while also encouraging the future development of the work. Kathleen's intellectual work is an inspiration to me and I am truly grateful for her continued enthusiasm, support, and encouragement.

At NYU, Lynne Haney's teachings were critical to my development as a gender scholar and Richard Arum motivated my commitment to a well-crafted research project and to stratification research. Many other members of the NYU community contributed to the development of this project and I owe a special thanks to Ruth Horowitz, Florencia Torche, Caroline Persell, Josipa Roksa, Sheera Olasky, Miriam Ryvicker, Pamela Kaufman, Monika Krause, Allison McKim, Jill Conte, Leslie-Ann

Bolden, and the members of the NYU Gender Workshop. I am indebted to John Mollenkopf, at the CUNY Graduate Center, for spending many hours working with me on the NYC Voter Registration database. Faculty from my undergraduate institution, Hamilton College, first inspired my love of learning and research and I thank the college and Peter Rabinowitz, Douglas Raybeck, Mitchell Stevens, and (post graduation) Dan Chambliss for this gift.

The postdoctoral program at Rice University provided me the time, funding, and intellectual support to complete this project. Jenifer Bratter was tremendously committed to this project and offered valuable feedback. Conversations with Elizabeth Long sharpened the arguments presented in chapter 7. Adrianne Frech became a dear friend, provided insightful feedback on many drafts, and shared our office with an open ear and a willingness to work across the methodological divide. For their support and encouragement during this process, my thanks go to all the members of the Rice Sociology Department, and, particularly, to Sergio Chavez, Elaine Howard Ecklund, Bridget Gorman, Holly Heard, Rachel Tolbert Kimbro, and Jeremy Porter. As I worked on finishing this book, I had the wonderful opportunity to meet my new colleagues at the Pennsylvania State University, where I will be an assistant professor in the Department of Labor Studies and Employment Relations. I thank my new colleagues for their enthusiasm for this project.

Several people read and commented extensively on chapters and drafts, providing thoughtful insights and constructive criticism. I am grateful for the extraordinary feedback and friendship of Adrianne Frech, Josipa Roksa, Sheera Olasky, Jonathan Knapp, Miriam Ryvicker, Pamela Kaufman, Sergio Chavez, Gretchen Webber, and the terrific members of my writing group: Julie Artis, Heather Jacobson, Kristin Schultz Lee, and Robin Hognas. Josipa Roksa shared many lengthy discussions with me about all things sociology and stimulated my thinking in many aspects of this book. A huge thanks goes to David Hughes for joining this endeavor to design figure 1.2.

I am extraordinarily lucky to have James Cook as my editor. His early interest in this project provided much encouragement during the dissertation-writing phase, and his insightful comments on early and late drafts were extremely beneficial as I worked to craft this book. Thanks also go to the rest of the Oxford team, including Jaimee Biggins, who moved the book to press, and to Karen M. Fisher for her copyediting work. Two anonymous reviewers for Oxford University Press gave tremendously helpful critiques, as did Naomi Schneider of California University Press and the wonderful work-family scholars and editors of the Families in Focus Book Series for Rutgers University Press, Anita Garey, Naomi Gerstel, Karen Hansen, Rosanna Hertz, Margaret Nelson, and their anonymous reviewer. Additional thanks go to Amy Johnson, former editor of *Contexts*. Dana Britton, the managing editor of *Gender & Society,* went above and beyond the call of duty in her review of an article taken from this book. I thank her and the anonymous *Gender & Society* reviewers for their time and insightful comments. Portions of chapter three were previously published in *Gender & Society* and Sage had kindly given permission to reprint them here.

Financial support for this project came from several sources, and I am grateful for the financial support of the National Science Foundation, award #SES-0703212, a Woodrow Wilson Doctoral Dissertation Fellowship in Women's Studies, the Rice University Sociology Department, and a New York University MacCracken Fellowship. Kathleen Gerson provided me with research funds for participant recruitment, and my mother, Frances D. Knapp, gave me a much-needed "computer grant." The Sociologists for Women in Society, the Eastern Sociological Society, and the NYU Sociology Department gave (much appreciated) awards to research from this book.

My family provided the foundation for this project. The love and encouragement of my parents, Frankie and Stephen Knapp, has been unwavering throughout my life and has sustained me over the years. My brother, Jonathan Knapp, is a talented academic in his own field, philosophy, and an incredible support in my life. My beloved nana, E. Lucille Nichols, was the first in her family to earn a college degree, and she always believed I would write a book one day. Much joy and support in my life comes from the rest of my family: my grandparents, Emile Nichols and Walter and Toni Knapp; my in-laws, Claire and Dick Damaske; my siblings by marriage, John and Janet Damaske; my nephew, Noah Damaske; and my second parents, Connie and George Hamilton. I am fortunate to have an extended family and many dear friends and I am thankful for them all.

My husband, Paul Damaske, has been by my side at every step for over fifteen years, and his presence has immeasurably brightened my life's journey. Paul thoughtfully proofread many drafts of this book, challenging my assumptions, improving the writing, reminding me when the language became too technical for a nonsociologist and providing constant enthusiasm for this project. He is a true partner— committed to gender equality both in theory and in practice. I am grateful for his unwavering support, his belief in me and my work, and his friendship.

FOR THE FAMILY?

1

THE NEED AND CHOICE MYTHS

VIRGINIA LAUGHED WHEN I asked her to tell me about her work experience. It was a difficult task because Virginia, a white working-class woman, started the first of many jobs at an early age. We met at her apartment on the second floor of a weathered three-story building in a neighborhood left behind by the city's gentrification. We sat at her kitchen table as she kept an eye on her two children, ages seven and ten, who popped in and out of the room hoping to participate in our conversation. She recalled her entrance into the workforce: "I started shampooing [at a local hair salon] when I took up my trade, which was the tenth grade. And then I, you know, worked different stores and I did that until I graduated high school, because that's when I could get my license."

Soon after, Virginia met and married her husband, a white working-class man, and they started a family of their own. A janitor, her husband worked nights and picked up extra shifts when he could. Virginia continued to work full time after the birth of their son, but, she said, a year after their daughter was born, "I started working part time. And then I stayed home to raise the kids." Virginia left the workforce to "be home for the kids," but after a few years returned part time. Asked about her changing work and family experiences, she explained, "A mother should be home with their kids," but added that this isn't possible today, because "financially, [women] have to actually work in order to make it possible for their kids to have more." Virginia said her family's financial needs prompted her reentry into the workforce.

Unlike Virginia, Cynthia, a white middle-class woman, had never taken more time off from work than her paid twelve weeks of maternity leave, and she had only one employer for her entire career. A month after she graduated from high school, Cynthia went to work as a legal secretary for a law firm. "And I'm still with the same company actually. It's about eighteen years," she explained. Cynthia went to work for two lawyers, and as they were promoted in the law firm, she was promoted, too. "My bosses became partners so they kind of took me with them."

Cynthia met her husband, an analyst at the stock exchange, in high school before she started work. "We went to the prom together. And we just stayed together through everything," she said. He worked a nine-to-five schedule on the stock exchange floor, spending a couple of evenings at work each week, making close to $250,000 annually. At twenty-seven, she became pregnant, and, she explained, "I kind of wanted to quit, but then since I had my mother and she kind of encouraged me, 'Oh stay at work,' . . . so I could make all the extras and everything. Because we could have managed on my husband's salary, but you know she was just encouraging me to stay at work, so I could do better for them [nodding at her children]." Even though her husband's salary was in six figures, Cynthia said that she stayed at work to earn "all the extras" for her children. Cynthia's "extra" salary of $75,000 was significantly more than the $60,000 combined annual income of both Virginia and her husband—what was considered extra for Cynthia's family would have covered the basics plus more for Virginia's. Yet like Virginia, Cynthia explained that her work helped fulfill her family's financial needs.

Although they lived very different lives, Virginia's and Cynthia's explanations of their work participation followed a common storyline about how financial needs drive women's decisions about working. In fact, almost all of the women I interviewed, regardless of income or whether or not they worked, explained that they made their work decisions *for the family*. But a closer look reveals a more complicated picture. Virginia first left the workforce after new owners took over the salon where she worked. "I hated working [there] at that time," she said. She had multiple conflicts with her new boss and he reduced her job flexibility, leaving her less time to spend with her children—"It just wasn't the hours that I wanted," she said. At the time, Virginia's financial situation was troubled. Her husband had lost his job, and several years of unsteady employment followed. Despite the family's mounting financial concerns, Virginia decided to leave the workforce in the face of growing dissatisfaction at work and reduced flexibility.

When she went back to part-time work, Virginia's family was doing much better financially—her husband had been employed in a stable job for two years. While the additional money from her new job added to the family income, her financial situation had actually improved from when she left the workforce—indicating that financial need alone does not explain her complicated workforce decisions. She returned to work after finally managing to find a job she really "loved," teaching at a cosmetology school. Her new job required shorter hours, giving her more freedom to care for her school-age children. Employment also affected her outlook on herself: "It makes me want to get up and go somewhere. Like, if it wasn't for work, I don't think I would even get dressed. I would be in my pajamas all day." While the language Virginia used to explain her workforce decisions focused on financial need, her actions did not—she left a job that she disliked when her family had no regular source of income but returned to work when she found a job she loved as her family's financial stability grew.

Cynthia experienced work very differently than Virginia: she had only one employer, received promotions, was paid better, enjoyed a high level of autonomy, was in charge of other workers, and felt recognized and appreciated for her work. As her bosses received promotions, so did she, until she was working for the most senior partners in the law firm. "Since [my bosses] are partners now, they have people, like a lot more people, available to them to help out so I could kind of pass [extra work] along to the associates' secretaries. You know, I can give them the work and kind of tell them what needs to be done. It's not all on me anymore," she explained. Cynthia had risen to a high level in the firm, able to pass along less enjoyable work to more junior secretaries. She also had good relations with her coworkers and employers: "I like the people I work with. The attorneys are really good to me. We've been together for a long time so we work well together." She also greatly enjoyed her work, explaining, "It just seemed very fascinating and I liked that it was fast paced and a lot of things happening. It was just very interesting to me."

While Virginia's husband experienced multiple challenges at work, Cynthia's husband, a white middle-class man, sailed through college and found great success at his first job. "He's really happy I think. You know, it's a really good job and he got a lot of promotions since he's been there, met a lot of people, and he could go into a lot of other areas at [his work]. So, it's really good," Cynthia explained. At age twenty-seven, they decided to have children, and both Cynthia and her husband stayed at their jobs. When we met, their combined income was $325,000, and they, too, had two children, a girl and a boy. Like Virginia, Cynthia's explanation of her continued workforce participation focused on her financial needs, yet her work and family circumstances suggested a more complicated picture—she greatly enjoyed her work and was financially secure at home.

Why did Virginia and Cynthia (and almost all of the other women in this study) tell such similar stories about the role of financial need in their workforce decisions, particularly when they had led such different lives? Today, women face competing obligations to work and family and neither leaving work nor remaining at work can completely satisfy these twin demands.[1] While women are pursuing diverse work and family strategies, they continue to face historically negative moral connotations about women's paid work; staying at home continues to suggest altruism, while working suggests selfishness.[2] In mid-twentieth-century America, the gender division of public and private spheres traditionally held that women were expected to focus on caring for others, while men pursued paid work.[3] Although many things have changed since then, these divisions linger today, as social norms that divide the work and family spheres are connected to powerful cultural beliefs that help define "what makes a meaningful and worthwhile life" for both women and men.[4]

Throughout this book, I suggest that Virginia and Cynthia told similar stories about the role of financial needs in their work decisions because traditional gender conventions oblige women to frame their labor market participation in terms of their families' needs and not their own. When asked to explain decisions to stay in or return to the workforce, employed women, like Cynthia, replied that their family "needed" them to work. When asked to explain decisions to leave the workforce, nonemployed women, like Virginia, said that their family "needed" them to be home. Most women said their work-family decisions were made *for the family*, although this shared language allowed them to remake gendered expectations of caregiving to fit diverse work patterns. By using a frame that stressed obligations to their families rather than the fulfillment of their own needs or desires, both employed and nonemployed women connected work to family rather than an individual pursuit.[5]

The women's explanations of financial need connect to a broader popular discussion that generally frames women's workforce participation in two contrasting ways: middle-class women choose whether or not to pursue a career, and working-class and minority women need to work at a paid job.[6] The popular media and sociologists alike have focused on middle-class women's withdrawal from the workforce and the inability of working-class women and women of color to do so, suggesting that financial resources allow middle-class women to leave the workforce, while financial pressures force working-class women to stay.[7]

If financial needs dictate women's work, we would expect to find higher employment rates among working-class women, who generally have less income and lower education levels than middle-class women, who generally have higher incomes and higher education levels. But just as Virginia's and Cynthia's accounts do not neatly fit these stereotypes, neither do national labor force participation trends. As women's income goes up, so too does their labor market participation.[8] Whether women work is even more highly correlated to education level than it is to income. Data from a 2008 U.S. Bureau of Labor Statistics report show that highly educated women are most likely to work—85 percent of women with postgraduate degrees work, compared to 80 percent of college graduates, 68 percent of high school graduates, and only 48 percent of women with less than a high school degree.[9]

National trends in women's workforce participation do not support what we think we know about choice and need. As we see in figure 1.1, stay-at-home mothers are concentrated in lower-income families. And more middle-class women have joined the workforce over the last thirty years, while employment rates of working-class women have declined.[10] Moreover, today, the majority of all women with children under age six are employed.[11]

The work-family axis has become the defining structure for most women's lives, as they attempt to manage work and family obligations and conflicts. Given the contradictions between the conventional wisdom about need and choice and the national trends of women's increased labor-market participation, we must unravel this puzzle to tease out differences in how women negotiate their work and family opportunities and obligations across classes.

I conducted in-depth, qualitative interviews with eighty randomly sampled women to better understand women's workforce trajectories, the nature of their work, and how they negotiate their identities as women, workers, and mothers. Discovering the process by which women move into and out of the workforce allows for

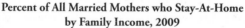

**Percent of All Married Mothers who Stay-At-Home
by Family Income, 2009**

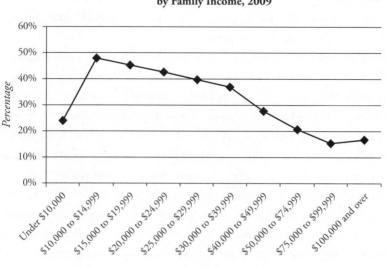

Family Income

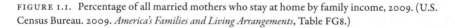

FIGURE 1.1. Percentage of all married mothers who stay at home by family income, 2009. (U.S. Census Bureau. 2009. *America's Families and Living Arrangements*, Table FG8.)

a more in-depth understanding of women's decisions about work, as well as a better explanation of why people continue to believe that financial needs determine women's workforce decisions. I found that the popular framework of need and choice is simply insufficient to explain the complex and varied paths that women pursue as social forces reshape their work-family options across classes. How these women perceived their workforce opportunities and constraints and how they negotiated the world around them provides us with a critical understanding of the way women work, why they work, why they leave work, and how they make sense of the social and cultural expectations of the twenty-first century.

The Need and Choice Myths

In October 2009, the *Washington Post* ran a front-page article exclaiming that a "new report" from the U.S. Census showed that "stay-at-home mothers tend to be younger and less educated, with lower family incomes."[12] *Post* reporter Donna St. George wrote that this finding was "clearly at odds with the popular discussion that has flourished in recent years" focusing on high-profile, professional women leaving their careers to take care of their children. But this is not the first time the Census has published findings showing that working-class women, like Virginia, are more likely to withdraw from the workforce. In fact, Census reports for the past ten years have featured similar findings. Still, though, the news media have remained focused on the so-called growing phenomenon of middle-class women who choose to leave the workforce, while academic studies using national data actually call into question the very existence of this alleged phenomenon.

The idea that economic needs propel women into the workforce even pervades sociological discourse, despite the fact that sociologists and economists have been finding evidence to the contrary for close to fifteen years.[13] Much economic and sociological research on middle-class women's work has propagated the need myth by suggesting that a family's financial resources are what "allow" women to leave work.[14] While scholars have brought attention to working-class women's workforce participation and their historically high levels of employment, there continues to be a presumption that working-class women's work is, first and foremost, driven by a family's financial needs.[15] At the national 2009 American Sociological Association meeting, many audience members at a work-family session—work-family scholars themselves—discussed how mortgages and children's college tuition ensured that working-class and middle-class women remained in the workforce, and that only upper-middle-class women could leave. Why do the media and much of the academic community have this issue so backward?

At the turn of the twentieth century, women's options for work were poor, and most married women did not work; many companies actually legally prohibited the hiring of women, particularly married women. Those married women who did work for pay generally did so as domestic servants or factory workers and were most often married to men who could not adequately provide financially for their families.[16] From an early point in our country's history, then, paid women's work was tied to the working class. But since the mid-1970s, women living in the United States have experienced dramatic social, political, and economic changes. In 1970, 43.3 percent of women over the age of sixteen worked, and today close to 60 percent do, as do 71 percent of women with children under age eighteen. In contrast, the number of men in the workforce has declined since 1970, when 79.7 percent were employed, compared to 73 percent today.[17] Men still remain more likely to have full-time, year-round work, but women are working more steadily than in years past.[18] Dual-earner families are now the norm among married couples, rather than the exception.[19]

These social and economic changes can help us understand how the connection between financial needs and workforce participation was cemented in the public understanding. While little consensus exists as to the causes of these changes, during this same period men's wages stagnated and declined, leaving fewer men able to earn a "breadwinner" wage with which to support a family.[20] The congruence of these patterns—lower pay for men and more working women—suggested to some that women were going to work to make up for their husbands' lost wages. Economists often contend that "income effects"—a husband's earning potential, in particular—influence women's work and childbearing decisions, so that, from this viewpoint, a woman's workforce participation is tied to her spouse's salary. Traditionally, economists have argued that women's ties to the labor market are weaker than men's and change as their husbands' ability to provide for the family changes. Some economists have challenged this notion, arguing that women may prefer to stay at home rather than to work for particularly low wages.[21] Recently, sociologists have added to this debate, arguing that "opportunity costs" are more important than "income effects," meaning that women with higher earning potential have a greater incentive to work and this is more important to whether or not they work than their husband's income.[22]

These economic arguments emphasize the importance of money in women's work decisions, but people may be employed or unemployed for many reasons.[23] In her book *Opting Out? Why Women Really Quit Careers and Head Home*, Pamela Stone shows that when middle-class women do leave the workforce, it is most often not because they choose to leave but because a combination of family and workplace pressures make staying employed impossible.[24] Many of these women find themselves in jobs that demand long hours and are married to spouses with similar schedules, leaving both with little time for the home.[25] While Stone and others provide convincing evidence to challenge the idea that women are simply choosing to be at home, considerably less attention has been paid to the need myth—the idea that financial needs (or even financial rewards) push women to work.[26]

But when we consider Virginia's workforce participation, we see that economic explanations, like the "income effects" argument, cannot easily account for her work decisions. When Virginia first left work, she did not leave because her husband's income had risen; in fact, her husband had lost his job, yet she left the workforce because she did not like to work for her new and disagreeable boss. Articles that focus on the "opportunity costs" of women's continued employment also cannot explain Virginia's return to employment. She did not return when she found a job with better wages; she returned when she found a job she felt she could "love" and that provided better hours.

The seeming neatness of the economic explanation is only partially responsible for the continued misperception that financial needs determine women's workforce participation. Continued cultural ambivalence about women's workforce participation also plays a role. Arguing that financial needs drive their work decisions implies that most women would prefer not to work.[27] This is a theme that is repeatedly found in popular media. In 2007, Donna St. George, again in the *Washington Post*, wrote under the headline "Part-Time Looks Just Fine" that most women would work part time if possible but that financial needs keep them from doing so. After 2008 vice presidential hopeful Sarah Palin decided to leave the Alaska governor's office, National Public Radio reporter Michel Martin explained that she envied Palin's decision: "I do not know a single working mother who does not dream at some point, even if just for a minute, about packing up that desk and heading for the homestead, even if that fantasy is about as realistic as the one about supplementing unemployment with Powerball winnings."[28] But while both of these examples again emphasize the role of finances in women's work decisions, they shy away from the other reasons that women may leave work or might remain. Think here of Cynthia—while her income was certainly important for her family's quality of life and total overall income, they could have led an affluent life without her salary. She remained at work for many reasons in addition to her salary.

The focus on financial explanations for women's work may reflect Americans' lingering discomfort with women being a part of the workforce in the first place. Although women have gained entry to the paid labor market in unprecedented numbers and men are now participating more in household chores and child rearing, women continue to be primarily responsible for the raising of America's children. Cultural expectations remain that women will dedicate themselves to their children, as Cynthia explained her mother did: "She was there to devote all her time to us." Sociologist Sharon Hays writes that the expectation that motherhood requires intensive interaction and selfless devotion has only risen since women entered the workforce.[29] As a result, culturally, it may be much more acceptable for women to need to work, than to want to work.

The current focus on need inaccurately pigeonholes the role of class in women's work and inadequately explains the workforce participation of women like Virginia and Cynthia. This popular discourse creates pervasive stereotypes in which middle-class women's work is understood to be a choice and, therefore, voluntary (and self-indulgent), and working-class women's work is understood to be a need and, therefore, involuntary (and unrewarding). Under this framework, the rewards of work are the province of the middle class, while the struggles are confined to the working class. Furthermore, the emphasis on economic concerns tells us little about why Cynthia and Virginia worked the way they did. Few comparative studies have examined work in both middle- and working-class women's lives in order to gain a better understanding of who is participating in the labor market and the role of financial needs in women's workforce participation, as well as other factors that might influence the role of class in women's workforce participation, such as whose work is valued and whose work is deemed necessary in our society.

Women from Diverse Backgrounds

If middle-class women like Cynthia actually work more, not less, than working-class women like Virginia—the opposite of conventional wisdom—it is necessary to reexamine the factors that lead women to remain at or leave work. Clearly, class played some role in their continued workforce participation: middle-class Cynthia appeared to have many more opportunities than working-class Virginia did. Yet the current economic explanations leave us searching for better answers as to why Virginia pulled back and why Cynthia remained.

Increasingly, women from all classes have more options for creating unique approaches to motherhood and work. Yet obstacles remain as women enter the workforce, begin to raise families, and juggle the two. And these obstacles may not be the same across classes. Middle-class women may have greater financial resources at home, incentives to continue working, and better access to child care, yet also face increased time demands at work and spouses working very long hours. Working-class women may work fewer hours and have spouses who are more available, but they may have fewer resources for child care, less flexibility, and less interesting employment opportunities. These differences raise several questions that will help us tease out the relationship between women's work and class: What are the different work patterns that women follow? How and why do some women follow one trajectory while other women, sometimes from the same class, follow a different one? How do women account for their workforce participation decisions?

I spoke with eighty women randomly sampled from New York City in order to find answers. As a group, the women all had had the opportunity to experience many of life's pivotal stages during which they made critical decisions—about education, marriage, childbearing, and work—that led them along on their life trajectories. All but one had spent some time in the workforce.[30] The participants came of age in the wake of significant cultural transformations surrounding women and work. They grew up hearing stories of women marching into the workforce and seeing images of women with a briefcase in one hand and a baby in the other plastered across the covers of magazines and books. These women were the ones who were supposed to have it all. They were to inherit the possibilities that the women's movement and the civil rights movement had created. In many ways, they are daughters of an optimistic time, but also of the conservative backlash that followed it.

Asking women detailed questions about their lives from birth to the present—what sociologists call a life history approach—reveals how women perceive and negotiate the constraints and opportunities they face in their work and family lives, as well as the processes through which they move into (and out of) the workforce and face different choices and obstacles. This kind of analysis examines the social structures, like class, schools, and families, that influence women's opportunities, as well as their individual decision-making strategies and the time period in which they occurred.[31] This method makes it possible to place women's rationales for their workforce participation in a social context and to chart changes in workforce participation over a lifetime.

All of the women participated in lengthy interviews, during which we discussed their family history, educational background, work history, current work circumstances, dating and marriage, childbearing and rearing, gender and family ideologies, work-family conflicts, household responsibilities, and future plans. All participants were between the ages of thirty-two and forty-two at the time of the interview, the average age being thirty-eight. As the women were fairly young, their lives were clearly unfinished and thus could not represent the entirety of their work-family experiences. I was, however, able to capture the first twenty years or so of adulthood—an important period during which key decisions about work, marriage, childbearing, and child rearing are made.

The women were a diverse group and, by design, closely resembled the larger American population. Fifty percent lived in middle- or upper-middle-class households, while the other half lived in working-class and working-poor households. But what does it mean to be middle class or working class? When President Barack

Obama was campaigning for election, he suggested that everyone who made under $200,000 a year was middle class. But this isn't a particularly useful measure of class. First, there is a big difference between a family making $195,000 a year and one making $50,000 a year, which is what the average American family made in 2007.[32] Second, social science research tells us that there is a lot more to class than just income. Many sociologists believe class is an indicator of inequality across multiple categories: income, education, and occupation can each tell us something about a person's social status. These are important measures of someone's class background, because people with higher education levels and higher status jobs may have access to more than just additional income. They often have connections to people who can help them find jobs (what sociologists call social capital) and an insider's knowledge about the ways that institutions like universities and workplaces function (what sociologists call cultural capital). These connections and knowledge can allow people to better maintain their social position for themselves and their children.

Class is a pivotal part of this study, requiring careful thought as to how it should be measured.[33] For this study, I divided the women into two groups: middle and upper-middle class (middle class) and working class and working poor (working class). I considered jobs middle class if they demanded a college degree or promoted a high degree of independence in daily tasks and work-related activities.[34] In this rubric, teacher, doctor, nurse, and small business owner were all considered middle-class occupations. Working-class positions also constituted a broad spectrum of jobs, including clerical positions (that required no higher levels of education), preschool teachers (without college degrees), store clerks, and women who received state assistance.[35]

At the time of the interview, 50 percent of the sample lived in middle- or upper-middle-class households, and the remaining 50 percent lived in working-class and working-poor households. I visited most of the women in their homes and saw their neighborhoods, which helped paint a portrait of their lives. Some women lived in large single-family houses, a couple in penthouse suites with views of Manhattan, still others in working-class neighborhoods of semidetached houses and small ranch-style houses, and a few in federally subsidized apartment buildings. They were also similar to the national population in their racial diversity; 11.25 percent of the women were African American, 11.25 percent were Latina, 6.25 percent were Asian, and 71.25 percent were white (table 1.1).[36]

The diversity of the women's race and class backgrounds was matched by the diversity of their family experiences. While 23 percent had never married, just fewer than 10 percent were divorced and 68 percent were married (including eight women who had been previously divorced at least once and were now remarried). Fewer than 25 percent had never had children, while the remaining 75 percent had at least one child.

TABLE 1.1.

DEMOGRAPHIC CHARACTERISTICS OF RESPONDENTS AND U.S. POPULATION

Characteristic	Sample (n = 80)	U.S. Population
Age, mean	38	N/A
Age, range	32–42	N/A
Marital status		
Married	58%	49%
Never married	23%	27%
Divorced	9%	11.6%
Divorced and remarried	10%	N/A
Children		
None	24%	20%
Employed	81%	75.5%
Race/ethnicity		
White	71.25%	76%
African American	11.25%	12%
Latina	11.25%	16%
Asian	6.25%	4%
Family social class		
Working class/working poor	50%	48%
Middle/upper-middle class	50%	52%

Negotiating Work Pathways

One of the reasons that sociologists have had a difficult time disentangling the role of class in women's work is that the way we measure women's work often does not accurately represent how women are working. Most studies of class and women's work ask whether or not a woman is currently employed, which leads to two broad categories of work: employed or not employed. But think about Virginia and Cynthia for a minute. Cynthia's work history certainly lends itself to this frame: because she was employed steadily for sixteen years, regardless of when a poll was taken, she would fall into the employed category. Virginia's work history, however, is a bit more complicated. She worked full time, then part time, then did not work outside the home, then returned to part-time work. One poll that asked if she was employed or not could not accurately represent her workforce participation over her lifetime. Because we are not accurately measuring women's work, we may be misunderstanding the role of class in women's work.

To make sense of the role of class in women's changing work decisions, I argue that we need to change our point of view, asking not whether women are currently employed, as the majority of sociological research on this topic does, but how women have worked across their lives. By changing the focus from employment status (whether someone works) to what social scientists call work pathways (how they have worked over the course of their lives), we can understand why women make different decisions at critical junctions and how these decisions shape their lives. A focus on women's work pathways allows us to trace women's life trajectories, examining the multitude of decisions women make that are influenced by personal motivations, structural constraints and opportunities, and competing cultural mandates. With this focus, I find that instead of just two categories (working or not working), the women followed three distinct work pathways: steady, pulled back, and interrupted. This distinction is important, because it lets us see more nuanced differences in class among women's work and, as we will see throughout this book, this viewpoint shows us important class differences that have been overlooked by past studies.

The women in the steady category, including Cynthia, spent the majority of their lives in the paid workforce. While they may have taken time off in search of new work, taken a maternity leave, or attempted to restructure their workforce participation to remain in the labor market, they were never out of the workforce for long. Forty-nine percent of respondents belonged to the steady group. The women who pulled back, including Virginia, had spent some time in the workforce, but left or greatly reduced their paid work after having children. Many of them switched fields at that point in an attempt to find part-time work that would coincide with their children's schedules. Nearly 30 percent of the respondents had pulled back at the time of the interview and had no plans to return full time to the workforce (and did not anticipate this changing in the next five years). The third group, the interrupted workers, spent much of their lives moving in and out of the workforce, experiencing at least two periods of unemployment. Unlike Virginia and Cynthia, the majority of the interrupted women faced significant challenges that made it very difficult either to work steadily or to withdraw from work. Slightly more than one-fifth of respondents—22 percent—were interrupted workers (table 1.2).

By focusing on the differences between these three longitudinal work pathways, I find that financial resources made it easier for middle-class women to remain at work full time during their twenties and thirties, while working-class women often found themselves following interrupted work pathways in which they experienced repeated bouts of unemployment. Finally, both middle-class and working-class women found themselves pulling back from work, but for vastly different reasons. In contrast to conventional wisdom, financial resources made it easier for the women

TABLE 1.2

CLASS AND WORK PATHWAYS (n = 80)

Work Pathway	Middle Class (n = 40) (%)	Working Class (n = 40) (%)
Steady (n = 39)	68	30
Pulled back (n = 23)	27	30
Interrupted (n = 18)	5	40

to remain at work, not easier to leave it. In fact, more than one of two middle-class women remained steadily employed, while only one of three working-class women did so. On the other hand, two out of five working-class women followed an interrupted work pathway, while only one in twenty middle-class women did so. Although the popular and sociological debate has focused on the role of class for the pulled back workers, I found that the middle class and working class pulled back at similar rates. Just under one in three middle-class women pulled back from work, as did one in three working-class women.

Tracing women's work patterns allows us to see differences across class in the women's work pathways and also in the mechanisms that led women to follow different work pathways (figure 1.2). The mechanisms that led women to follow steady pathways were fairly similar across classes: positive workforce experiences, good pay, and opportunities for advancement were all key components of good jobs that kept women employed. These experiences were more common for middle-class women, although some working-class women did find success and stability in the workforce. The mechanisms that led to interrupted pathways were almost solely confined to the working class and working poor, whose lesser workforce opportunities, low wages, low education levels, and few resources meant they could not adapt to unexpected challenges. However, the mechanisms that caused women to pull back differed according to class background: middle-class women were more likely to leave work in the face of a time squeeze caused by inflexible work demands and a similarly busy spouse, while working-class women left work when they felt unappreciated, unrewarded, and even demeaned by employers, or when their fragile care networks failed.

Class matters because it influences women's expectations about their future workforce participation, the opportunities available to them in the workforce, how they perceive these opportunities, and what family support is available to them. Variation remains because class influences these processes, but other factors, such as women's expectations about work and their work and family experiences, do too. As we will see in chapter 3, on the cusp of adulthood the women had formed opinions about

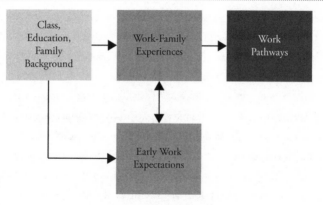

FIGURE 1.2. Tracing women's work pathways.

their future work—how they would work and whether or not they would remain employed. The majority of middle-class women expected to work throughout their lives, while working-class women were evenly divided in expecting either continual or occasional employment. Yet workforce experiences can change or reinforce these early expectations. While a slight majority of women who expected to work steadily did so, close to 45 percent did not, and the majority of women who expected to pull back ended up on a different path than they originally planned. Workforce and family experiences mediated women's expectations about work, changing some women's pathways while paving the way for others.

A Language of Need

The final section of the book returns to the puzzle of how Virginia's and Cynthia's different lives could have led to such similar stories about the importance of financial needs. Today's institutional structures and cultural paradoxes leave modern women facing deep conflicts and dilemmas about work and family. Work-family conflicts are difficult to avoid because women, most of whom now work while continuing to do most of the housework, must navigate demands from both the public and private spheres. How, then, do women manage the reality of their working experiences and the idealized images of selfless mothers?

Virginia's and Cynthia's conflicting accounts of their work histories were part of a larger trend in which the majority of participants emphasized their families' needs to explain their decisions about work. Most women used this language of family need to account for their decisions, although this shared language of need actually allowed them to make different choices. Yet family needs could not explain women's work trajectories because it was used to justify a range of different work trajectories.

Instead, the language of need masked the other factors, such as class, race, workforce experience, work expectations, and family support, that shaped the women's work pathways. Cultural constraints obliged women to frame their workforce participation in terms of their families' needs, not their own.

The public debate about women's work is stuck on need, in part, because women themselves describe their workforce participation by emphasizing the importance of financial need, even though it does not reflect all the factors that influence their work decisions. Writing over fifty years ago, Betty Friedan argued that in the 1950s, the traditional female dichotomy—either virgin or whore—had been supplanted by "the feminine woman, whose goodness includes the desires of the flesh, and the career woman, whose evil includes every desire of the separate self." [37] While women have made significant progress in the labor market, there remains a cultural ambivalence toward women's workforce participation, and today's institutional structures remain ill equipped to accommodate dual-earner families—there is no national day care system, little work-hour regulation, nor mandated paid parental leave. [38] Given the remaining ambivalence toward women's work and the lack of public support for mothers in the workforce, it is no wonder women remain reluctant to talk about how work may be important in their lives and instead focus on how their work is important to their families. While the language of need might likely provide protection from cultural criticisms, it also reinforces the idea that women work for selfless, not self-interested or structurally constrained, reasons.

In the following pages, I untangle claims about need and choice—and the underlying claims about women's work—to understand how women form attachments to the labor market, how these attachments are supported or challenged, and how women participate in the labor market as a result. As we take a closer look at Virginia's and Cynthia's lives, we see why Virginia expected she would only occasionally participate in the workforce, while Cynthia planned to work full time. We also see how a bad workforce experience suggested to Virginia that she was right not to expect much from the workforce, while Cynthia found a good job early in her career. Finally, I consider why they both returned to a language of need to explain their workforce participation, each emphasizing that their decisions stemmed from family needs.

At the turn of the twenty-first century, much social progress has been made in advancing women's rights. Increasingly, women from all classes have more options to create unique approaches to work and motherhood. Despite the overwhelming cultural mandates about motherhood, women continue to forge divergent routes for dealing with work-family conflict in their lives. They also continue to face constraints as they enter the workforce, begin to raise families, and attempt to weave both. In recent years, there has been little progress in resolving this tension, but the women I met were resilient in their ability to negotiate these challenges and seek new opportunities. Neither working-class nor middle-class women conformed to the images that dominate the current debate. The majority of working-class women did not base their workforce decisions on their financial needs, nor did the majority of middle-class women feel awash with choices. But middle-class women enjoyed more social and financial resources to seek careers, while working-class women faced a more uncertain set of pushes and pulls. At the end of the day, some women, particularly those from the working class, found themselves left out.

1

Expectations About Work

2

THE SHAPE OF WOMEN'S WORK PATHWAYS

SITTING ON COUCHES, at kitchen tables, or on living rooms floors playing with their children, women told me about their experiences at home and at work. As they recalled their lives, the eighty women described facing a complicated series of decisions about their workforce participation—not one turning point, but many that helped shape the course of their lives. Angela, a white working-class woman whom we will meet more fully later in this chapter, considered leaving work after the birth of both her first and her second child. Instead, she remained employed full time and left only after a corporate buyout led her to feel forced to leave by work circumstances. She did not work for two years, then returned to work part time, after which she and her husband decided to have a third child. I came to realize that, like Angela, the majority of the women in this study made a number of difficult decisions, shaped by their circumstances, at pivotal moments in their life trajectories. This realization convinced me that it was necessary to use what sociologists call a life course approach to understand the women's lives. Life course scholars argue that to understand the decisions people make, it is necessary to study the course of their lives, putting key moments of decision making in a broader structural context and examining the cumulative effects of different turning points across the life course.[1]

Yet the majority of research on women's work, including most of the research on the topic of financial needs, is most often based on a snapshot of women's lives.[2] This snapshot asks whether women are currently employed or not employed, capturing a particular period in time. It does not tell us much about how women might move into and out of the workforce over their life course. But the snapshot approach cannot adequately explain women's work experiences, as women are less likely than men to follow straightforward work trajectories.[3] Moreover, focusing on whether or not women are currently employed rather than on their work patterns over time may obscure important class differences. First, approximately one-third of women employed in the United States are employed part time and they are primarily from the working class.[4] Second, men and women across classes are facing increasingly unstable employment.[5]

The snapshot approach suggests that women's workforce patterns are stable—one either works or leaves with little room for ambiguity.[6] But today, fewer and fewer companies offer the type of steady, lifelong employment opportunities that middle-class men and unionized blue-collar workers at manufacturing jobs enjoyed only a few decades ago.[7] Given the rapidly changing workforce, we must also consider the possibility that either remaining in paid work or leaving it are stable pathways to which some women may not have access.

In contrast to the snapshot approach, a life course approach takes a longitudinal look at how women enter work, the decisions they make about remaining at work, and their expectations about how they might return to work in the future. Much of the current life course research divides work pathways into three groups: employed, intermittently employed, and not employed.[8] The employed category includes all full-time steadily employed workers; the intermittent category includes women who work part time and women who work full time, but experience multiple bouts of unemployment; and the not-employed category includes all women who have left the workforce entirely. I argue that these categories are not conceptually useful for understanding women's work in the twenty-first century. Including women who work part time in the same category as women who are out of work may mask important class differences. Moreover, it has become less common for women to exit and never return to the workforce, making the not-employed category too exclusive. Entering the twenty-first century, women's work patterns have changed and we need to change how we measure them.

The Pathways

In this chapter, I examine women's *work pathways*—how women move into and out of the workforce over the course of their twenties and thirties, which are prime job-finding, career-building, and childbearing years for both women and men. By examining how important periods of transition, such as work entrances and exits, childbearing, or marriage, make up a person's life, we can better understand their significance and see the larger pattern formed by individual decisions and the structural context that shapes women's opportunities and constraints.[9] The majority of respondents had long employment histories, although for some, like Cynthia, a long employment history meant time served at one company; for others, like Virginia, a long employment history meant full-time and part-time work at a variety of jobs.

Instead of two options—working or not working—my research finds that women followed three different work pathways: the steady work pathway, the pulled-back work pathway, and the interrupted work pathway. While there were minor differences between women included in each group, we will see culturally meaningful differences in the way the women in each group related to paid work, as steady workers actively maintained their connection to the labor market, while pulled-back workers changed their relationship with work at some point after having children, and interrupted workers found themselves unable to maintain a steady presence in the labor market. Because these categories are based both on a longitudinal perspective of women's work and on analysis of detailed qualitative interview data, they better describe twenty-first century work patterns by capturing the dynamic between women's expectations, goals, and work-family circumstances. The categories that I developed and describe in this chapter place both part-time workers and stay-at-home respondents in the pulled-back category. I create a new category, interrupted, for those women who experienced multiple periods of unemployment. This differentiates between women who work part time and those who work hours closer to full time and experience at least two bouts of unemployment. Finally, I have renamed the category for steadily employed full-time workers the steady category.[10]

Those whom I considered steadily employed had worked more than thirty hours a week almost every year before I met them.[11] Although their jobs and their work strategies were far ranging, the women in this category actively made decisions to remain employed at crucial periods in their lives, strengthening their ties to the labor market. In the steady category I include women who had changed careers multiple times, taken maternity leave, and left work (no more than once) for a period of no longer than one year. Also included are women who pursued careers, as well as those in working-class jobs.

Pulled-back workers included both women who left the workforce entirely and those who returned or remained part time. While these women may have worked in different settings, in the end they all reduced their ties to the labor market in significant ways, which not only impacted their financial futures but also represented a notable shift away from their steady peers. At the time of the interview, none of the pulled-back workers spent more than twenty hours a week in the workforce and most spent less than ten; some are likely, when their children are older, to return to the workforce, perhaps even full time.[12] All had dramatically altered their relationship with the paid workforce. I depart from prior research by broadening this category to include all women who have had steady part-time work, those who delayed entry into the workforce, and those who entered (much like their male counterparts) demanding professional jobs but left.

The interrupted workers straddled both pathways but could not maintain access to either. Almost all worked full time when they were employed but also experienced multiple periods in which they did not work, with at least two bouts of unemployment. It is not simply that these women modified their original steady or pulled-back strategies. Most had attempted both, yet workforce and family circumstances made it impossible for them to follow a more stable trajectory. Their inability to access a stable path defined their lives and their work pathways, making their pathway clearly distinguishable from the other two. Unlike the steady and pulled-back workers, the interrupted women's lives were defined by instability so great that it affected their most basic work decisions. But like the other women, the interrupted women continued to hold a desire to conform to one pathway or the other despite their previous failures to do so. This pathway operated at the nexus of gendered work-family strategies and classed workforce experiences.

In the following sections, I provide greater detail about the differences between these three groups and introduce six women whose experiences illustrate the different pathways and common findings I explore throughout the book.

Staying Steady

The women who worked steadily, 49 percent of the total sample, were a diverse group. As we see in table 2.1, women's work pathways varied according to class and race. One-third of all steady workers were working class, while two-thirds lived in

TABLE 2.1.

WORK PATHWAY BY CLASS AND RACE (n = 80)

Class and Race Characteristics	Steady (n = 39) (%)	Pulled Back (n = 23) (%)	Interrupted (n = 18) (%)
Middle class (n = 40)	69	48	17
Working class (n = 40)	31	52	83
White (n = 57)	61	82	78
African American (n = 9)	18	0	11
Latina (n = 9)	13	9	11
Asian (n = 9)	8	9	0

middle-class households at the time of the interview. Just under half of the steady workers grew up in working-class households. Overall, they were more racially diverse than the larger sample: 61 percent were white, 18 percent African American, 13 percent Latina, and 8 percent Asian.

They also reported different successes and challenges. Many struggled over the years to find good work, adequate child care, or family support. Their work also had varying impacts on their families. Some women were primary breadwinners, some were dual earners, and some considered themselves secondary earners, despite their full-time work (and felt their families did the same). Their lives were similar, however, because of their ties to the workforce and their unrelenting attempts to find a space for themselves in the paid labor market.

LAUREN: MEETING EXPECTATIONS

A thirty-six-year-old black woman, Lauren grew up in Brooklyn, New York, the daughter of immigrants from the Dominican Republic, who moved there hoping to find better economic opportunities: "They dropped out at eleventh grade because they [had the chance] to move to the States." They had three children and Lauren was the middle child. Her parents worked long hours: her dad as a construction worker and her mom as a seamstress in a factory. Her father found great satisfaction in his work: "He love[d] construction. . . . I do not recall him jumping around from job to job. I remember him being steady in one job." Although Lauren's father found work he loved, her mother was less fortunate: "I do not think she liked the job at all. I think she did her job because she knew how to sew and she knew how to do patterns. And besides that, I do not think she liked it—like this [was not] a career for her."

Her parents' fortunes improved as Lauren got older. Her father's talent for construction work grew, and he became better paid and finally started his own business. They moved from a "poor neighborhood" to one that had a "good" school district. Her parents emphasized education above all else: "They always instilled in us that education was important, and they always wanted us to go to school. I think that part of it was because they did not finish high school that they wanted to make sure that we completed our education." Lauren felt this emphasis on schooling gave her a head start on her future employment: "I had a good education and I knew that I went to great schools and I knew that I was going to college, so I did not think that [finding work] would be a struggle."

Lauren went to college straight from high school and graduated with a degree in communications that she did not know how to translate into a job. Four months after graduation, still jobless, Lauren decided to expand her job search to nonprofits. She found a job, "went to work for a nonprofit organization," and quickly made her way up the ranks: "I was an assistant, then I became an assistant director, and after I became the director of the [larger project], and then I became the director of the [entire] program that oversaw everything else." After eight years working her way up, Lauren decided it was time for a change and moved to a comparable director's position in a larger national nonprofit organization, which paid better and also paid tuition for her master's degree.

When she was twenty-three, Lauren met her husband at a "club, dancing." They both were out with friends and they hit it off right away. Lauren wasn't sure she was looking for a serious relationship, but her husband was persistent and charming. They married three years later. She explained, "You know, in the early years, it was good, bad—we have gone through a lot as a couple. But the relation is definitely stressful at times. There are good days and there are bad days." They considered divorce, but, for the moment, were trying to work on their problems.

MARIA: HER OWN TWO FEET

The eldest of seven daughters, Maria, a working-class Latina, lived in a New York City housing project for the majority of her childhood. She never knew her father— her parents divorced when she was four and her mother remarried twice more, having two daughters with her second husband and three with her third. Her mother's third marriage stuck, thirty-five years and counting. Maria was seven when they married. She had lived with her stepfather for the majority of her life and considered him her dad: "I always had my stepfather and my mother. . . . He did everything for us even—I walked with him down the aisle when I got married."

Maria worried that outsiders would judge her humble beginnings, which she saw as an unjust way of viewing her parents, industrious people who cared about their children's upbringing.[13] Maria's dad, as she called her stepfather, had a hard time finding steady employment. "He went from cab driver to limo driver. It was always something driving, and that was it." Her mom had more stable workforce participation: "My mother was the one that always worked; she never changed. I think that is where I get that from. I stayed at the same place seventeen years. So, I think we got that from my mother. She is more stable. She still works." Maria's mom "barely graduated" from high school and "barely could do any schoolwork." In fact, she asked her daughters to help her when she applied for new jobs. But she started a job in a nursing home, cleaning bedpans and changing the sheets. Her persistence paid off and ten years after Maria left her childhood home, her mother became a supervisor at a nursing home, overseeing the nonmedical staff.

Although her parents worked hard, they lacked the resources to find good-paying jobs, and they found it challenging to feed seven mouths: "Many nights we had peanut butter with banana or rice with egg, and then she made this famous thing: the rice with milk. It tastes good but you get tired of it after a while as a kid." Surviving was such a struggle for Maria's parents that they had little time to give to their children. They also both had barely graduated from high school and felt unable to help with homework: "Education was not big in the house. [School] was a struggle, very bad, because they could not help us. How are they going to help us?" The family's financial situation also made it necessary for the children to work at an early age. "They would prefer us to get a job to help out in the house financially [instead of focusing on schoolwork] because we had jobs about the time we were twelve or thirteen. We were all helping."

Maria dropped out of school when she was sixteen: "I decided I would not go anymore and I just decided to leave. . . . [I] actually worked in [a] grocery store and then I became a waitress." During this period, Maria met and married her first husband, with whom she had a daughter. Through a combination of multiple jobs, Maria managed to carve out enough hours to work full time. "I worked at the old drugstore and I delivered the newspaper. I remember having three jobs and then I used to work at [a diner] . . . and I did that part time on the weekend." Although Maria worked full-time hours, she wanted more job security than her three different jobs gave her. After her divorce from her first husband, she also needed additional income to support herself and her daughter.

Maria met and married her second husband, Pablo, soon after her first marriage ended. They had two children, another daughter and a son. Pablo, a mechanic, was a very hands-on dad and did a lot of work around the house, too, which Maria considered an added bonus. Both his mother and Maria's mother-in-law from her first marriage doted on all three grandchildren, actively providing daily child care for them. Pablo's mother helped Maria get an interview at a local hospital soon after they met. "I got the job. I have been at the hospital for seventeen years now. This September, I will be there eighteen years." The hospital hired Maria as a nurse's aide, and when we met she had worked her way up to be a unit clerk. Maria earned her GED, which allowed her to make the change to unit clerk. This job paid "more money to do less physical labor. You are just using your brain a little more." When we met, Maria had gone back to school to earn an associate's degree in nursing. With two daughters grown and out of the house, she finally had time to go back to school, while still working full time and caring for her youngest child. She was secure knowing that she could stand on "her own two feet."

The majority of steady workers had strong incentives to stay at work. Rewarding jobs, financial incentives, and family support all served to encourage their steady work. Like Maria, many partnered with spouses and other family members to find ways to weave motherhood and work. Like Lauren, about one-third of the steadily employed women grew up in working-class homes and found themselves firmly ensconced in the middle class as adults. Like the majority of the steady workers, Lauren and Maria were married and like just over a third of the steady workers, Lauren had not had a child. The steady worker category was more racially diverse than the other two groups, and the vast majority of African American women, like Lauren, worked steadily.

Pulling Back

Were the women who pulled back from the workforce, 29 percent of the respondents, similarly diverse? There was, in fact, more class diversity in this group than among the steady workers. Just under half lived in middle-class homes and just over half lived in working-class homes. But there were some striking commonalities that were not found in the other two groups. The vast majority, over 80 percent, were white. None was African American. They also shared a similar family structure—all of the pulled-back women were married and had at least one child.

TRACY: INFLEXIBLE INSTITUTIONS

Growing up in a blue-collar neighborhood, Tracy, a white woman, her twin sister, and their younger sister had a comfortable childhood. Her parents met shortly after completing high school and soon started a family; their family grew faster than expected with the birth of twin daughters. Twelve years later, they had a second surprise when Tracy's youngest sister was born. After finishing high school, Tracy's father went to work for a telephone company and her mother became a secretary. She left work when she had her twins. Tracy's father, an Irish American, labored for the phone companies, installing phone lines. Her father worked steadily throughout her childhood, but his family was his primary focus: "I don't think—he didn't hate [his job] but, it wasn't, like, his first priority. I'm sure it wasn't." For her father, work "was just a means to make money to support a family." After Tracy and her sister entered kindergarten, her mother went back to school to earn a BS in nursing. After earning her degree, she began work "in an emergency room hospital." Unlike her father, Tracy's mother loved her work. Tracy explained, "Where my father would be more inclined to call in sick or take time off if there was something going on, my mother wouldn't switch it." Tracy appreciated the importance of work in her mother's life: "I was proud that she had a good job, she liked it and everything."

Tracy's parents had high hopes for their daughters: "I just remember, when I was young, my father just told me to be a lawyer, be a lawyer, be a lawyer. And I am a lawyer. I don't know why he always said that—to me and my sister. And she's a lawyer, too." True to her father's predictions, Tracy was an all-star in high school. She earned grades in the nineties every year and loved school, even though she thought that it made her a bit of a "weirdo" to enjoy school so much. She was the editor of her yearbook, in the French club, and on the school newspaper. She wasn't big into sports, but she still tried cheerleading and basketball, although, she explained, "I wasn't very good at that." From high school, Tracy went straight to college, where she continued her high achievements, earning a scholarship to a state university and keeping it by maintaining a high GPA throughout her college years. Her professors thought she stood out from the crowd. One was particularly encouraging: "This one professor kept telling me to be a senator some day." She then "went right to law school, straight to law school when I left [my college]."

After completing her law degree, Tracy went to work for an organization known to hire dozens of new law school graduates. "It was really, like, fun. It was a lot of young, new people. We had a really good time." Tracy's husband was one of the young people hired along with her. They married two years later, and three years after that they had their first child. Soon after Tracy learned she was pregnant, her company offered her a promotion. She explained her situation to her bosses and was told her options were either to accept the promotion or leave the firm. Both Tracy and her husband worked long hours, and the promotion would demand even longer ones from her. In the face of the ultimatum, Tracy said, "'No.' I wanted to go less not more. So I quit."

Tracy quickly "found a job with a law firm," but there were pluses and minuses to the new job: "The biggest plus was really they were very flexible. Whatever days you wanted, they were very easygoing. They were so happy just to have the good help. The biggest drawback was that they paid nothing, really pretty much nothing." In her new position, she worked thirty hours a week, down from fifty, and earned one-eighth of her previous salary, an enormous pay cut. After a year, Tracy switched firms again, starting a position working full time from home, which gave her additional flexibility and allowed her to have her second and third children. But this schedule also had problems: "I would have to, like, work a whole week through and then I didn't have [child care]—then I'd have to be asking my husband or I'd be working at night because I didn't have anything set."

After three years, Tracy switched positions yet again, this time working for a judge. Although she had been promised better hours, she worked full time and was only able to "leave, like, around four" every other Friday. Of all of the jobs Tracy had had, this was her favorite. She enjoyed the opportunity "to act as a lawyer" and appreciated the social contact she had missed while working from home. But this job, too, was unsustainable: "I worked there for eighteen months but it was just too much full time, with the three kids." When we met, Tracy was working part time at the same organization she had worked for right out of law school. They had agreed to hire her back on a part-time basis, working two nine-hour days a week. She went back at a much lower pay scale and without benefits, but she was able to negotiate vacation days as part of her package.

Although she had struggled for many years to find a full-time position that would allow her to reduce work-family conflict, Tracy finally came to believe that this was not possible. She and her husband had a good relationship that had no more than "the everyday stress. He was very supportive with me working. He said, 'You should try it and everything.' But the fact of the matter is—is that . . . there's just not enough time in the day or the weekends with the three kids." And while her husband encouraged her to "try it," he certainly did not participate in the household chores or child care work in a manner that would have reduced Tracy's workload at home. Tracy said she accepted his inability to do more at home because, "He's as helpful as any husband could be or anything. The fact of the matter is that the whole burden would always shift to me because [of his job]."

ANGELA: DISMISSED AT WORK, REWARDED AT HOME

A thirty-two-year-old white woman, Angela grew up in a traditional working-class, breadwinner-homemaker family. Angela's dad worked as "a butcher in the meat department." Although he didn't have a high school diploma, his work brought him a decent salary—enough money to buy a home and support his family. He tried to make sure he spent time with his family: "He would come home around dinner time." Angela's mom was one of eight children and she also did not finish high school, because she had to go to work to help out her family. After she had her children, she stopped working. She stayed at home until her son had graduated from high school and Angela had two years left in school: "She worked at [a hospital], yeah in the radiology department," where she typed "radiology transcription reports." The family's financial situation was tight, but never desperate.

Unlike Tracy, Angela did not shine in high school. She explained that her parents did not expect her to do so:

I probably had like maybe C-plus, B-minus average through my years. I was always a [well-behaved] student and I think that's what they enforced. [My parents' attitude was:] "If this is the best you can do then that's great. Don't slack off. Do what you have to do," and pretty much that's what their importance was.

In fact, education was often seen as selfish ambition. Angela attended community college for one year but decided that she was only going to school for herself: "I guess it would have just been for me, to know that I had it." She expected that her degree would not be used for work, because she hoped to marry, have children, and leave the workforce. Given that college was a personal pursuit, Angela felt obligated to take a more practical path, leaving college to go to a secretarial school to earn a legal secretary certificate.

After nine months, Angela completed the program and joined a law firm. One year later, Angela asked to be reassigned, and the school found her a position working for a large corporation: "I started there and it was the best eight years; I'll never forget. I loved the company." Angela contributed significantly to the corporation and was given the opportunity to grow in her position:

> In the beginning, I was like a junior secretary. It wasn't major things; obviously, I was answering the phones and stuff like that and doing expenses for the analysts and the associates. But I felt it was very exciting when they would give me, like, documents that they had to do for certain deals and projects. . . . I felt it was very exciting because I felt really useful.

Angela enjoyed her work so much that when she met her husband, married, and had a child, she decided not to leave the workforce as planned. Her husband, an electrician, who injured himself and was confined to desk work at his electric company, supported her decision to remain employed. She continued to be promoted. "[I worked first for] an analyst and [then] I worked for associates, then I was promoted in 1997—no the end of 1996—and I started working for vice presidents and directors." Finally, she became the administrative assistant to a managing director, the highest administrative position in a very large multinational corporation.

Her family worked to make her continued employment possible. Her father stepped in to take care of her son while she was at work, and her husband did more work around the house. She had her second child and continued working, but after the company was bought out, her new employers moved Angela from her position as assistant to the managing director back to the secretarial pool.[14] This demotion meant that she was back working in the position she had started in, but for new employers who did not respect her lengthy work history or her storied contributions to the company. The new position was "frustrating" and she "felt very uncomfortable," so after three months in her new position, she decided, "It was just time to be home and that was it."

Angela spent two years at home with her children and then returned to part-time work after she and her husband decided they could "really use the money." This time, Angela found a part-time job working for the company that had employed her mother to transcribe radiology reports. New technologies now allowed the work to be done from home, which allowed Angela to spend time with her children and gave her the needed additional income. She and her husband decided that her time at home and their extra income provided the cushion necessary for them to have their third child, and Angela gave birth to their youngest one year after returning to part-time work. Angela felt proud of the income she earned:

> Not that I treat myself all the time but it makes me feel a little more at ease to say that we could. I could do some extra stuff and not feel like I'm just taking my husband's money, you know. And I do have a friend that it's like his is his and hers is hers, and then when she has a baby and she's home, it's like his is his. You know he'll leave like $20 on the counter because she's going to the movies with the kids. You know you can't even rent a movie and get a pizza for that money. So—and you know my husband—he's not like that in the least, but it makes me feel better. You know it's Father's Day, like, I really did pay for it [chuckling]. It's not that it's all his income and I'm just taking out of it.

Although Angela had pulled back from the workforce, she felt strongly about her continued participation. She enjoyed the money that she earned and the contribution she made to her family.

While the women in the steady group tended to continue working for similar reasons, the women in the pulled-back category followed two distinct trajectories. One group, like Angela, pulled back when faced with poor work conditions. The other group, like Tracy, pulled back when they found themselves unable to manage the time demands of work and home. Like Angela and Tracy, the majority of the pulled-back women remained in the workforce part time and the vast majority reported that they wanted to work. And some of the women who had left the workforce entirely reported that they would prefer to be working but could not find a job. As chapter 1 suggested, and as we will see in later chapters, the "choice" to leave work was made within fixed boundaries and constricted options.

An Interrupted Life

While the pulled-back and steady workers generally followed similar patterns in which they entered the workforce, worked for a period of time, had a child (or decided not to), and then made a decision about whether to remain in the workforce, the interrupted workers, 22 percent of the total group, had lives that looked little like their contemporaries'. Almost 50 percent of the interrupted workers had never held down a steady job, so deciding to pull back or stay steady after childbirth was never an option. In fact, they often lacked access to the resources that would have provided more stable work pathways. The vast majority, over 80 percent, of the women in this category lived in working-class or working-poor families. Just over three-quarters were white and the remaining quarter was evenly divided between Latina and African American; there were no Asians in this category. Many had grown up in working-class or working-poor families—families that sociologist Joseph Howell would have called "hard-living," because they lacked stable finances or even a consistent roof over their heads.[15]

SHERRI: SEARCHING FOR RESPECT

The second of four children, and the oldest girl, Sherri, a white woman, grew up in a working-class home that was fraught with hidden tension. Her father, an Italian American, was a policeman, who had earned his GED while on the force. Her mother, an Irish American, finished high school and then stayed at home with her children until Sherri was in middle school, at which point her mother went back to college to earn an LPN degree. They seemed like a perfectly typical family with a boisterous set of four children. Once Sherri's mom went back to school and then work, they hired "the greatest babysitter," who made sure everything got done: "The dinner would be ready, laundry would be done, baby would be down." On the surface, it seemed like they had it all: "We all went to Catholic school. . . . We had all had a great education. We all had the best of everything. A great house and the great neighborhood we grew up in. I'm very fortunate, that's for sure."

Sherri's dad "was a police officer. New York City's finest." He often worked a second shift on the weekends and earned extra money for the family as a handyman. Her father cut back on his work hours after Sherri's youngest sister was born. He wanted to make sure he had time to see his children, and her mom welcomed the chance to move back into the workforce, working "nights, yeah mostly nights." Her mom would see everyone off, hand the baby off to the babysitter, and drop off to sleep. But below the surface, Sherri's mom suffered from a drug addiction. It started simply enough: "She was taking pills to stay awake at night. By the time it was a problem and she realized it, it was too late." Sherri's parents stayed together until after their children left home, but their family life was deteriorating around them. Her mother's addiction "took away from all of us. You know what I mean? 'Cause she was tired—it made her old. It made her feeble. Then a lot of responsibilities were mine as an oldest girl."

Between dealing with her mother and caring for her siblings, Sherri didn't have a lot of time to focus on her schoolwork. As a result, she did poorly in school and felt dismissed by her teachers, who called her "a stupid little girl." She explained, "I was always labeled that I always had problems at school. I hated school." She left school as soon as she could, at age sixteen—an act that she later came to regret. "I should have went back but I didn't." When we met, Sherri was taking GED courses to pass the math portion of the exam.

Sherri had a career plan mapped out from an early age: she would become a chef. But without a high school diploma, it was difficult to gain entrance to the city's culinary schools. She found work at Burger King, but she knew she didn't want to spend the rest of her life working in a low-paid position. She thought she could aim higher: "I could be running the place. That's all I want[ed] to do [was] run the place 'cause I knew what I was doing. I knew everything about it, but I wasn't getting paid for it because I didn't have the education behind me."

So, Sherri applied to a culinary program through work. "[I] lied my way through [the application process], telling them I had a diploma, which I didn't." She "finished culinary school," but with no actual diploma, it was difficult to find a position with a reputable employer. Sherri spent the next twenty years working at a number of organizations, spending anywhere from six months to a year in a position and then leaving the workforce for a period of time. She found it difficult to find a job where she was respected. She went to work at a local hotel restaurant, "But people there at that time . . . really didn't want me there." From there, she moved to another restaurant, then to a local branch of a national chain restaurant, then to another branch of that chain, then to a diner, then a catering company, then a high school cafeteria, and multiple other locations, too numerous to recount or for Sherri to remember in great specificity.

When asked why she cycled through so many positions, Sherri explained, "Once I get tired of things, I usually leave 'cause I had enough." When pressed to explain what things tired her, Sherri said that she hated that everyone always acted like she didn't know how to do her job. She felt micromanaged and expendable, as if her work was not valued. Her employers would boss her around, acting as if they expected her to be stupid. "They just [would say], 'Do this.' [So, I said,] 'Okay, I can do it. Goodbye.' Then they would [make mocking noises at me]. So, I'm like, 'What up, what up?' Don't demean me and talk down to me like I'm shit. I hated that, I hated that, just hated it." At one hotel, employees who dropped a dish were made to perform a task in the freezer to atone for it. "I just thought that was so cruel." Sherri was asked to do this once. "[My boss] made me stand in the freezer once to make whipped cream." It was not uncommon for her employers to attempt to embarrass employees who made mistakes or even those who had stellar employee records.

Over the years, Sherri "worked so many places," but she never thought about leaving the workforce, despite her many frustrations with it. She would be fired or leave work after a particularly frustrating employment situation and then reenter the workforce six months or a year later, after securing a "better" position, in the hope of finding that dream job. She met her husband a couple of years after she dropped out of high school. They were not careful with birth control—"We didn't use protection lots of the time"—and three months into their relationship, Sherri was pregnant. Three months after that, she was married. Her husband worked as a painter for the city and had a few side jobs. Sherri worked part time after the birth of her son and then took a couple of years off before returning to work (and then leaving it again repeatedly) when her son entered school. Despite her many workforce challenges, Sherri still held out hope that gainful employment in a good workplace, where her workforce contributions would be acknowledged and her skills respected, could be found.

ERICA: WHEN PULLING BACK DOESN'T WORK

At forty-one, Erica, a white woman, felt that she had lived several lives by the time I met her. She was just beginning, she explained, to try to live on her own. Erica's parents divorced when she was quite young and her mother remarried a few years later. While her mother and stepfather did not have any more children, her stepfather had three children from a prior marriage, who would visit on the weekends. Since her mom remarried when Erica was still in preschool, Erica formed a close relationship with her stepfather, his children, and their extended family. Although her parents maintained a "relatively good relationship" after their divorce, her father was not particularly involved in her childhood. She explained that her father "was not very much a family man." She recalled that he was not like "other fathers," who, she imagined, "worked normally from nine to five." These fathers "came home when dinner was on the table." Instead, he was largely absent or drinking heavily: "He was pretty wild. When I was younger, from what I remember, he drank." Erica's father dropped out of high school and never earned his GED. He often went without work when he was drinking heavily and did not help out financially: "My own father did not really think it was important to contribute to that."

Erica's stepfather played a significant role in her upbringing. She explained, "He is my dad. I am closer to him than I was to my real father. So, he is really to me, he is my father, my dad."[16] Her dad, as Erica called her stepfather, dropped out of high school and had an unstable workforce history: "He drove a truck. He was a truck driver, so he had jobs. But then the place he had the job closed down." After that, her dad found it difficult to find work. Out of desperation, he started working for a large trucking company that required its drivers to show up and wait every morning for assignments, but employment was never guaranteed: "He would get a job here and there in between but there were times where he go without. . . . There were large periods where that happened."

Although money was always extremely tight and food for the adults lacking at times, Erica's mother did not work until her children were both in high school. When she went back to work, she worked nights as a telephone operator. Looking back, Erica regretted that her parents did not take a more active role in her education or her plans for the future. "I think that they could have done more to push me a little bit. I do not think that they did. I did very well in school when I was younger so, I mean, they were always proud of me, but I do not think they ever pushed me to be inspired to do anything." When Erica was fifteen, she became pregnant, unexpectedly. Because she was born into an Irish Catholic family, abortion was not an option, nor was completing high school. Both sets of parents demanded that the teenagers marry and drop out of school; Erica stayed at home with her son and her new husband was sent to work at an auto shop. "So that kind of put all my aspirations on the back burner because now I was a mother and that really needed focus."

As happens with many marriages between such young adults, Erica's marriage failed. Her husband found a new girlfriend and left his family.[17] "I dropped out in freshman year of high school to have my son. Several years later, probably when [my son] was around four or five years old, my marriage obviously was not working out and I was going to be getting a divorce, probably about nineteen or early twenty." But Erica left school during ninth grade. "I did not have the education—what type of work would I do? Where was I going to work at nineteen?" she asked. Erica also had no idea what types of opportunities would be out there for a person with her skill level—she had only ever thought of being a veterinarian or a psychologist.

It was difficult to find steady work as a single mother, particularly as one who did not have a high school diploma. Erica first worked "part-time retail jobs." She moved into a full time job as a receptionist and "was there a couple of years." But the receptionist job paid poorly and had no benefits, so Erica went back to school and earned her GED, which she hoped would lead to better employment. She quickly learned, however, that a GED did not guarantee stable employment. "I did a little waitressing in there and got a little extra money when I was waitressing. I decided to check into being a stenographer and being that I was waitressing I realized that I could not do it because I had carpal tunnel." Erica's work options seemed very limited. She also had a hard time finding someone to care for her son, as her son's father had no interest in the task.

She continued to work from time to time, finding employment at a gym and in other workplaces. But she was unable to maintain a steady level of employment, and finally she took time off and moved back in with her parents. "I had to move back home to my parents' house for three years until I could get back up on my feet." After Erica had saved enough from her hairdressing and waitressing work, she and her son moved back out on their own. He was in high school at the time and more independent, and Erica decided it was time for change. She went back to school in a paralegal program and worked multiple jobs to pay for it:

> My schedule, I never knew what it [was] going to be. It is like, "Where was I going to be now?" And I would come home from school and jump in my car at the train and head with my supplies to get to somebody's house to do a haircut. Saturday, I would go through like three haircuts, then I would go to the restaurant. It really was insane throughout.

After she graduated from paralegal school, Erica spent five years working in a law firm. She started the job after her son turned eighteen and joined the navy. It was the longest period of time she had ever spent in one job, and she hated it. She missed the hustle and bustle of the hair salon and the social interaction at the restaurant. She quit her job and went back to school to earn an associate's degree to become an LPN. When we met, Erica had three months left to go in her training, and she hoped that her interrupted work pattern had stopped. Her son had long since left home— she had been on her own since she was thirty-six. She hoped that her luck was changing and that her workforce participation would become more "normal."

The interrupted workers' lives were defined by structural forces that prohibited them from following steadier paths. Almost all of the women who followed this pathway were from the working class or working poor. They were slightly more racially diverse than the pulled-back group, although less diverse than the steady workers.

Conclusion

The focus on need and choice has led us to expect that women follow two work pathways: working or not working. Because middle-class families are so often the model for longitudinal life course studies, we have also ignored an important third pattern: the interrupted pathway. By asking how women have worked across their adult lives, rather than whether they are currently employed, this chapter finds three distinct work pathways that reflect significant differences in women's lives.

This chapter advances prior research on women's work by providing a conceptual framework for understanding women's longitudinal work patterns in the twenty-first century. I contend that the current focus on employment status (whether or not a woman is currently employed) masks important nuances in women's work, as it does not capture the ways that gender and class shape women's work over their life course. This chapter identifies three conceptually distinct work pathways: steady, pulled back, and interrupted. By conceiving steady work as any workforce participation over thirty hours a week, this reconfigured category measures a high level of labor force attachment while acknowledging that women often do have slightly lower levels of paid work than men because of their relatively high levels of unpaid work in the home. By including both stay-at-home mothers and part-time workers in the pulled-back category, I acknowledge that the majority of women do not leave the workforce permanently when they withdraw after having children and also identify the important ways that these women's ties to the labor market change at some point after they have children. Finally, by adding a separate category for all women who experience at least two bouts of unemployment, I identify a group of workers whose unique work pathway was masked in other categorizations and who experience higher levels of socioeconomic distress than their contemporaries.

The women's pathways suggest that their gender constrains how they make decisions about work—these decisions are generally made when their continued workforce participation is in question and they must consider leaving the workforce altogether. Gender beliefs continue to structure women's workforce participation by framing women's work as a choice, although this frame often ignores the structural constraints that shape these choices. The women in the study repeatedly evaluated their workforce participation choice. The choice to work is a frame that overshadows women's, but not men's, workforce participation. While men may likely expect to work as adults (and then may need to deal with the ramifications of this expectation if they face a job loss or an economic downturn), women's continued workforce participation is never assumed. For women alone, work is not taken for granted, although making a choice about work is.

In the chapters to come, I explore these differences in greater detail, as I investigate why women came to follow these different pathways. We saw in the stories of Maria, Lauren, Tracy, Angela, Sherri, and Erica that even at a young age, the women had expectations about their future workforce participation. We also saw that their lives often did not go as planned. In the next chapter, I ask how women developed early expectations about their workforce participation. In the following chapters, I ask what happened when these expectations met the realities of their workforce participation and family lives.

3

A "MAJOR CAREER WOMAN"

How Women Develop Early Expectations About Work

CASSIE, LILA, AND Angela grew up in a time of expanding opportunities for women. But they had very different expectations for themselves after they graduated from high school. Cassie, a white woman from a working-class background, felt she had to decide between either becoming a professional or staying with her high school sweetheart. Lila, an Asian American from a middle-class family, never considered anything other than becoming a long-term member of the workforce. Angela, a white woman from a working-class family, decided she didn't want to invest too heavily in a profession because she wasn't cut out to be, in her words, a "major career woman." To understand why Cassie, Lila, and Angela had such divergent expectations at a young age, this chapter asks: How do women develop expectations about their future in the workforce?

The women who participated in this study came of age in the 1980s and 1990s—they are the "children of the gender revolution."[1] These were women who grew up seeing daily images of a woman with a baby in one hand and a briefcase in the other.[2] During their childhood, women marched into the workforce and Murphy Brown joined Mary Tyler Moore as icons of working women. Given these changing norms, we might expect that all women would anticipate a lifetime in the workforce. But, as we see in Cassie's, Lila's, and Angela's explanations, this was not the case.

During the 1980s and 1990s, media coverage of working mothers almost always portrayed them as white middle-class women.[3] When women of color were portrayed in the media, they found themselves most often depicted as workers, but not mothers, or as mothers on welfare.[4] While the woman with the baby and briefcase may have been emblematic of women's hopes to have it all, this dream was popularly portrayed as being specific to a particular race and class. Given the underlying subtext of these images, the intersection of race, class, and gender may play a central role in women's expectations about work. Are some women less likely to expect to work than others? How do race and class inform women's expectations about work?

It is necessary to understand how women develop early ideas of work, particularly given the national trends that show working-class and working-poor women are more likely to spend time out of the workforce. In this chapter, I consider how the respondents, when they were young adults, formed expectations about what their future work lives would be like. We will see that while some of the women planned to be lifelong workforce participants, others thought that their workforce participation would be occasional and not a primary focus of their lives. Expectations about workforce participation varied across classes, education levels, and family experiences. Interestingly, women's thoughts about their future work were not necessarily connected to their plans about family formation. In fact, the majority of all women, regardless of their expectations about work, expected to form families.

Who Works Full Time?

Women's expectations about the way that they will work may be shaped by the opportunities that they perceive will be available to them (or the constraints they expect to face) and their expectations about their own abilities.[5] Life experiences may shape women's expectations about their lives, including decisions about workforce participation and about marriage.[6] Family pathways—how families respond to change and traverse unexpectedly choppy waters—influence children's outcomes and their expectations for their own adult lives.[7] Interactions with parents shape, to an extent, women's expectations about work, but schools, work, and social experiences appear to play an even greater role.[8] Work pathways are constrained not only by the options available to women, but very clearly by how women perceive these options. In her research on law firms, sociologist Jennifer Pierce found that there are cultural expectations about how different jobs are gender specific; that is, we expect doctors and lawyers to be men and secretaries and teachers to be women.[9]

The decision to stay at home or work full time is something that is only available to those women who have another adult in the household who can financially support the family, typically a division of labor found only in families where the husband is the primary breadwinner and the wife the primary caregiver.[10] This division of private and public spheres has been less common in lesbian, black, and working-class households, where families historically have been more dependent on the earnings of female workers.[11] Since black men historically earned much less than their white counterparts, African American communities depended on working mothers and never embraced motherhood as an acceptable alternative to full-time paid employment.[12] Working- and middle-class women, as well as women of color, may also receive differing types of kin support for their workforce participation.[13] I argue that these differing experiences of women's work may mean that expectations about women's responsibilities as workers may be constructed differently across race and class.[14]

Early ideas about working influence decisions women make at crucial transitional periods in their lives.[15] Expectations about future workforce participation also influence women's decisions to gain skills necessary for long-term work.[16] Since there are lifelong economic consequences for full-time versus part-time work, it is important to understand how these decisions are made.[17] To distinguish between these two conceptions of work, here I discuss *continual* or *occasional* work.[18] Women who expected to work full time for the majority of their young adult lives are in the continual work category. Women who expected to work part time or not to work once married with children are in the occasional work category. This framework does distinguish between the types of workforce participation that women expected to have, but it should not signal that continual is more socially valuable than occasional work or that careers are more important than jobs. Instead, this approach allows us to better understand when class influences women's expectations about their future work and what other factors may also play important roles in women's development of ideas about work.

Early Expectations About Work

Most women, including 100 percent of my participants, now expect to spend at least some part of their young adult lives in the paid workforce. In itself, this suggests a remarkable transformation has occurred over the last forty years, as none of the women anticipated a lifetime entirely in the private sphere. When asked to recall their expectations about work when they were on the verge of adulthood, 64 percent of the participants reported that they expected they would work continually, while the remaining 36 percent reported that they expected that they would work more occasionally in the paid labor market.[19]

Women's perceptions of the opportunities available to them influenced the development of their early ideas about work. Class origins, race, education, and family experiences shaped women's perceptions of those opportunities (and quite likely, the opportunities themselves). For women growing up in both working- and middle-class homes, the combination of parental expectations about continual work and school successes (for themselves and their peers) created strong early expectations that they would be continual workers. These expectations also developed when women rejected the traditional breadwinner/homemaker model—a path some associated with great financial risks. The women who expected to be occasional workers often perceived that there would be few opportunities for them in the workforce. These women experienced school roadblocks, familial pressure to focus on the family, and unstable family lives that led them to develop expectations that they would participate in the workforce only sporadically. While the factors that motivated women to be continual workers were shared across race and class, the factors that motivated women to be occasional workers were far more likely to be found in white and Latina working-class and working-poor families. The only middle-class women who expected to be occasional workers were those from families with religious or cultural objections to women's workforce participation.

Expecting Continual Work

Prevailing explanations of early expectations about work and family emphasize class differences. Researchers who study working-class women have suggested that because working-class women need to work, they don't experience work and family as opposing factors, the way middle-class women do.[20] Since middle-class women have better workforce opportunities, they are likely to expect careers and long-term workforce participation. This would lead us to expect fairly homogenous expectations among classes and large differences between working-class and middle-class women's early work expectations. Instead, I find that the women from working-class families were divided in their expectations about their workforce participation, with 58 percent expecting to work continually compared to 42 percent who expected to work occasionally, while over 80 percent of women who grew up in middle-class homes expected to be continual workers (table 3.1).[21] In other words, most women from both groups expected to work continually, although a sizable minority of women from working-class homes expected to work only occasionally.

Women from middle-class homes, regardless of race, were highly likely to expect continual work. Class and race influenced not only early expectations but also the process through which expectations developed. The vast majority of women from middle-class origins, of all races, gave little consideration to their desire to be continual workers. In fact, when questioned about their early expectations about work,

TABLE 3.1

EARLY WORK EXPECTATIONS BY CLASS OF ORIGIN (n = 80)

Expectations	Middle-Class Origins (n = 21) (%)	Working-Class Origins (n = 59) (%)
Continual (n = 51)	81	58
Occasional (n = 29)	19	42

many of the women from middle-class homes seemed puzzled to think that there could have been an alternative to continual work.[22] On the other hand, the majority of women from white and Latina working-class origins felt that at a young age, they needed to decide whether or not they would work continually or occasionally.

The majority of middle-class women did not feel burdened by this choice at the end of high school. This is, perhaps, because their class position allowed them to delay adulthood until after college.[23] Middle-class white, black, Latina, and Asian women described growing up with a strong sense that they would work and while many of them found these expectations challenged later in life, they did not explicitly experience an early period of choice the way the working-class women did. Similarly, working-class blacks anticipated a lifetime of workforce participation. In contrast, working-class white and Latina women articulated a conscious calculation of continual versus occasional work. Women from white and Latina working-class families described a process in which parental expectations or school success were generally experienced as an alternative to pressures to stay at home. The time delay of grappling with these issues is, perhaps, a gendered advantage of the middle class that has been previously underexplored. This suggests that structural factors played an important role both in women's expectations and in the process through which expectations developed.

MIDDLE-CLASS PRIVILEGES

The white, Asian, African American, and Latino middle-class parents, almost unanimously, promoted the importance of education and future professional employment to their daughters. Eighty-one percent of women from middle-class homes expected continual work, including all but one of the six middle-class women of color and twelve of the fifteen white women; the only exceptions were women from families with religious objections toward women's paid work, including three white women and one Asian woman. This supports findings that middle-class parents prepare their children for the middle class.[24] In fact, several recent studies find that women raised in middle-class families are brought up to achieve excellence in the classroom and the workforce.[25] Women from middle-class families received a significant amount of encouragement from their parents to focus on their schooling in preparation for their entrance into the workforce. Although they reported their parents "did gender" as it pertained to their dress, the household division of labor, and their restrictions on children's extracurricular activities, the middle-class girls reported their parents took a gender-neutral approach to schoolwork and future employment.[26] They were expected to be the rival of any male in the classroom and at work. This focus on excellence in school led the middle-class women to hold high expectations about future education and labor market opportunities when they completed high school.[27]

Parents' expectations created an atmosphere in which the middle-class women believed long-term employment was the normative experience for all women. Lila, an Asian American middle-class woman, recalled her parents' attitude:

[They] wanted [us] to get the most education that we possibly could in order to do what we wanted. And, of course, they stressed thing like—*what most families would stress*—like, try to get into the medical field or go into something that's going to land you a job that's going to provide for you, in medical field or engineering.[28]

Lila's parents expected that all of their children—Lila and her two brothers—would excel in school and go on to become doctors or engineers. Lila did not believe that her parents held different expectations for her than they did for her brothers, just as she believed that all families held similar beliefs about their daughters' workforce participation.

White children from families in which at least one parent has a college degree often expect to go to college.[29] Jodi, a white woman, felt her middle-class parents weren't explicit about their expectations that she would excel in school and enter the workforce, because they took both steps for granted: "[The expectations] weren't vocalized, but I was expected to go to school and do well in school. And it was just a given that I would be going to college and then to work. There was nothing more to it than that." Sheila, a white woman from a middle-class family, agreed: "Oh, it was just—it was without question." Indeed, for most of the middle-class women, there was nothing more to it than the expectation that they would excel in school and enter the workforce. While excelling in school or attending college and entering (and then remaining in) the workforce are clearly different stages, the majority of the women conflated the two, arguing that finishing high school or expectations of college attendance were part and parcel of their early formation of continual workforce participation expectations.[30] While middle-class families in earlier eras may have expected their daughters to go to college to earn a "Mrs.," the majority of the middle-class women described parents who expected that their daughters would have life-long workforce participation.

Like Lila's family, many middle-class families stressed the importance of being financially independent. Both of Lucille's parents worked.

> I think it was always assumed I would go to college, which is a good assump-
> tion. I was an accountant because I'm from a family of accountants. I think—I
> don't know if that was expected. I mean, I fit that personality type anyhow but
> it was more geared toward business and working in New York versus the arts.
> So the arts wouldn't be acceptable because you can't earn money in the arts.

Lucille's parents highlighted her need to find a job that would be financially re-warding, not a job that could leave her financially vulnerable. As with Lucille, women's workforce participation, and even their need for financial stability, was considered independently of marriage for most middle-class women.

The women who grew up in middle-class families, with very rare exceptions, were focused on continual workforce participation from a young age. Their parents expected they would work; their peers and their teachers did, too. There was little consideration of another pathway. Middle-class origins privileged women by delaying the influence of gender expectations about workforce participation. While they may have been expected to do gender in the home, they were given free reign at school and formed dreams about continual workforce participation.

WORKING-CLASS FAMILIES PREPARE WOMEN FOR WORK

I found the working-class white and Latina women evenly divided in their expectations about work. As table 3.1 shows, 58 percent of the women from working-class backgrounds expected continual work, including half of the white and Latina women. The African American working-class women, on the other hand, were united in their expectation that they would work continually. Working-class white and Latina women formed hopes for good paid work when their parents encouraged it as the best way to be financially secure. Working-class African American women grew up in households in which women's work was taken for granted.[31]

While continual workforce participation was a way to maintain financial security for women from middle-class origins, it was often considered a strategy for upward class mobility for women from working-class families. Many working-class women's parents encouraged them to focus on continual workforce participation. These parents saw education as an opportunity for their children to better themselves. Cameron, a black woman who grew up in a working-class family, recalled, "I don't remember my mother not talking about education. School was always a priority, always number one, always good grades. It came first; nothing happened until the schoolwork was done [laughter]." Like her middle-class counterparts, Cameron grew up with the expectation that she would enter the workforce and be a steady worker.[32] Her mother had strict rules about schoolwork and workforce participation, and encouraged her to always work part time after school.[33]

Some working-class parents hoped to have their daughters adopt the practices of the middle class, so that their children could have opportunities that had been denied to them. As more and more young women are aiming higher both in high school and in college and graduate school, they are gaining greater skills to enter the workforce.[34] Claudia, a Latina who grew up in a working-poor family, had parents who expected her to work continually. "Well, they always stressed that I should continue going to school, especially my dad. He never went to school. So, he always wanted us to go to school, and I was my dad's favorite girl. I would always listen to him," she said. As a result, "[I] always expected to work. I only expected not to work maybe later on in life when I retire." Like the middle-class women, the working-class and working-poor women associated long-term workforce participation with high educational goals.

Financial insecurity during childhood led some women to focus on full-time work. Amy grew up the daughter of Asian immigrants who owned a corner store. While her family "never worried about food, not having food," there were a lot of "ups and downs" for her family. This financial instability led Amy to want to never "worry about money. To be able to make sure that my kids have everything they needed." Growing up, she said, "[I] definitely wanted to work and make money. . . . I wanted to take [the experiences] and see where I could go from there."

Some women from working-class origins were inspired by their mothers' work. Maria, a Latina from a working-poor family, felt she should match her mother's continued workforce participation:

> It was nice to see that my mother works. It gave me the inspiration to work myself as a kid. I have always worked because I saw it as important for a woman to work and have their own bank account and never rely on a man just bringing the money.

Although Maria loved her stepfather, she also appreciated that her mother was not dependent on him, because she knew how vulnerable this would have made her family after her mother's first two divorces.

Anita, a white working-class woman, explained, "They wanted me to get good grades and go to college. You know, that's what they wanted." But this was not the path that she wanted for herself, as she had always dreamed of a career in radio. Her parents worried, because they saw it as a financially unstable field: "They wanted me to get into a different field. They were unhappy. 'You are going to go nowhere. It's hard to get into.'" Although Anita and her parents differed in their expectations of how she would work, they were in complete agreement that she would work. She recalled, "Honestly, I just never thought of not working, you know."

In many cases in my study, working-class whites and Latinas seemed very similar to each other, as some expected to work continually and some expected to work occasionally (figure 3.1).[35] Working-class African American women were the exception, as 100 percent of the black respondents expected to work continually. The majority of African American women (from both classes) expected either that their spouses or partners would be unable to earn a breadwinning wage or that they would not marry.[36] This reminds us that women who expect to work only occasionally must also expect a future marriage or partnership in which the partner is able to earn, throughout the course of their lives, a wage that can support, at minimum, two adults, and likely children as well. Most African American women expected that they would need to be primary earners in their family, regardless of their expectations about marriage.

Few of the working-class African American women explicitly connected their race to their desire to be continual workers, but the vast majority of them grew up in homes in which their mothers and the other mothers that they knew worked full time. Aisha, a working-class African American woman, described her mother's workforce participation:

> I would say she worked for pay all of the time. My memories of my mother's work were her sewing; that's what she did. She made costumes for a dance company. I just remember there being a lot of fabric around the house and she had a major project, it spilt over into the dining room, on the dining room table with all of that sort of thing and you know she was pretty much always paid. She was the costume mistress for a dance company so that's what she did and they always paid her.

Tina, an African American woman from a military family, explained that even though her family moved frequently from base to base following her father's job, her mother worked "all the time." Like Aisha, Tina felt that her mother enjoyed her work and would not have wanted to do anything else: "She's always worked. . . . She liked working. I mean I don't think that my mom's the type of person to stay with something that she doesn't like to do. She likes what she does."

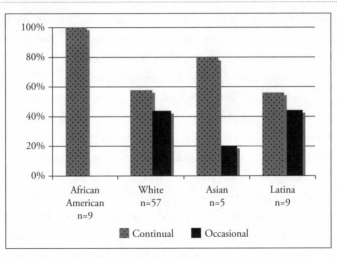

FIGURE 3.1. Early expectations by race.

Cameron, an African American woman, was puzzled when I asked her if her mother had ever considered leaving the workforce:

> I don't know, not work at all? I don't know; that's sort of complicated. She liked her job. [Might she have wanted to] do something different? I'm not sure. She just said she liked her job because it fit the needs of the family at the time, so it's not like she had great aspirations to be something else. She just felt like the job was good for its purpose.

Her mother's job inspired Cameron's own work pathway: "It influenced me to do what I am now, an occupational therapist, and she works in the rehab department, so that's how I was introduced to it."

Because there were few black homemaker mothers, African American women's continued workforce participation faced fewer questions. I asked Tina about her mother's continued workforce participation:

> SARAH: How did you feel about her job when you were growing up?
> TINA: I really didn't have any feelings in regards to that at all. Because I mean, everyone around me, their parents worked; so it wasn't like—there were people who had stay-home moms—they were—generally everybody worked.
> SARAH: So it just seemed like everybody did?
> TINA: It was normal.

Aisha, a black working-class woman, said that not only was continued workforce participation assumed, but success in the workplace was, as well: "I think for the most part, success wasn't an option for me or for any of us. It was more something that we knew was tangible, that we would just work for, that we would get." Sandra, an African American working-class woman, explained that she always expected to work, which was tied to expectations that she would provide for her family: "I definitely wanted to be able to provide for my family, what I was given, like everyone else. Do even better."

The normalization of continual work for black women led their daughters to expect that they, too, would work. Like their African American, white, Asian, and Latino middle-class counterparts, working-class blacks explained that continued workforce participation was taken for granted. Discussion about future workforce participation was not necessary, because working continually was the only option. As we will see in future chapters, this did not mean that all black women then took steady work pathways, as some struggled to find steady work, spending years moving in and out of the workforce. But they did all start out expecting to work continually.

THE PERCEPTION OF OPPORTUNITIES

While parental expectations were important, high school successes also played a role.[37] Life contexts shape women's expectations about work, and my research suggests that during adolescence, experiences in schools play a pivotal role in shaping women's expectations about what awaits them in the labor market. The education system remains an important site of gender, race, and class divisions and because education remains closely tied to workforce participation, women's experiences in schools helped to define their expectations about work.[38] Good grades, positive feedback from peers and teachers, and integration into school programs developed women's self-confidence and led them to believe that they could find success in the workforce. For middle-class women, high school successes confirmed early work expectations and cemented them within their peer groups. Success was particularly important to working-class girls, as it encouraged women to explore different interests—interests that could lead to future careers.

Katya, a white middle-class woman, explained that while her middle-class parents did have high expectations for her, "It wasn't like [I needed] somebody pushing me to study. I was like that myself. I liked it all the time." She elaborated that even though she felt socially awkward with classmates at times, she felt at home when "getting knowledge." Katya always expected to work, because she assumed she would find the self-fulfillment in the workforce that she found in school. Norma, a working-class Latina, expected continual workforce participation and also a lifetime commitment to higher learning. "I was always looking forward to like going to school. [Laughs.] My husband is like, come on, you'll still [be going to school] when the kids go to college." Norma's enjoyment of school combined with her parents' high expectations of her: "I would say that it just made me stronger. I always believed that I would have my career."

While the middle-class women often felt more prepared for the challenges in the classroom, many working-class women did well in school, and these successes often encouraged them to seek future success at work. School successes allowed working-class women to see themselves as potentially successful workers and focused their attention on long-term workforce participation. Others participated in vocational training programs that led them to see the possibility of long-term pink-collar work, particularly in secretarial programs, which were the predominant form of vocational training for women when the respondents were in high school.[39] Molly, a white woman, felt that her classmates looked down upon her because she grew up working poor. Additionally, living with a physically abusive father further distanced her from her peers. But in school, Molly began to find a place for herself:

I was a very good student. [There] I felt like I could do anything I wanted to do. I had the ability, like the intelligence to study, you know, whatever. . . . Like everything I did I saw myself taken to the top of whatever it was.

Molly's high achievements at school led her to gain acceptance among her peers and to expect to be a continual worker. When Molly graduated from high school, her goals centered on her continued workforce participation, through which she hoped to find future successes.

Amanda's working-class parents had "very basic" goals for her life, and she felt disappointed by their lack of interest in her schooling, because she "would have liked a little bit more guidance back then." Although Amanda, a white woman, received little encouragement at home, she found an abundance of it at school. She described multiple teachers who took an active interest in her education, because of her promise as a student. Amanda "always expected" that she would work, she said, "because in my grade school years I did very well." As Amanda began to identify more with her middle-class teachers and less with her working-class parents, she developed a strong expectation that she would work continually.

Not all of the working-class women who had school successes developed expectations about middle-class jobs. And positive educational experiences in high school did not necessarily lead to college. For many working-class women, they led straight to the workforce, but positive experiences at school or in vocational training programs were closely linked to early expectations of continual workforce participation. Some saw the possibility of continual employment in pink-collar work. Cynthia's working-class parents encouraged her to go to college, but she was uncertain if that was the right move for her. Instead, she looked for other opportunities provided by her high school and found a high school intern program.[40]

> Through my school. There was a career day. So we just picked up interviews. Some of the companies came and I interviewed with them. And then I went to the city for a second interview. And they just picked me and I'm still there.

Cynthia, a white woman, firmly believed that the intern program had helped her develop her commitment to continual workforce participation.

REJECTING THE HOMEMAKER MODEL

For some women, the decision to commit to the workforce was an explicit rejection of the breadwinner/homemaker division of labor. For these women, this decision stemmed less from the opportunities that they saw in the workforce than from their perception of the lack of opportunities for women who became homemakers. Some women described this rejection as stemming from their disillusionment with their parents' relationship. Others described feeling that the breadwinner model was untenable, so they decided to focus on work as an alternative. For all of these women, committing to the workforce meant that they would not have to rely on anyone else for financial security. Interestingly, the choice between work and family was most explicit among these working-class women.

Lindsey's working-class parents divorced when she was thirteen. The fragility of her parents' marriage left Lindsey, who is white, determined to be able to support herself. "I just wanted to be financially independent without a husband, by myself, you know? Just to be independent whether or not I was married . . . to be able to take care of myself and do what I want." Lindsey's father encouraged her to follow this path after his wife's decision to leave the family challenged expectations of a traditional gender division of labor in the household.

Like Lindsey, Anya, a white woman, was skeptical of the promises of marriage. Growing up in a working-poor family, she never wanted marriage, because she had "never seen a good one." The daughter of Russian immigrants who divorced when she was twelve, Anya was determined to support herself so that she could avoid the cockroach-infested apartments that plagued her childhood. Anya attributed her impoverished years to her father's departure and her mother's inability to support herself without him. Starting at age twelve, Anya found work whenever she could, often working under the table—all in the hopes that one day she would be able "to stand on [her] own two feet."

While Cassie's working-class parents remained married, she, like Anya and Lindsey, rejected the possibility of following in her mother's footsteps:

> I think that she gave a lot, but she never charged for her services. She fell short of her potential. The rest of my family are women and we have rather good jobs now. I think my mother was more than capable to do what we do. I think we have the same work ethic as she does. I really think she could have done some more for herself and maybe helped support her family. I am proud of what she did, but, of course, I always wished that she could have done more.

Cassie focused on steady work to avoid what she saw as her mother's disappointments from being a homemaker.

Sallie, a white working-class woman who is gay, did not decide to focus on work due to concerns about marital insecurity or her mother's unfulfilled potential. But she knew that it would not be possible for her to rely on a husband's success: "I think subconsciously I knew that for me [marriage and kids] was never really going to be the road that I went down." As a result, Sallie rejected the homemaker model at an early age, not from fear that such a model would disappoint her, but from her expectation that her sexuality would preclude her from participating in a traditional gender division of labor.

Developing Occasional Expectations

Half of the white and Latina working-class women, 50 percent, developed expectations that they would work only occasionally. Even fewer middle-class women, only 19 percent, three white and one Asian, expected that they would work only occasionally. Low opinions about their chances for good work often led women to expect to work only occasionally.[41] Many working-class Latina and white women grew up in families in which women had poor work opportunities or where women's workforce participation was not valued. Women also developed occasional expectations when they faced poor experiences in the school system and when starting a family seemed like the best alternative to a chaotic home life. Finally, a small number of both working-class and middle-class women grew up in families in which traditional family forms were expected.

WHEN WORK IS LIKELY TO DISAPPOINT

Working-class hopes were tempered by the doubts raised by the very real constraints working-class girls saw around them. They doubted, as Angela did, that they could be "this major career woman." These doubts stemmed both from families' inclination to downplay the importance of women's paid work and from the structural constraints of finding good work. Because full-time work was associated with a middle-class life, many women grew up thinking it was out of reach. The association came, in part, because women saw their own working-class mothers as workers, but as not full-time, essential workers. Like most working-class women growing up during the 1970s and 1980s, these women lived in households in which women were expected to work. Thus they expected to weave workforce participation with caring for family.[42] But a long line of research also suggests that working-class households consider women's workforce participation secondary.[43] In fact, women often deliberately reduce the significance of their own workforce participation to maintain peace in the home, by adhering to more traditional gender divisions.[44] Growing up in a household in which the significance of women's work was diminished suggested to some women that even though working-class women work, they play a "helper's" role in the family.

Working-class women described mothers who went back to work to help out the family, but whose work was characterized as secondary, both by the family and by the mothers themselves. Audra, a white working-class woman, explained:

> She enjoyed making brownies and cupcakes, the whole thing. We always had home-cooked meals. . . . I think she really felt the family unit is you're supposed to be home, raise your own kids. So I think she would think the other women that were working, when the kids were young, would be almost selfish or not the right thing to do. . . . So she went back to work, like I said, when my brother was in junior high school. . . . That's when you start finding out that everything costs money. But it was either my father got a second job or she went back to work.

Although her mother stayed in the workforce long after the family's financial strains were less pronounced, Audra explained that her mother worked to "help out" her dad.

Working-class mothers' work was often framed as "extra money" for the family or for the mother herself. This led some girls to view their mothers' workforce participation as insignificant. Wanda, a white working-class woman, explained:

> She never had an actual job. . . . She cleaned houses. She was, like, a maid [for] people in the neighborhood, like, and she made some extra pocket money for herself . . . and she'd go into the beach club because there was a beach club close by. She'd clean their bungalows and cottages and then she'd clean like a couple of houses in the neighborhood.

Although Wanda remembered that her mother cleaned houses and also worked for the local beach club as a maid, she also explained that her mother "never really worked."

Working-class women also saw their mothers work in jobs in which they were not highly rewarded. Women saw that their mothers did not have good workforce opportunities and did not want the same poor workforce options for themselves. After her parents divorced, Virginia's mother started to work even longer hours: "She was always cleaning. . . . She was the cleaner. She cleaned in buildings. . . . She always worked that four-to-one shift. . . . She was never around. She worked two or three jobs but it was to work and to . . . [voice trails off] to support us." Virginia's mother always told her what would happen if she didn't gain a college degree: "If you don't go, well, you are just going to be [a] cleaner. So, it's like if you go, then you advance, or you stay where you are and do what she did." But since Virginia "didn't like school," she knew that that meant she would end up having a career like her mother's if she had to work full time.

Janice's mom worked odd jobs part time when her children were young. "I think she went back to work when I was maybe five or six—waitressing. It was like off and on—then she had side jobs cleaning apartments or like little—here and there she cleaned a dentist's office." She was poorly paid and had a hard time finding steady employment, and she also felt guilty about leaving her children: "I think my mom says she wishes she had been home more." This painted for Janice, a white working-class woman, a picture of women's work that was unrewarding and coupled with guilt about being away from the home.

Unlike their middle-class peers, working-class women's participation was often classified as "help" and not crucial income for the family. Some working-class mothers worked in low-status, low-paying jobs that they found unsatisfactory. These contradictions left women who grew up in working-class homes more divided about their future workforce possibilities than their middle-class peers.

SCHOOL ROADBLOCKS

Just as perceiving opportunities led women to expect continual work, perceiving constraints could make continual work seem impossible to achieve. Women most often faced these roadblocks to full-time work in their school experiences. Facing roadblocks at school led some women to expect little from the workforce. When schools offered few rewards, women saw the tangible emotional and personal rewards that could be found in the home. Some women described these rewards as stemming from the personal benefits of motherhood, while others saw marriage and motherhood as a place where they could retreat from the rejections of their schools and, later, the workforce. Other research has found that women working in jobs with poor earnings, few benefits, and little chance of advancement may prefer to retreat from the workforce.[45] Most expected that they would still have to spend some time in the labor market, but they hoped to be occasional workers who would participate less often.

Working-class white women often believed they could not live up to the image of the steady worker—whom they saw as a middle-class woman. Those who expected to work continually and those who expected to work occasionally attributed steady work to the middle class (continual workers saw themselves, as Cassie described earlier, moving up through this steady commitment—"the best progression to a profession"). Angela, a working-class white woman, struggled to fit in at school, felt discouraged about her skill sets, and gave up on her schoolwork.

> I worked very hard. I did my studying and I passed. I probably had like maybe a C-plus, B-minus average throughout my years. . . . But starting around fourth, fifth grade, I got a little insecure, you know embarrassed, boys versus girls, and I was never this popular kid or whatever. So, I think I started to get very intimidated and I don't think I put my whole self into it.

Her school experiences led Angela to believe that she would not be successful as a professional and to believe that, as a result, she should focus on family rather than attempt (and likely fail) to become a "major career woman."

Christy, a white working-class woman, didn't see the point in investing in the school system. She thought her classes were boring and her teachers uninterested in her. Her high school experience was disjointed, at best:

> I didn't go an awful lot. I didn't go down the time where normal people go. I would go and meet my friends and leave. I mostly went to summer school for four years and I went to night school for two years, on top of going to day school.

Christy's lack of interest in school did not lead her to focus on working-class jobs. Instead, she developed an expectation that she would not need to find continual employment, because, she said, "[I would] find somebody who would support me and take care of me and my family."

Many working-class women didn't see the possibilities of full-time work, as Cassie had, but the perils. They thought that they would not be qualified for good work or would be unable to achieve high goals. Darla didn't expect to be a full-time worker. She explained that those workers went to college, and so she never considered full-time work, "because in my brain I was not going to college. I didn't need all the academics. You know, your reading, writing, and your math. . . . It was like useless to me." Darla, a white working-class woman, struggled in school growing up: "I hated school—always." She never had a favorite teacher or subject and spent most of her time trying to "get around the system. So, you take the classes you need to take during the day. . . . You are free the rest of the day." Like Christy, Darla turned to occasional work: "I was always more family oriented than career oriented. So, I was going to be the housewife." Darla decided to focus her plans on marriage and believed that if she needed to earn extra money, she would become a hairdresser.

When parents appeared disinterested in schooling, this lack of interest encouraged some women to divest from their own education. A divestment from the education system almost always led to a subsequent disinterest in long-term work. This suggests that the "natural approach" to child rearing found predominantly in working-class homes may also have gendered disadvantages.[46] Kathy, a white working-class woman, did not experience the same type of parental support for work and education that the women with continual workforce expectations described. Instead, she described an environment at home and school in which school and work were less emphasized. "In my lower years, we had to study, do our homework, not as much now as then. Now, we go over our kids' homework. They didn't do that," said Kathy.

Some also faced discouragement in school explicitly because of their gender. Growing up in a working-class neighborhood, Linda, a white working-class woman, knew lots of women who worked, but as "helpers," not breadwinners. Her guidance counselor encouraged her to realize that her workforce participation would conflict with her duties as a mother:

> Unfortunately when I was in high school, my senior year, my guidance counselor said, "What do you want to be a doctor for?" And I graduated number one in my class in high school. And she told me, "Ha, you're going to grow up, get married, have kids. What do you want to be a doctor for? That's just going to hold you back." And I changed my profession; I went into pharmacy instead. I mean, I like it; it's a good job for a woman—you [can] balance your family life and work life. But I wanted to be a doctor.

Linda's parents had little interest in her education, and the formal advice that she received in school was to focus on a career that would allow her to "balance" her work and family obligations.

FAMILIES IN CRISIS

While the majority of the working-class women felt that they needed to make a conscious decision between continual and occasional work, some women, particularly those who grew up in families in crisis, felt that active consideration of their future plans was beyond them.[47] This turmoil led a minority of women to turn to building a new family in an attempt to escape the chaos of their family of origin. Many of these women also perceived few opportunities for them in the workforce and reasoned that a new family was the only way to experience a change of fortunes.[48] Other research has also found that women living in poverty and in search of a fresh start often form new families rather than seeking employment, since good work opportunities are virtually nonexistent.

Women who faced a high level of chaos in their everyday family life did not turn to work for escape. Instead, they wanted to form their own families, hoping to create stability there that had been lacking in their own early lives.[49] Miranda, a working-poor Latina, never knew her father, and her mother passed away when she was eight. An older sister and an older brother helped raise her, but their struggles with drugs made them unreliable caregivers. She explained that these struggles made it difficult to think about future plans:

> There was more important things going on in my life around me than to think about what I want to do and where I want to go, you know, and stuff. Lotta things going on [laughs]. . . . It's just a lot of things, you know. If it wasn't one thing, it was the other, you know, and I was focusing on my sister [a drug user who was Miranda's primary caregiver] and what she was going through, so I didn't really have time to think about what I wanted.

Miranda was held back in school repeatedly and decided to drop out at the age of eighteen when she found out she was pregnant. While she had never taken the time to think about what she wanted for herself, focusing on raising a family became her default position. She was able to escape the drama of her sister's household by moving in with her son's father and his more stable parents.

Dawn, a white woman from a working-class background, similarly felt unable to think about what she wanted from life. Her stepfather's drinking binges made life at home "miserable," and when asked what she wanted to do after high school, Dawn explained, "I wanted to go away. Wanted to get out of the house—that's all I wanted." When she became pregnant, she decided to marry her boyfriend as a means of escaping her parents' house. Likewise, Laura, a white woman who grew up in a poor family, felt unable to concentrate on herself because of, she said, "the chaos going on in my house. Just not being able to get there [to a place where she could focus on herself]. There was just so many things." She dropped out of school to go to work as a secretary at the age of sixteen, but knew that once she had a child, she "wasn't going back [to work]."

Sharon's parents divorced when she was young and she had a chaotic young adulthood, moving multiple times every year, as her mother searched for work and for new husbands. Sharon wanted out of her family as soon as possible and thought that the best way out would be marriage. "The old saying, 'If I had to go back and do it again,' knowing what I know now, had I known what I know now I would have stayed in school. I would have geared myself more toward my education and my life [rather] than gearing it toward a man, which is what I did. I guess searching for [an escape] made me look in the wrong direction."

Even high expectations and support from parents were not always enough to subvert the extreme stresses of poverty. Isabel, a Latina from a working-poor family, was the eldest of ten children. While her parents had "very high expectations" of their children, Isabel found it difficult to focus on those expectations given the demands of her younger siblings and the challenges of growing up in poverty. She explained, "It's always so hard to have to be so poor—and we were too many kids, we had not enough attention to each one. So I was [voice trails off]—it was hard for me. But I tried my best." When asked if she had ever thought about what she might do for work as an adult, she explained, "No, I really was so confused; I never thought about it."

For these women, focusing on starting a new family provided hope that they could have a fresh start. Work was largely absent from their plans, despite the poverty many faced. This was, perhaps, because stable employment was not a realistic goal for the majority of this group of women.

REINFORCING THE TRADITIONAL FAMILY

The only women from middle-class origins to expect occasional work lived in homes in which traditional religious and cultural practices were prominent. Regina, a middle-class white woman, explained that her Catholic father made it clear that "they were not paying for college" for a daughter. Her parents had helped her older brothers: "My brother Andy was the brightest of all of us. He has a doctorate in meteorology with a minor in oceanography." Although Andy received financial support, Regina would not.

> When it came time for college and I really didn't know what I wanted to do, I met my husband. That played a big role in my decisions, too. I was a senior and I had a very steady boyfriend who was three and a half years older than me. . . . So, I didn't go to college.

Regina's lack of support from her parents coupled with her loving and supportive relationship with her high school boyfriend convinced her that she should focus on family, and work would take a backseat.

Gurneet, an Asian American woman, was one of the four women from middle-class origins who expected to work rarely. Her family's expectation that she would marry and raise a family were very clear:

SARAH: Now, did you want or expect to work when you grew up?

GURNEET: No, I was not expected to work, no. Just to get an education, that was the expectation.

SARAH: And once you completed your education, were there expectations about what you would do after that?

GURNEET: Well, yes, my parents only wanted me to get married. And then it's your husband's responsibility. Whatever he tells you—it's up to your husband and whatever he decides.

Strong family objections to workforce participation made it difficult to imagine continual work even for women growing up in middle-class families.

Conclusion

This chapter focused our attention on an important transitional period in women's lives to investigate how women develop expectations about their long-term workforce participation. Women's perception of the opportunities available to them strongly influences their expectations about continual or occasional work. Significantly, all participants expected to participate in the labor market as adults, and over 60 percent expected to be continual workers.

This chapter shows how women's class and race intersects with gender schemas to influence the processes through which women form opinions about their future work. The majority of white, Asian, African American, and Latina middle-class women described a process in which expectations that they would enter the workforce were so strong that they gave little consideration to other options. Similarly, African American working-class women described growing up in communities in which women's continual work was taken for granted. On the other hand, the vast majority of white and Latina working-class women described a process in which they considered the possibility of working full-time or part-time, and half expected to work occasionally while the other half expected to work continually.

The women who grew up in white, Asian, African American, and Latina middle-class families, with very rare exceptions, were focused on continual workforce participation from a young age, regardless of whether or not their mothers worked. A study of longitudinal trends in mothers' and their daughters' gender attitudes toward employment finds sizable differences in the mothers' attitudes toward work from

1956 to 1986, with most mothers holding less traditional gender ideologies and holding higher identification with paid work in the 1980s than they did in the 1950s.[50] This suggests that as norms have changed about women's work, women's attitudes about work have changed too, and, regardless of their own workforce participation levels, mothers might hold different expectations for their daughters than they did for themselves.[51]

Sociologist Annette Lareau's research on the parenting styles of middle- and working-class women certainly suggests that middle-class parents treat their sons and daughters similarly and prepare both for entrance into middle-class institutions, such as education and professional employment.[52] My findings extend this by suggesting that middle-class families are better positioned to help their daughters take advantage of the cultural shifts that have made women's workforce participation more acceptable. The middle-class women did not simply benefit from delaying the consideration of work-family conflict; they also benefited from an early expectation of workforce participation, which led them to gain important work skills. The time-delay of grappling with these issues is, perhaps, a gendered advantage of the middle class that has been previously underexplored.

Unlike their middle-class peers, women from white and Latina working-class homes grew up with a conflicting picture of their potential workforce participation. The structural pushes and pulls of workforce opportunities and constraints and the continuing prevalence of the traditional division of work and family spheres was much more present in their lives. Many had parents who emphasized long-term workforce participation as the key to economic success and economic independence. On the other hand, working-class white women's participation was often classified as "help" work and not crucial income for the family. Some white and Latina working-class mothers worked in low-status, low-paying jobs that were unstable. These contradictions left white and Latina women who grew up in working-class homes more divided about their future workforce possibilities than their middle-class peers across races, and their African American working-class contemporaries. Building on Annette Lareau's findings that working-class families develop a "natural approach" to child rearing, in which working-class parents grant their children more freedom and do not structure their daily activities, my research suggests that there are also gendered disadvantages to this approach, as some white and Latina women whose parents were disinterested in school found themselves turning away from paid work entirely.[53]

Class and race influenced not only women's expectations about paid work, but also the process through which these expectations developed. The vast majority of women from middle-class origins, regardless of race, gave little consideration to their desire to be continual workers. In fact, when questioned about their early expectations about work, many of the women from middle-class homes seemed puzzled to think that there could have been an alternative to continual work. Just as white, Asian, Latina, and African American middle-class women rarely questioned the possibility that they would work continually, African American working-class women similarly believed that they would work continually throughout their adult lives. Historically, black women have had less of an opportunity to withdraw from the workforce than their contemporaries, and my research suggests that this has translated into an expectation of full-time work in women's lives. On the other hand, the majority of white and Latina working-class women felt that at a young age, they needed to choose whether or not they would work continually as adults. The women who articulated a conscious calculation of continual versus occasional work were white and Latina working-class women.

Finally, I found that some women faced pivotal moments in their upbringing that shaped their expectations of future workforce participation. Women who were brought up by homemaking mothers and whose families hit hard times were particularly devoted to the idea of not being homemakers. These women saw the bad times faced by their families and thought that their mothers' lack of employment left the family in peril when facing other challenges, such as a father's job loss or divorce. Women who grew up in families in which staying at home was a strong cultural imperative followed this tradition. Finally, women who grew up in families in turmoil turned toward forming new families at a young age—and not toward work—to escape their families of origin. These women saw themselves as having particularly poor workforce opportunities and hoped that starting a family at a young age would give them a reprieve from the challenges they faced in their own families.

In the next chapters, we will see how these expectations guided women's decisions after high school. While they did not determine whether or not these women would work (the majority of the respondents were employed at least part time), their early expectations helped to shape their work pathways. While early expectations have been shown to be poor predictors of whether or not women work (Gerson 1985), my research suggests that they may influence women's perceptions of their workforce opportunities and the skills that they gain as they prepare to enter the workforce.[54] This was particularly important for steady work, as 60 percent of the women who expected to be continual workers went on to become steady workers, while only 32 percent of the women who expected to be occasional workers went on to work steadily in the paid labor market (figure 3.2). This suggests that expecting to work continually helped women prepare for future steady labor market participation. But this research also suggests that future life experiences did cause women to change course.[55] A full 20 percent of the women who expected to be steady workers found

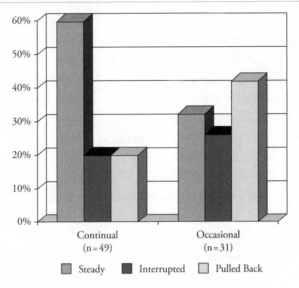

FIGURE 3.2. Workforce expectations by work pathway.

themselves pulling back from the workforce, while only 42 percent of the women who expected to be occasional workers went on to do that.

While early expectations clearly do not explain the entirety of women's workforce commitments, they have an underexplored role in workforce pathways. Once in the workforce, however, other factors—such as opportunities and barriers at work, and changing family structures—played a much larger role in women's formation of workforce ties. Part II explores how workforce opportunities further shaped women's work pathways, changing some women's early expectations and cementing others' early goals.

Work Pathways

4

WORKING STEADILY

Good Work and Family Support Across Classes

WHILE WOMEN HAVE participated in the workforce in growing numbers over the past century, their steady employment is a relatively new phenomenon.[1] Many researchers point to men's declining wages (and women's need to work) as a key component of this changing phenomenon, but labor shortages, occupational growth, the women's movement, and a growing acceptance of women's employment also played key roles.[2] In the wake of these changes, sociologist Anita Garey writes that popular discussions about why women work "dichotomously categorize women as either those who have to work for economic reasons or those who choose to work for reasons of self-fulfillment."[3] As we saw in chapter 1, this categorization is tied to assumptions about social class; working-class women need work, while middle-class women choose work. This categorization creates a class distinction about the voluntary (middle-class) or involuntary (working-class) nature of women's work.[4] It also suggests that middle-class work is more rewarding and that working-class work is less desirable or less sought after.[5]

Sociologists have suggested that the meaning of work varies greatly by class. For the working class, "a good job is a means to a good living, but achievement in a specialized vocation is not the measure of a person's worth, not even for a man."[6] For the middle class, the "devotion-to-work schema" demands a "single-minded, emotional intensity that fuses personal and professional goals and inspires [one] to meet these goals."[7] My participants' lives suggest that both these analyses of women's ties to the labor market miss key components of women's approaches to working.

Drawing such broad distinctions between middle- and working-class work decreases the complexity of women's work and simplifies the reasons that women might find themselves continuously employed. It also unnecessarily dichotomizes the financial rewards of work and the personal and social rewards of work. Women who search for fulfillment at work are likely to appreciate the financial rewards that their work brings, and women who might have begun work out of financial necessity may find themselves remaining at work for many reasons, particularly when they find "good work." Sociologists Margaret K. Nelson and Joan Smith suggest that (working-class) employment can be divided between what they term "good work" and "bad work." While Nelson and Smith use this term to refer to working-class employment, my findings suggest that good work is similarly defined across classes. Nelson and Smith explain that good work must be full-time and year-round and likely provides benefits or workplace stability.[8] I build on their terminology, suggesting that, additionally, in order to maintain long-term employment, good work must engender a worker's interest, provide a sense of positive accomplishment, garner peer or employer recognition and respect, include the possibility for advancement, furnish adequate financial remuneration, and, at times, lead to an improved social status for women's families.

While good work had similar traits across classes, these traits were most often found in middle-class jobs. Over two-thirds of the women who worked steadily were middle class, and just under one-third of them were working class. Importantly, the mechanisms that led women to remain employed were shared across classes. While it was easier to find good work in middle-class jobs, about one-third of the working-class women were able to find working-class jobs that had good work characteristics. I found little evidence that the working-class women who worked steadily felt differently about their employment than did their middle-class peers. Because working-class women, particularly those who were mothers, often faced a greater struggle to maintain full-time employment (they often had more precarious child care strategies), this suggested that their continued work was important to them. It was important to them because of the financial benefits that it brought and also for the social rewards of paid employment.

As chapter 3 suggests, women's early expectations also played a role in their continued employment. The majority, 72 percent of steady workers, had expected to work and experienced bad jobs as road bumps in their search for good work; a smaller minority, 28 percent, had expected to leave work and changed their minds when they found good work. This suggests that it was much easier to follow a steady work pathway if it had been anticipated; the women in this group gained higher levels of education, on average, and were more likely to participate in technical and vocational programs if they were from the working class. Although women's early attitudes about work framed how they made sense of their work opportunities, it was positive experiences—at work, with child care, and with household support from their families—that were the most important factors in determining their ability to maintain a steady place in the workforce.[9] Almost all of the steadily employed women eventually found good work and managed to craft an effective strategy for managing work-family conflict. All the women who remained employed despite expecting not to work found good work—which they and their families often considered great work—and strong support at home, which encouraged them to remain in the workforce. As women spent years working steadily, they often grew increasingly attached to the paid labor market and continued having positive experiences, which reinforced their attachment to it.[10]

Women of color were overrepresented in the steady worker pathway. While non-white women made up 29 percent of the total respondents, 39 percent of the steady workers were women of color. As might be expected from their early expectations about work, African American women were most likely to work steadily, with 80 percent of the African American respondents in this category. Fifty-five percent of Latinas worked steadily, as did 60 percent of Asians. In contrast, only 42 percent of whites worked steadily across their lifetime. It is necessary to be cautious of these findings, because in the overall group of eighty women, a large majority (fifty-seven) were white. Only five women identified as Asian, nine as black, and nine as Latina. While these numbers are small and suggest that further research must be done on this topic, these findings do support other research which suggests that women of color are more likely to participate in paid labor than their white counterparts.[11]

Just under half of the study participants worked steadily. Most had children and most were married. Their incomes positively contributed to their lives and the lives of their families, and most found good work. Table 4.1 shows the family characteristics of the three groups. The majority of all women had children; two-thirds of those with steady participation had children, as did over four-fifths of those with participation gaps. Not having children may facilitate steady employment, as more steady workers were childless than were either the pulled-back or the interrupted workers. But the majority of steady workers did have children, which suggests that having children does not prevent steady workforce participation. The majority of all women were married and the steady workers had much higher marital rates than the interrupted workers.

Women's steady workforce participation was not only personally important; it also had far-reaching consequences. Continual workforce participation often allowed women to hedge against the unexpected. Although health challenges and

TABLE 4.1.

FAMILY CHARACTERISTICS BY WOMEN'S WORK PATHWAYS (n = 80)

Family Characteristic	Steady (n = 39) (%)	Pulled Back (n = 23) (%)	Interrupted (n = 18) (%)
Married (n = 54)	70	100	22
Have had at least one child (n = 61)	64	100	72
Working at time of first pregnancy (n = 59)	100	99	99
Left work following birth of child (n = 11)	0	30	30

individual losses often felt like very personal challenges to the women in the study, millions of Americans face the possibility of family illness or job loss every year.[12] Copious sociological and economic research shows that men's average wages have declined over the last thirty years.[13] Workers, particularly in the working class, face "a long-term squeeze" in which the average wages for men have dropped; health insurance is more difficult to obtain; hours at work have increased; and pensions for the retired have become less common.[14] The women in the steady category often described themselves as better able to withstand outside pressures than their counterparts in the pulled-back and interrupted groups. Continual workforce participation allowed the women in the steady group to prevent financial crises in the midst of familial and economic change.

Finding Good Work Across Classes

The majority of steady workers, 69 percent, were middle class, and most had expected to work steadily. The remaining 31 percent were working class, and, like their middle-class peers, they largely expected to work full time. Very few women worked steadily who had not expected continual work. Women who expected to work continually forged strong ties to the labor market at an early age, and finding good work cemented their attachment to it. Women also noted that jobs could bring important gains in status for their families—some had middle-class jobs while their husbands had working-class jobs; others had secretarial work that provided access to higher-status networks and institutions. Not all women found good work immediately upon entering the workforce, but these women switched jobs multiple times, confident that they would eventually find good work.

INTERESTING WORK AND JOB SUCCESSES

Why did middle-class women stay employed when most had financial resources that would have allowed them to leave work? Almost all had expected continual work, and finding good work simply moved them along on their expected journey. Most of the steady middle-class workers did not describe a particular moment when they decided to work full time. Instead, they described a series of events in their work histories and home lives that led them to remain employed full time. For some, companies made it clear that they would be highly valued workers. For others, it came at the end of the work day, when they experienced a sense of accomplishment in the tasks they had completed. For still others, it came in the recognition that they received from their employers or peers for the work they did.

Interesting work made women more invested in working. Lucille, a white middle-class woman, explained: "[This] job was a great plus because it was a great industry to get into. I get to work with a lot of really intelligent, smart people. . . . I deal in all aspects of running a company." Lucille's rapid rise to the top reinforced her decision to maintain steady employment. Finding work that was interesting or rewarding encouraged women to invest in their careers. Liz, a middle-class black woman of Dominican descent had a hard time finding employment when she first graduated college. "I was getting frustrated, so I just took whoever hired me first," she explained. While her first job was not in her chosen field, she grew committed to the work she did. After a few years and several promotions with a nonprofit organization, she said, "[I realized] that I was able to give back and that was when I started to realize that my job was really important."

The sense that a job was good work often stemmed from external recognition of the value of a woman's work. When women's expectations that their employers would recognize and reward their hard work were met, they felt their work was important—a factor that was missing in the work of many pulled-back and interrupted workers, as we will see in the next two chapters. Vivian, a white middle-class woman, explained that her employer rewarded hard work and talent. This increased her satisfaction at work:

> You can perform there, based on your ability. The more you know, the more they trust in you, the more you can do—various legal documentation, doing various research, and very detail-oriented work. And, the more you learn, the more you show the ability that you have, the more responsibility you get.

As Vivian's responsibilities increased, so, too, did her commitment to her company and to her continued employment.

Working-class women also benefited from management that recognized the work of employees and promised future opportunities. Tina, a working-class black woman, started out working minimum wage at a welfare agency. Tina felt her job was interesting, but she found herself wanting more. "I liked the work but it wasn't challenging enough for me," she said. Her boss made it clear that if she did a good job, he would find a better placement for her. "They put you where they thought they could use you," she explained. Eventually, Tina received the training necessary to do work that she found stimulating and very important to society. "Now I work with the family to resolve whatever issues that brought the children into foster care," she said.

Work successes that promised a bright future and the likelihood of promotions and further rewards led women to develop stronger ties to the labor market. Cameron, an African American middle-class woman, had grown up in a working-class family (that at times was working poor after her parents' divorce), earned a scholarship to a prestigious local university, and chosen a career in physical therapy. Halfway through her college degree, she learned that several companies would assume her college debt and pay for the rest of her bachelor's and master's degrees if she would commit to working for them.

> A lot of people come to the school and tell you about the scholarships they have, because they will pay for your schooling: "Come work for us." So they kind of recruited you. Even though you had to go through the interview process, they recruited you.

Finding herself heavily recruited by a number of programs was the confirmation Cameron needed to forge ahead with her plans for work.

Maritza, a working-class Latina, did not enter her chosen profession immediately. Having grown up in a working-poor family, she needed to find full-time work after high school to pay for her associate's degree. While she ultimately ended up as a preschool teacher, her early work in retail supported her early expectation that she would work continually. She received a promotion within months of her hire:

> Then I did—I was a section manager. So I used to place orders for like—it was a children's store. So I used to place orders for all the baby supplies, bottles. I used to have to contact the salesperson and then we used to meet and then place orders. Yeah, it was pretty good. The owners loved me. They still want me to work with them, but I just don't want to. I don't want retail.

Although Maritza decided against pursuing a career in retail and went to work as a preschool teacher instead, she found her first workforce success in this retail store, which increased her confidence that she could readily find other work opportunities.

Some women's first jobs were more clearly the building blocks of their future careers. These experiences not only confirmed expectations that good work was available but also gave women additional skills to aid in their pursuit of these jobs. At thirty-two, Parul had graduated from an Ivy League school, worked her way up the corporate ladder, earned a six-figure income, and expected to graduate from a top MBA program. A middle-class Asian American woman, she described her entrance into the workforce:

> I learned a lot of the foundation of market research. I did, like, survey development and discussion guide development and also analysis and report writing, stuff like that. . . . I liked looking at the data and analyzing it. Also, I liked understanding what people thought about things and kind of applying that. That was fun.

Her job was both fun and filled with future potential, providing further confirmation that her decision to work full time was a good one.

Working-class women also benefited from opportunities to gain skills on the job and the promise of promotions. Molly, a white working-class woman, explained that her employer saw the pride she took in her work and offered her opportunities to grow with the company:

> But I think, I take pride in whatever I'm doing, doesn't matter what it is. Even when I was doing retail, I enjoyed working and I like to do the best job that I can. And this company really, as much as I complain, they gave me opportunity to change. When I got bored with the admin thing, they let me move into the billing. They gave me opportunities that maybe other companies wouldn't have because of my degree.

When we met, Molly was determined to remain employed and to go back to school to create new opportunities for herself.

Women also found that full-time employment benefited their self-esteem. Lori, a white middle-class woman, explained that working increased her "self-confidence": "I think it makes me a more independent person. Not only that, it . . . I feel like you raise your head higher when you're a working woman. I'm doing this. I don't need . . . [voice trails off] I don't need you to support me."

Just as working increased self-confidence, staying at home lurked as a shadow that could rob women of such confidence. Helena, a white middle-class woman, explained that she could never stay at home: "I can't stay at home. . . . I would feel—I still have to go somewhere, do something for somebody, get myself looking positively, because when you are at home you kind of start looking down. When you go to work you're more disciplined."

FINANCIAL REWARDS

For almost all of the respondents' families, the steady worker's paycheck played an important role in their finances. For many, the ability to be financially independent, to sustain their families, or to offer more for their families was itself a sign that they had chosen the right path. Tangible financial rewards further strengthened the ties these women had formed with the labor market. The financial benefits of women's work were shared across classes, as both working- and middle-class women felt that their household contributions were important to their families and their own sense of security.

African American women often expected that they would need to be primary or dual earners in their families. Tonya, an African American middle-class woman, always expected to be the primary earner in her family. Tonya and her husband met in college and married at a young age. While they both graduated from the same college with the same degree, it quickly became clear to both that he faced more barriers at work than she did. His career took a backseat to hers, and she became the primary breadwinner. They never discussed the possibility of Tonya leaving work. As we will see in chapter 5, white working-class families sometimes took the opposite path even when women substantially out-earned their husbands.

Women who grew up with very little money often started working at a young age. Seeing the financial benefits of their work for their families often convinced them to remain employed. Maritza, a working-class Latina, explained:

I always worked, since I was fifteen years. When I was fifteen, the first job that I had [was] at [my mom's factory]. My first paycheck—I said, "Wow." It felt good helping my mother. Because I was still, like, in high school. . . . So, I helped her, like, pay some of my tuition. I had braces. I paid for my braces.

Maritza was able to lighten the load for her mother and she felt the significance of her financial contribution to her family.

Gabra, a black middle-class woman, had always wanted to dance professionally, but an early injury sidelined her from her chosen career path. To make ends meet after her injury, she took a job as a computer tech because she had always been talented with computers and needed a job that provided health insurance. "[One of the firms] offered me a job on their support desk, which was very cool. So, I took it. I said, 'Oh hey, I need benefits, I need steady work.' It just started going up from there. I went from writing code to doing software applications to analyst work and from that I became a project manager," she said. While Gabra had originally expected to take the job temporarily to pay the bills and give her health benefits, the firm continued to offer her promotions and raises and she found herself becoming more and more invested in it. What started out as a temporary job became long-term employment for Gabra.

A woman's salary was not always a breadwinning salary for her family, but it often provided a needed sense of financial independence. Maria, a working-class Latina, grew up in a working-poor family and remembered that the "fire escape in the projects" where her family lived "was the refrigerator for a little while when we were younger." As a result, she said, "I wanted to make sure I always had food on the table for my kids." Her mother's and her own failed first marriages made her acutely aware of the importance of self-dependence. At the age of nineteen, Maria decided to leave her first husband because he became "very physical" with her, but she was working at a drugstore and had no benefits. A relative helped her find a position as a nurse's aide at a local hospital. After her divorce and subsequent remarriage, Maria worked her way up to being a unit clerk at the local hospital. While her husband's job (as a mechanic for an airline) provided the bulk of the family income, Maria's job was also financially significant to the family and it provided her with a safety net.

Having a job that provided a sense of financial independence, even if breadwinning responsibilities were shared, often increased women's ties to the labor market. Anya, a white middle-class woman, had a well-paying job as an auditor in a large corporation. She explained that this job gave her long-term financial security in a way that marriage, or a high-earning spouse, did not:

> I think it's very important to stand on your own two feet. It's not so much that I frown upon things supported by a man but, not only do they leave, which is fine, but they also die . . . even the best. You can have the best choice [in a man]. You don't know what's going to happen. And it's very important to be able to maintain, not that I have a certain lifestyle, but it's very important to me [to] maintain for myself and my son.

Anya reported that her job was "very challenging and the people [were] terrific," but most importantly it gave her the financial security that she desired.

IMPROVING FAMILY STATUS

Women's employment also had the ability to raise the family's status.[15] It often gave the family access to social and cultural capital that they might not have had otherwise. Steady workers explained that their jobs gave their families, particularly their children, access to more opportunities. While marriages tend to pair up people from similar class backgrounds, the study respondents who married high school sweethearts were particularly likely to have different levels of higher education. Since women are now more likely than men to earn a bachelor's degree, some of my respondents found themselves with bachelor's degrees in middle-class jobs while their husbands were in working-class jobs.[16] Women without bachelor's degrees also could find themselves in higher-status positions. Some of the working-class women worked in secretarial or other office positions (often termed pink-collar jobs), while their spouses were employed in more manual labor, blue-collar jobs. Women in pink-collar work often had access to status that their husbands in blue-collar jobs did not have.

Lori, a white middle-class woman, and her husband met in the twelfth grade and married soon after. They earned similar salaries, but Lori worked as a teacher and had a master's degree in early education while her husband worked as a firefighter and had only completed high school. Her educational background clearly established the family in the middle class in a way that his job as a firefighter (and his high school diploma) did not. As a teacher, Lori said, "[I have] a lot of children who come from, how can I put it nicely, low socioeconomical backgrounds, who don't understand how important an education is, and neither do their families." Her position as a teacher, however, gave her access to better schools for her children and to knowledge about what school districts she wanted her children to attend. "It also gives my children a better outlook: 'My mom's a teacher.' They know it's important," she said.

Researchers sometimes determine if couples live in dual-earner households based on the percentage of income that each spouse contributes. Couples are considered dual earners only if both spouses contribute close to half of the family income, regardless of whether both members work full time.[17] But this system ignores the other benefits, such as social capital, that can be brought to the family by the lower-earning spouse. In contrast, the women in my study reported that the benefits of their work went beyond the financial. Cassie's husband, Jim, earned 55 percent of the total family income compared to Cassie's 45 percent. While Jim was a blue-collar worker, a mechanic who finished his education when he earned his high school diploma, Cassie earned a master's degree in urban affairs. She worked at a local university and had access to university resources. Cassie and Jim often told people that he was an "engineer" who worked for the city, rather than admit he was a mechanic. Cassie explained, "[His job] is something I do not like. I mean, he is, like, embarrassed to say what he does. Nobody knows. . . . I was expecting more. . . . He says [that] I expected myself. I always expected more." Cassie's job, on the other hand, in the communications department of a local college, gave them a higher status and allowed them to pass off Jim's claim to work as a city engineer.

Middle-class women were not the only ones to field this sort of advantage, as working-class women in pink-collar jobs found unexpected access to middle-class capital. As a pink-collar employee in a large white-collar corporation, Irene, a working-class Latina, had access to middle-class networks for her children. "It's your environment that you are in. You grow up and you realize, the way you need to speak and the way you need to carry yourself," Irene said. She had access to internships for her children. "When [my son] gets out of school I make him get on the train and come to work with me. And he works in the office, just making copies, but he is not out hanging out on the street." She explained that her firm also had opportunities for her daughter, a college student:

> My daughter is majoring in economics and she wants to be a corporate attorney. I told her, "I will pay for your education and I will get you into a December internship in the company and I will get you into the legal department."

Irene's position in a white-collar firm, even though she was not a white-collar worker, gave her access to social networks that were out of reach for her husband in his job as a prison guard.

Maritza, a working-class Latina, and her husband each earned about $25,000 a year and lived in a split townhouse in a working-class neighborhood. In New York City, this income (and their occupations as a preschool teacher and a truck driver) put them solidly in the working class—a giant step up from the factory line poverty-level wages earned by their parents. As immigrant Latinos, their parents had often worked illegally and often earned less than half of the minimum wage.[18] In addition to her salary, Maritza's workplace also offered her free child care in the after-school programs it ran. Although her husband left high school before graduation, Maritza completed her high school diploma and was working toward "an associate's degree in early education," she said. Her status as a preschool teacher enhanced the family position, giving them entry into a more middle-class world. Her position was a stark contrast to her husband's hard days of manual labor, which were much more similar to their parents' factory work than her daily tasks.

SEARCHING FOR GOOD WORK

Early expectations of continual workforce participation led some women to pursue good work when they were unable to find it immediately upon their entry into the workforce. Some found that the fields they chose did not meet their expectations. Others moved into fields that were not as lucrative as they expected. But most of these women expected their fortunes to change and worked to achieve that goal.

While sociologists continue to find evidence that women are stuck in the "occupational ghettoes" of feminized fields, most of the steady workers expected freedom in their choice of work. Even those working in feminized occupations expected to have opportunities, although high expectations that good work could be found were most predominant in the middle class.[19] Middle-class women's high expectations were a form of privilege, encouraging them to gain important workforce skills, including higher education, and allowing them to delay consideration of work-family challenges. If the companies that hired them did not provide opportunities, they expected to find new work opportunities without much difficulty. Their expectations were not always the reality, but this did not diminish them. A small group of women held such strong expectations about the importance of work in their lives that they continued as steady workers without ever having found good work. Expecting continual work led women to view early obstacles as temporary rather than permanent setbacks, and it made pulling back from the workforce a more distant option than it was for other women.

Women who expected to find steady work often had clear expectations about what this work would be like—financially remunerative, personally and intellectually rewarding, and carrying the potential for future promotions and opportunities. Jasmine, a middle-class black woman who described herself as a "Jew with an African American father," started out as an optician, but, she said, "By the time I graduated [from college] I had already reached the pinnacle of my career. I was working in one of the top shops in Manhattan. . . . The next step would have been for me to open up my own shop." With no viable next step in sight, Jasmine decided that she needed to find a field that would give her more possibilities. She changed to real estate, quickly moving up the ranks and switching to ever-larger companies. Her confidence that better-paying work was around the corner allowed her to leave the field she had trained in for one that eventually led her to be one of the best-paid women in this study, earning more than $250,000 annually.

Some women felt certain that the work they aspired to would be available to them. Mary, a white middle-class woman, always expected that she would have an easy time finding a job in her chosen career. "There are always PR jobs around. Sometimes you settle. I mean, it is not always exactly ideal for what you want. But there are always PR jobs to be found," she explained. Mary experienced great success in public relations, rising to a high-profile position in a large, multinational corporation.

Expectations that multiple doors would be open to them gave women the confidence to search for better employment opportunities. These women kept going when others did not, fueled by optimism even in the face of obstacles. They also often had college educations, which opened many doors for them. Jodi, a white middle-class woman, explained that her first job wasn't great, which led her back to school for an advanced degree. She didn't know which advanced degree to get at first, but felt confident she would earn one and that it would provide positive employment opportunities:

> After I graduated from college, I had a first job with the city that I wasn't so crazy about. So I returned. So I went to graduate school, and that was out in California. And after about a semester there I decided to return to New York, and I was faced with this decision about what type of graduate degree I would get, so I— and it was either going to be psychology or social work, or education—so I picked education.

Jodi didn't like her first job or her first graduate school, but she didn't leave the workforce when she faced these roadblocks. She didn't change her expectations about the workforce because she believed other opportunities would be available.

Some women spent years in mundane work searching for a better opportunity. Cassie, a white middle-class woman, graduated from college and started work as a paralegal in a large law firm. The hours were long and she found the atmosphere of the law firm "just miserable," so Cassie decided to quit before she had found another job. She quickly found work in the public sector and spent ten years with the city government until she realized promotion opportunities were not opening up for her. She decided to move into a college admissions office because she was able to "see growth" there that she had not seen in her other job.

Asked about job satisfaction at her first job, Katya, a white middle-class woman, explained, "Compared to what I do right now, no [I didn't enjoy it]. I just worked." While she did not find much enjoyment in her first job—it was "just work" and nothing more—Katya never considered leaving the workplace. She found her current job much more satisfying and said, "I love it. I love the company and the work." Some women remained employed even when they didn't find satisfying work. Amanda, a white middle-class woman, explained, "I have a strong work ethic, so, I mean, I think work is important to me. But I'm, just, I'm still . . . I don't feel completely satisfied with what I'm doing." Amanda said she had recently left her job of seven years for a new position because "I wasn't really all that happy with what I was doing. I thought maybe, when I left, after the job I had seven years, I thought maybe I might find something different in a new company." While she remained unhappy in her new job, Amanda had not given up hope that she would find good work.

The expectation that work conditions might improve was not confined to the middle class. While some in the working class may have faced challenging work situations, many passionately believed work was an integral part of a woman's life and did not give up this belief, even in the face of significant challenges. Leslie, a working-class white woman, found the least success and satisfaction at work by far. Reflecting on her job, she sighed, "How I got to where I am, I've no idea. Just punishment." At the time of the interview, Leslie had been at her current job for almost fifteen years and, she recalled, "So my mom died the same day I started this job. I said, 'You would think I would look at signs that are coming at me' [chuckling]. It was like she was telling me, 'Don't do it.'" While Leslie's comments reflected how deeply unhappy she was at work, she had not given up hope that she would find good work someday. Her husband had decided to defer a job transfer so that Leslie could start taking college classes with the hope that she might one day earn a degree and "do research—biomedical research." Their combined commitment to her employment gave Leslie the enthusiasm she needed to stay on her chosen path.

Like Leslie, Claudia, a working-class Latina, had remained employed without good work for close to ten years. "I started applying for jobs and I got accepted at the Department of Social Services, and ever since, I've been stuck there," she said. She explained that she took the job because "it was paying more than what I was getting paid, because I was making only $8 an hour [at a student job], and so, this job was giving you a little bit more than $8 [it paid $10 per hour]. So, that is the main reason why I took it." Claudia's pink-collar position provided little status, a low salary (even after ten years of employment), few opportunities for advancement, and little personal satisfaction. Despite these challenges, Claudia had not left the workforce to stay at home with her son. Instead, she decided to go back to school to forge a new career path. She explained, "I hope that I will be a teacher later on. So, I am trying to [attend classes] at the same time, while working, paying for my degree in special education."

UNEXPECTEDLY REMAINING

Just as some women entered the workforce and remained in search of good work, others anticipated leaving the workforce, but never did. A minority of the steady workers, 28 percent, expected to work only occasionally when they entered the workforce. These women did not expect much more than poor opportunities for employment. They all expected to participate in the workforce for a time and then to leave to care for children full time. But great opportunities changed their minds. Most steadily working women who originally expected to be occasional workers described a watershed moment in their young adulthood, a point at which they realized they wanted to remain in the workforce. This was in contrast to those who expected to work continually and described a more linear progression toward steady work, rather than a turning point at which they actively decided to work full time.

For many, this moment came at a time when their prior workforce experiences coalesced into good work they found extremely rewarding. This realization made them change course and commit to staying in the workforce.

Irene, a Latina working-class woman, planned to be a secondary earner in her household and expected to stay at home with her children when they were very young. But she was working at a great job when she became pregnant at twenty-one:

> My husband said, look I don't think it's a good idea [for you to quit]. You have a great job. Why would you leave this job? And my mother was so against me leaving my job. . . . And you know when you go out to make a salary [no one] can tell [you] what to do. I can go out and buy whatever I want, because I earned it.

At the time of the interview, Irene had worked her way up from secretary to a position in the research analysis division of a multimillion-dollar corporation. She outearned her husband, a corrections officer. She believed that a transfer to a white-collar job was in her future when she completed the four-year college degree her corporation was paying for her to earn.

Like Irene, Cynthia, a white middle-class woman, expected to be a secondary earner in her family and to work part time when her children were young. As a young adult, she had no clear work plans. "I wasn't sure what I wanted to do. . . . I just wanted to go out and see what it was like to work," she said. When her high school hosted a career day, Cynthia interviewed with a law firm and was hired as a legal secretary. She spent some time in the secretarial pool and then became the primary secretary for two young attorneys. As they received promotions, so did Cynthia, and she moved out of the secretarial pool permanently, earning increases in salary and responsibility. Cynthia's unexpected successes prompted her to reevaluate her earlier expectations. She realized that she "really wanted to work." Once this became clear, Cynthia explained, when she married and had kids, "It didn't affect my work at all," because she wanted to stay with her employers and the opportunities they provided her. Once Cynthia had made her decision to be a steady worker, she never looked back. Eighteen years later, she was still with the firm and those two lawyers.

Sheila, a white middle-class woman, had only a high school diploma when she started working. Her father encouraged her to complete a computer programming certificate program at a local community college, and she soon found herself employed in a better job but still unsure about her future prospects. She found the work boring, but after several promotions her work changed, and so too did her feelings about staying in the workforce long term:

I was changing my roles, because there was programmer and then I was—my position, my title was changing all the time. But now my responsibilities were changing as well, so I acted more as the subject matter expert. I had offshore people working as programmers, so it was not just assigning work. It changed a little bit and started being more interesting.

The combination of the success in the form of a promotion and the satisfaction she experienced on the job convinced Sheila to remain employed full time after the birth of her two children.

The importance of work did not always become clear while women were in the labor market. For some, taking a maternity leave revealed the differences between working steadily and pulling back from the workforce. This pivotal moment showed how important work communities had become for some participants. Ellen, a white middle-class woman, had always expected her work would "help out" her stockbroker husband. She reasoned that as an elementary school teacher, she could leave the workforce when her children were young and go back once they were older. When her oldest son was born with autism, Ellen was convinced that leaving work was the only thing to do. She took her maternity leave just before summer vacation. By July, she knew she wanted to go back to work. She missed "her kids," that is, her students, and received great services from the city and state to help care for her son. Now a mother of three, Ellen busily balanced full-time work and caregiving and said she was amazed that she once thought she would prefer to work part time.

Regina, a white working-class woman, went to work for a law firm when she finished high school and found success at her job. She received several promotions and earned a higher salary than her husband, a blue-collar city worker. In light of this success, she decided to remain at work after having her two sons. But after many years with the firm, Regina and her husband discovered that their oldest son was autistic, and she left work. Regina was home for only a few months before she found a new position and returned to work full time. She explained, "I guess you do want to work, but you don't at the same time. . . . You get torn when you have children, but I definitely feel rewarded a lot of times. Like I have one client, they just love us. They call us for everything. And it feels so good to just be relied on." Regina's enjoyment of her work convinced her that she needed to try to weave her workforce participation with her son's unexpected needs.

Interest in paid work was particularly surprising to women who had never excelled in school. Many women associated workforce success with school success and, as we saw in chapter 3, when they had little success in high school, they had little hope that work would be any different. Jamie, a white working-class woman who didn't enjoy school, found her first job as an administrative assistant "really exciting. I mean, I would work very long hours, but, it was just great." Jamie enjoyed her job so much that it encouraged her to take chances and look for more challenging work. She left her first job after four years to seek out better opportunities:

> Because I was just there too long, I felt, and it was not going anywhere. There was no room for advancement at that point, so I needed something a little bit more challenging at that point, and an agency, like always, called you up and says there's this great opportunity, come and take a look.

This was a pivotal moment because Jamie's father and her first boss convinced her to find a new position that would expand her opportunities. It was her next job that gave Jamie the chance to start "learning about the business more, getting out there more, getting [her] feet wet." Jamie never revisited her decision to stay employed.

Family Support

For most of the steady workers, weaving work and family was part of their daily lives. The majority of the steady workers partnered with family members or hired child care providers to find ways to weave motherhood and work. One-third never had a child and felt relatively unburdened by these difficulties, although they too struggled to find enough time for their lives outside work. Ultimately, the women who found a balance reported fewer challenges to their workforce commitments than the other women.[20] They also were less likely to report being "mommy-tracked"— pushed to the side at work after bearing children—or experiencing financial losses after having children. Child care costs were often high. Even women who made six-figure salaries worried about the cost of work, but these women were better able to manage such costs. Working-class women often relied more heavily on family members or friends for child care, or sometimes worked split shifts with a spouse, so they each could be home with the kids. Regardless of how steady women managed child care, the effort that it took suggested that it was a task that was only done for good work—the job needed to be worth the task of finding and managing child care.

Women who worked steadily often relied on an egalitarian division of labor in the home. Tonya, an African American middle-class woman, felt that her husband was very equitable in this area. Because she was the higher earner, she often worked long hours and depended on her husband to help care for their household. But, she explained, he did not resent this division: "He is very responsible. He is a great father. He gets involved, like, we share all of the responsibilities. There is no, like, 'You did the cooking last night.' He does the cooking. He does everything [I could want him to do]." Irene, a working-class Latina, and her husband were both invested in her continued employment. To tend to their kids and keep their jobs, Irene explained, "He worked nights and I worked days. He had a shift where he would work sometimes from eleven o'clock at night to seven o'clock in the morning. So, I slept along with the kids. And that's the way we had to do it in order to balance out the babysitting."[21] While this arrangement was demanding, both Irene and her husband felt it was best for their family. Once their children were older, they started a tradition: "[We] go out every Friday night to dinner and it's like we've just met each other all over again," she said.

Families sometimes reorganized chores and hired help when they realized that a woman's steady workforce participation demanded greater household participation from all family members. Sheila, a white middle-class woman, realized that when she was at home during her maternity leave, no one recognized her contribution to the family. At home, she worried and was always, she said, "Stressed about that I'm not doing anything. I didn't feel that I'm being important, needed. I mean, except for the cleaning the house and doing all these things." Paid employment made her feel like she gave more to the family. "I'm more responsible—more dedicated to my family," she said, and it was more tangible to her family. When she went back to work, her husband realized how much work she had been doing at home. In addition to finding full-time day care for their children, they hired someone to clean the house every other week. They also divided the family chores—both became equally responsible for cooking, cleaning, and child care. The resources available to Sheila—and her middle-class contemporaries—sheltered her from some of the toughest strains of balancing work and family.

For a minority, husbands acted as the primary homemaker and caregiver. Gabra, an African American middle-class woman, explained that when she and her husband had their first child, "I made four times what [my husband] made, so it wasn't even a consideration. We couldn't live off his salary. So we just switched and he became a stay-at-home dad." Gabra and her husband switched because of her higher earning potential. While Gabra had originally expected to take the job temporarily to pay the bills and provide her health benefits, her firm continued to offer her promotions and her husband continued to be the primary caregiver. Vivian, a white middle-class woman, laughingly interrupted me when I began to ask who took care of a list of household chores: "My husband, everything." She explained that I didn't need to read my list because he performed the household chores.

Circumstances sometimes conspired to create the need for women's full-time paid work and men's work in the home. Helena's husband, an engineer, lost his job when he was being treated for cancer and thereafter was unable to find work in his chosen field. At the time of the interview, he worked in an unskilled security job, while

Helena, a middle-class white woman, held a prestigious position as the head of a medical school library. She explained that her husband did more of the "second shift"—a term sociologists use to describe household chores and child-rearing activities that are done after the first shift, paid work, is over—than she, but he did not resent her success or their gender-role reversal. "He always lets me shine. That's another good part about him. He is never jealous about it," she said.

When women could not find an egalitarian division of labor with a partner, they often sought external support for their child rearing. Relying on parents or paid child care was a common strategy for all steady workers, but it was particularly necessary for those whose husbands refused to participate in household or child care chores. Not all women found family support or the leverage to demand household participation from spouses, despite the importance of their income. While scholars have speculated that the importance of the income contribution changes the power dynamic in the household, other research finds that women who out-earn their husbands spend more time, not less, doing housework.[22]

Support from extended kin allowed women to face challenges at home while remaining employed full time. Maritza, a working-class Latina woman who was a preschool teacher, reported that her husband refused to participate in household activities. Despite her inability to find an egalitarian division of labor at home, Maritza said that she "never" considered not working. She managed to carve out a caregiving strategy—a combination of day care and her parents—and thought that her job was worth the extra effort. Maritza's ability to depend on her parents left her better able to withstand her husband's expectation that she be the sole caregiver and homemaker in the family.

Cynthia, a white middle-class woman, explained that while her husband supported her decision to work, he left almost all the household and child care work to her and that his chores focused on "the backyard. He maintains that. That's his thing." Cynthia noted that her husband did not actually do the outdoor work, but that he was responsible for hiring a "landscaper to come for lawn work." Like other women with a spouse reluctant to participate in the home, Cynthia came to rely on her mother as the primary caretaker of her children. Before her kids started school, Cynthia's mother "would watch them . . . for the whole day," and once they entered the school system, her mother watched the children after school. "Pretty much she gets them until about five o'clock, so from three to five every day, except for Wednesdays," she said. This level of support allowed Cynthia to decide to remain employed full time. Without it, she explained, "I probably wouldn't have went back to work [after my maternity leave]."

Familial resources buffered the financial and social costs of raising a child alone, allowing some women to weave single motherhood and a career.[23] When Aisha, an

African American middle-class woman, found out that she was pregnant midway through college, she considered dropping out to marry her daughter's father and raise her child. Instead, her parents and siblings helped with child care so she could finish her education. While early pregnancies are often considered a roadblock to future successes, family support prevented Aisha's pregnancy from derailing her career plans, and she completed college and an advanced degree. Eventually, using the skills she had gained through her education, Aisha found employment in a school system.

The ability to hire caregivers was also an important strategy for women who worked full time. This was particularly important—and more financially feasible—for the middle-class women who were less likely to live near a family member who could act as a surrogate while they and their spouses worked. The ability to hire paid caregivers also helped ease the time bind that women experienced in keeping job commitments while also completing their work in the home. This may explain, in part, why middle-class women, who were more likely to report a time strain, also were more likely to work—they had the financial means to acquire external help for their household and child care chores.

Full work days, commutes, and other daily pressures led most steady workers to wish for more time, but access to paid child care and paid household labor reduced these demands. Vivian, a middle-class white woman, explained that her husband was fully involved in the lives of their children and in household tasks. Still, though, they had "women coming in" to take care of the cleaning. When this was not possible, Vivian explained, "If it's not them, then it's myself and my kids." Paid workers helped ease the time crunch, and paid child care was an essential part of their daily lives when the children were young. Vivian and her husband lived too far from extended family and friends to rely on them for child care. In general, Vivian said, "I'm satisfied. . . . I think [my life's] pretty much in perfect condition now."

Consequences of Steady Work

Women who remained steadily employed reported feeling more financially secure than the women in the other two groups. Not only did working steadily give women more financial independence, but they also experienced an increased sense of financial security. Steady workforce participation gave some women a better chance to weather unexpected storms. The women who worked steadily reported feeling a time bind at a much higher level than the pulled-back women, although it was similar to what interrupted workers experienced. But these women also reported developing acceptable strategies with which to manage their time commitments. Overall, the vast majority of steady participants, 95 percent, were satisfied with their workforce participation.

HEDGING AGAINST THE UNEXPECTED

When life changed unexpectedly, women felt steady work eased the transition. While these women had long committed to their steady paths, they saw these occasions as further proof that they had chosen wisely, most often because they were able to curtail financial crises in the midst of family change.

Women who had been steady workers discussed the importance of these positions in times of great family change. Just under one-quarter of the steady workers unexpectedly found themselves the primary earner in their household for a time. This is not surprising; given the changing relationship between employers and employees, more and more employees find that the workplace does not provide the same safety net for them that was available to their parents.[24] Lindsey, a white middle-class woman, became the primary earner when her husband injured himself in an on-the-job accident while working in a public sanitation department. After his injury, he found work at a deli as an hourly employee, but Lindsey's job as the project manager of a large corporate sales department became the primary family income. Unexpected illnesses forced women who had worked steadily, but considered their work secondary or the helping portion of their family income, to reconsider their economic role. Jamie's husband started taking multiple days off from work and then finally quit his job. "Because he began getting these ailments. And . . . I found out later on it was anxiety. But he ended up, like, quitting his job, and I was the moneymaker." Jamie, a white working-class woman, felt ill prepared for this role, but her salary staved off financial devastation and she managed to continue paying their mortgage.

Unexpected health challenges can rock the foundation of a marriage, and most bankruptcies in this country can be traced to the costs of a family illness.[25] When Anya, a white middle-class woman, gave birth to her son, she was tested for HIV as part of a battery of tests the hospital ran. She learned she was HIV positive and that her husband had had an affair, contracted the disease, and passed it to her. As she faced their illnesses and her suddenly rocky marriage, her job (which was always the higher income) became increasingly important to her. At first, Anya thought she might divorce her husband and that she would need her salary to support herself and her son. Instead, the couple decided to remain together, and Anya felt that he was "trying very hard." Her salary became the family's primary source of income when his health deteriorated, forcing him to scale back his work commitments. Anya and her husband found themselves very financially dependent on each other—even their health insurance was interdependent. "I have great medical insurance and bad prescription insurance. He has great prescription insurance and bad medical insurance," she said. In the ensuing years, her husband became the primary caretaker for their son while Anya increased her attachment to the labor market.

Although health challenges and individual losses often felt like very personal battles, these are precisely the types of roadblocks that face millions of dual-earner couples every year.[26] And women's employment is often the primary safety net for families in financial trouble.[27] Lori, a white middle-class woman, explained that her husband was "on medical leave" at the time of our interview. When he went to the doctor's office to complain about chest pain, "They found an irregular heartbeat—led to other things and now he's been out [of work], about a month. He just had surgery on his sinus cavity. So, we're just waiting—he actually is at the medical office today." As a firefighter, he was entitled to benefits from the city and a reduced salary while on medical leave. But because he was not injured on the job, when he returned to work it would be at a reduced salary, as he would only be allowed on light-duty work, per city policies for people with heart conditions. Light-duty work meant a lower pay-scale position and no overtime. Lori's job became ever more crucial to the family as they realized the long-term consequences of her husband's illness.

EXPANDED MARITAL OPTIONS

The steady workers also felt that full-time workforce participation expanded their marital options. Like the majority of women in America, the majority of respondents married at some point before the age of thirty-five. Of the women who were steadily employed, twenty-seven were currently married (including several who had divorced and remarried), two were divorced, and ten never married.[28] Of the twelve who were not married, half were involved with steady boyfriends and half were not currently involved with anyone. Almost all hoped for a relationship, but also expressed concerns about the challenges that come with marriage and partnerships. Although some scholarship suggests marriage would be financially beneficial for women, particularly working-class women, many of my respondents worried that marriage would bring new challenges.[29] For most of the single women, concerns about the costs of divorce and the availability of acceptable partners fueled their reluctance to marry.

As most steady workers had always expected to work, they experienced little financial pressure to marry. While conservative scholars traditionally focus on how women's better career choices might lead to increased divorce rates, they have not highlighted that these same options may also prevent women from making poor marital choices that would eventually lead to divorce. The single women in this study clearly drew this conclusion. Jodi, a white middle-class woman, explained that while her boyfriend wanted to get married, she didn't "feel that comfortable" about the possibility. She worried: "There is a lot of risk involved, you know, like a divorce, and, ah, you really open yourself up to being liable for things." For now, Jodi was content to remain single, supporting herself in a high-level position in a large education system. Similarly, Aisha, a black middle-class woman, worried about the costs of marriage. When she became pregnant, she said, "I really had to grow into parenthood and adulthood, and I don't think that [my baby's father] took it at all as seriously as I did." She decided against rushing into a marriage that her child's father was not prepared to handle. At the time of our interview, Aisha had been in a long-term relationship with another man. While she hoped that marriage would be "in [her] very near future," she had taken this relationship very slowly because she worried about the emotional and financial costs of divorce for both her and her daughter.

Many of the unmarried women explained that they were single because of the lack of an acceptable partner. A few, like Jasmine, a black middle-class woman, suggested that their single status was linked to a fast-paced job and an inability to find similarly positioned men. Anie, an Asian American middle-class woman, said, "It's hard to find someone who is as educated as yourself or from the same background and economic situation." Both women believed that men in their dating pools were not looking for women who were as educated or as committed to the workforce as they were. Given the choice between their current workplace commitments and the expectations of the available pool of men, neither was willing to pull back from work to make herself more marriageable.

WORK-FAMILY CONFLICT

The steady workers consistently felt they could not find enough time in their days to do everything they wanted. A few felt frustrated that their husbands did not contribute more in the household. While more than 90 percent of the steady women were in jobs that they enjoyed and wanted to keep and an additional 5 percent wanted to find such jobs and remain in the workforce, most wanted more flexibility. But unlike the women we will meet in the next chapter, for these women the time strains were not strong enough to drive them from the workforce, and for the most part they managed to find ways to partner with family members or hire external support to allow them to remain steadily employed.

Deciding to have both children and a career left some women anticipating a time strain. These women wanted to have children and wanted spouses who would participate fully in the raising of these children. Helena, a white middle-class woman, explained that she knew "you have to juggle or you have to make a choice: career or child." In other words, the only options were to juggle child and career or to choose between them. She decided to "have arrangements to have both." In the end, "it was really, really tough" to have both, although she was glad she did. Asked how much leisure time she thought she had in a week, Helena replied, "I don't think anybody has leisure." Helena's husband's participation in the home helped to ease the burden.

Women whose mothers had not worked often felt the difference in time available to them quite keenly. Meredith, an Asian American middle-class woman, estimated that she had "maybe like ten, twelve hours" of leisure time each week and that her husband had "about the same, depending, but sometimes around the same or sometimes less." On the other hand, she thought her mother had about "twenty or thirty" leisure hours a week and that her father had "probably about the same, 'cause we always had dinner together." She explained that they had "much less" leisure time than her parents: "I think today, we have to work a lot harder."[30] Meredith and her husband used a combination of day care and hired nannies to ease child care burdens, but still found themselves pressed for time.

Women who wanted to have an egalitarian division of labor and were unable to find one with their husband delayed having children. Lauren, an African American woman, felt reluctant to add children when her life and her husband's life were already so busy:

We do not have time together. We work so much. I am in school, he is in school. We both work. I have a business and I work and he works a lot of hours also. I just think we do not have time together. I think part is I feel like I am always under the microscope because his family lives here. His parents live here.

Not only did both Lauren and her husband work and go to school, they also lived with his parents and provided care for them. Providing care for older family members is a growing demand on working men and women, particularly women.[31] The possibility of adding child care to the demands of elder care weighed heavily on Lauren.

Conclusion

Historically, men's labor market participation rates increase as they finish school and remain at similarly high levels until they retire.[32] While it is presumed that men will be employed continually, women's employment has been expected (and subsequently proved) to be less steady, typically dropping slightly when women enter their childbearing years.[33] Women's continued employment is almost never assumed—it is, in fact, almost always questioned, and questioned throughout women's lives. Law professor and work-family scholar Joan C. Williams notes every woman brings the possibility of motherhood (and its attendant possible challenges) with her to inter-views and promotions.[34] Because women must work harder to attain steady work and must fight off challenges to their continued full-time employment, all of my steadily working respondents, including working-class women, attributed a significant amount of meaning to their continued employment. Although a job may simply be a job for working-class men, it is rarely just a job for a woman, particularly when it is a steady job—or series of jobs—she has held throughout her life.[35] Women who worked steadily saw their continued employed as an accomplishment they had achieved, often despite challenges.

Just under half of all participants were steady workers, making them the largest group by far. This pattern is part of a larger trend over the last thirty years in which women's workforce participation has come to more closely resemble men's. It was easiest for participants to work steadily if continual work had been anticipated. Women who expected this gained more job skills, had more confidence about work, and were more reluctant to turn toward home. This was not true of the other work patterns, as we will see in the next two chapters.

Middle-class women were privileged not only in their origins (as we saw in chapter 3) but also in their workforce opportunities. They had access to jobs that were more remu-nerative and had higher status than those of their working-class peers. They had greater job flexibility, job skills, and a stronger belief that better jobs could be found, which led them to seek out new work when they were unhappy with their jobs. They faced greater time challenges than their working-class contemporaries did, however, when it came to balancing work and family. Middle-class women were more likely to be employed as salaried workers, of whom longer work hours were expected. The increase in work hours over the last thirty years has been experienced primarily by the middle and upper-middle class, who also have more flexibility in their jobs. Challenges were also tempered because middle-class women had the financial resources to absorb the cost of child care through day care or a private nanny.

Working-class women had more constrained options. Even those who sought steady work did so because they believed it would enhance their lives, not because they believed good work would be easily found. However, working-class women were not without resources. They were more likely to live near relatives who could help provide child care—women of all classes continue to express a preference for relatives to care for children if both parents work.[36] Working-class families often operate with the expectation that extended family members will provide support.[37] This is particularly true for black families, who often provide both monetary and nonmonetary support to members of their community.[38] Working-class women also partnered with husbands to devise time-sharing strategies so that a spouse would always be at home with their children.

The experiences that led women to remain steady workers were fairly similar across classes. The steady workers found good work that wasn't necessarily confined to the middle class. Women who worked in pink-collar jobs found much to appreciate at work when their work was appreciated. Even those working low-wage jobs derived rewards from them, as long as they found stability, benefits, and respect at work. Certainly not all women had such positive experiences—the women in the next two chapters often did not. And women did face roadblocks at work and lived with daily frustrations created by employers or coworkers. But most remained because they believed work could be enjoyable and was an important part of adult life.

5

PULLING BACK

Divergent Routes to Similar Pathways

ANGELA, THE WHITE working-class woman who, in chapter 3, explained that she could never be a "major career woman," found she enjoyed working more than she expected. She enrolled in a community college hoping to earn an associate's degree, but after several classroom frustrations she withdrew to attend a secretarial program. "Part of me always felt that I gypped myself for not at least having an associate's degree, rather than just getting a certificate," she told me. Yet she also believed that she made the most of the degree she did earn: "You know I did well with it." Angela joined a large investment bank as a junior secretary and was promoted several times until she reached the highest level for a secretary in the company. Angela hadn't expected to go so far, but said, "The head of the group, this very intimidating female, her secretary was leaving and she came over to me out of nowhere and she said, 'You're working for me in one week.'" In this new position, Angela "definitely felt intelligent. I felt like I had stuff to offer. I liked that kind of environment; I liked working for the bankers."

When Angela had her first child, and then her second, she decided not to leave work as she had originally planned. Her husband made some changes to his schedule so he could be home with their children more and her parents also pitched in. But three years after Angela received her big promotion, the investment bank was bought out. Although she had worked her way up, as a result of the buyout she was demoted to a floater position. "The [merged] investment bank was so big that sometimes you would be put in positions where people really didn't know you. So it's like I started all over. I was very uncomfortable because I would walk in in the morning—and I know what I'm doing—and they would talk to you like, 'You're a temp and the phone is here and you can answer it.'"

Angela, a mother of two at the time, decided to leave the workforce. Her father had recently become unable to care for her children, and it seemed like too much effort to find a replacement for him so she could stay in a job with an employer who treated her like "a dingbat that doesn't know how to answer a phone." Angela's husband had been quite active in child care and housework, but he was forced to find a second job when she left work, so his participation at home dramatically declined.

Donatella, a white middle-class woman who earned both a law degree and an MBA, said that being a career woman was the only type of employment she ever considered. "I guess I'd have to say that I wanted to be a professional, and I guess I was raised where professionals were doctors and lawyers and pharmacists and some kind of a scholar in that arena," she said. Even in graduate school, Donatella was clearly on the fast track to a career as she juggled her MBA program with her already-busy course schedule in law school. After earning both her graduate degrees during a three-year period in which she lived away from New York City, Donatella moved back to the city confident she would find a plum position. She stayed two years with her first law firm and more than five with the second, where she made great strides working ninety hours a week and earning a six-figure salary. Over the same period she met her husband, another "workaholic," and they had two children. After the birth of their second child, Donatella switched to legal consulting to reduce work-family conflict but still felt guilty because she saw too little of her children. "I busted my butt to get my higher degrees, and I did them with honors, and I'm proud of it, and I was finally at a [place in my] career where there were people beneath me, and I was in a good place, and I just didn't want to give that up," she said.

Donatella's mother had been providing child care for her toddler son, but when Donatella became pregnant with her second child, her mother decided watching two children would be "just too much for her." Donatella hired a nanny and changed jobs yet again to reduce work-family conflict. When she attempted to engage her husband in the household work, they had "some serious fights" about child rearing: "He is, um, obsessed with work. When he's involved, he needs to be dragged out." When she found herself unable to engage her husband more fully in rearing their children, Donatella decided to leave a job that she enjoyed to stay at home full time.

While steady workers described similar factors across classes that led to their continued employment, the pulled-back women left work for disparate reasons across classes. Angela and Donatella had different experiences at work, different financial resources, and different levels of support from their spouses, yet both left the workplace. Angela had enjoyed her work but left when she was demoted and became discouraged by institutional changes. Donatella loved her job and did not want to give it up—she switched firms four times in an attempt to resolve work-family conflict. At home, Angela's husband's working-class job left them with few financial resources and unpaid bills, but he spent time with his family. Donatella's husband's high-rolling tech firm gave them financial comforts most people could only imagine, yet his presence in the family was minimal at best. Donatella was clearly "home alone," but Angela was not—her husband played an active role in raising their children. Donatella had access to the security of a husband's high earnings, but Angela did not—her husband's salary barely covered their bills, even when her parents helped out by putting some money into their mortgage.

Unlike the steady workers, the pulled-back women were almost evenly divided between middle-class women who all had expected to be continual workers and working-class women who all had expected to be occasional workers. This raises some important questions: Why did the women who expected to be occasional workers go on to do just that? Why did the women who expected to be continual workers pull back? Did they face larger roadblocks? Have less family support? Were they less committed to the workplace than they originally thought?

Why Pull Back?

Cultural expectations about women's work have changed dramatically over the last thirty years. While it was once common for women to pull back from work, the majority of women now work, including the majority of mothers with young children and women in their thirties and forties, like the study participants. Why, then, did a full third of the participants pull back? It is important to note that these women did not necessarily leave the workforce entirely. Fifty-seven percent continued to work part time and a handful worked as many as twenty hours a week, but they had significantly altered how they worked and the hours they devoted to work. Unlike their steady or interrupted peers, all the pulled-back women were married with children.

The media commonly frames women's workforce departures in two ways: as the fulfillment of their devotion to family or as the natural position for a married woman with a well-off husband. But there are fundamental problems with these approaches. The majority of respondents did not pull back in response to long-held traditional beliefs. Close to half had expected to spend the majority of their adult lives at work, and although a slight majority did expect to be occasional workers, very few of these women actually left the workforce upon the birth of a child.

Instead, like Angela, many entered the labor market and found good work that caused them, at least temporarily, to set aside their original expectations. They left only when work ultimately disappointed them. Only one-quarter of pulled-back women, a tenth of the larger sample, pulled back because they believed only a mother could adequately care for children.

While the cultural expectations of motherhood remain strong, they did not drive workforce participation for the majority of women, or even for the majority of women who left the workforce. In fact, my findings suggest that devotions to family and work often develop in response to women's positions within this framework.[1] Women who expected to be continual workers, but due to circumstances pulled back from the workforce, became more devoted to family commitments after they had pulled back from the workforce. Family devotion did not lead them home, but being home increased their devotion to family.

It is quite tempting, then, to point to the women's marital status and the presence of children to explain their retreat from the workforce. But this facile answer cannot explain why only four of the twenty-three women left the workforce after the birth of a child nor why many continued to work for years after their children were born. Further complicating the picture, the majority of the steady and interrupted women were also married with children. Moreover, there was a diverse range of incomes among the pulled-back women (in fact, there were poorer women in this group than in the steady group).

A well-off spouse cannot explain the pathways of the women who pulled back from work. While many of the women described themselves as "lucky" to be able to pull back, many others had no sense of economic security. Although half of these women lived in middle- or even upper-middle-class families, the other half lived in working-class or working-poor families, and two received government assistance. Sociologist Pamela Stone argues, "Husbands' income was certainly a necessary condition of [affluent women] quitting," but "not a sufficient one."[2] She goes on to contend that "how much husbands earned enabled their wives to quit," although women's decisions to leave work were likely related to job satisfaction and family support, not motivated by their husbands' salaries. However, I find that how much husbands earned per se was less important than the presence of a spouse, even if his earnings were below the poverty line. The presence of a spouse creates a socially acceptable environment in which to leave work, even if it does not provide the financial security with which to do so.

Class differences were pronounced in the pulled-back women's access to child care, family support, and job satisfaction. Although researchers often argue that middle-class women's workforce retreat can illuminate why women of different classes retreat, I find that white and Asian middle-class women left the workforce for different reasons than their white and Latina working-class contemporaries.[3] The one-quarter of women who left the workforce with traditional ideologies in mind were the exception, and both working- and middle-class women did so. The pulled-back women's experiences varied along the intersection of race and class, as white and Asian middle-class women were more likely to leave work in the face of a time squeeze caused by inflexible work demands and a similarly busy spouse, while working-class white and Latina women left work when they felt unappreciated, un-rewarded, and even demeaned by employers. No African American women pulled back from the workforce.

When working-class and working-poor women left the workforce, their families keenly felt the loss of their income. Most families responded by sending the husband out to work a second job or by having him work longer hours at his current job. While middle-class families had larger financial cushions, they, too, felt the pinch when someone left the workforce. Unlike their steady peers, women who pulled back from the workforce felt unprepared for crises and sometimes found themselves unable to return to the workforce if a family emergency demanded that they do so.

Lacking Solutions to Work-Family Conflict in the Middle Class

Why did some middle-class women pull back from work at a time when others were joining an expanding workforce, particularly when they had expected to be continual workers and spent years training for employment in prestigious jobs?[4] The women who expected to be continual workers but ultimately pulled back were entirely from the middle class and mostly white; no middle-class Latina women pulled back (no black women pulled back in either class). These women faced multiple challenges. They faced pressure at home, where they did not have a spouse who was willing to contribute to the daily household work and child care. They faced pressure at work, where full-time often meant working fifty or sixty hours a week instead of forty.[5] These were women who wanted to work. They enjoyed their work, and often its demands, particularly before they had children. They also enjoyed their time at home and felt rewarded when children came, expecting that they could find a way to weave the two together. Most middle-class women left the workforce when they could not negotiate the time bind between work and family. All struggled to reduce work-family conflict before leaving. Most switched jobs at least once, negotiated with current employers, implored parents to help, and attempted to reengage their husbands. Only when these attempts failed did they leave.

THE TIME BIND

At first, middle-class women found work enjoyable, as they had expected. Amy, an Asian American middle-class woman, explained that she took her first job in graphic design, because the pay was "unheard of" at $60 an hour. She also felt confident in this move, because she "knew that if [she] didn't like the job, [she] could always quit later and look for something else while [she was] working." Amy's success in her field led to several rapid promotions, as her high-flying career quickly moved her away from her working-class origins to, in Amy's words, the "upper-middle class" by the age of twenty-five.

But for these women who hoped to work continually, the good times did not last.[6] The time demands on these women's schedules made long-term goals of workforce participation seem unbelievably naive to them in retrospect. Most worked more than forty hours a week and experienced little help at home. Although many of the women expressed frustration that their husbands did not participate more fully in family life, they did not blame their husbands for their absence. Nor did the majority blame the institutions for which they worked.[7] Instead, most framed their workforce participation decisions as personal choices that came in response to inexorable demands. Most believed that these institutional norms could not be changed to accommodate a changing labor force, made up of more women who had both family and work responsibilities. They also accepted that their husband's career would come first.

Even privileged women often felt unable to directly confront the time bind challenges. Tracy, a white middle-class lawyer, left her firm after it became clear to her they would not provide job flexibility. It also became clear that her husband wouldn't either. She explained that for her husband, a lawyer, putting children before work was not a consideration. While Tracy's husband refused to act in a way that would have helped Tracy keep her full-time position, he did not vocally oppose her workforce participation. While they had met at work right after they both graduated law school and Tracy received a promotion there before he did, it was her job that was considered secondary. She switched jobs several times, working as a law clerk for a judge and full time from home for a company as their counsel, but ultimately pulled back to part-time work. Tracy pulled back from the workforce because it became clear to her that he would not. She explained, "Men have a very different perspective" about raising children:

> That's how I think men are. [Putting children before work] just is not even a thought. Like work is the first thing first, and then if [he] can help out with the kids... whereas the kids are always the first thing for me and then the work is after.

Barbara, a white middle-class woman, did not leave work immediately after having her daughter or her twins. Instead, she left when work and family challenges combined to prove too challenging. First, a corporate takeover created much longer and less flexible hours, then her husband started his own business and worked close to eighty hours a week, then her father fell ill and her mother stopped acting as her primary caregiver. In the face of overwhelming work-family conflict and with her mother no longer able to act as a surrogate, Barbara withdrew from the labor market. Barbara contributed approximately 43 percent of the total family income when she decided to leave the workforce and she also lost her ability to qualify for the company's pension plan, as she left the company one year before she would have qualified. Barbara's decision to leave was financially hard on the family, and she considered them now more middle class than upper-middle class, as they were in the days when they were a two-income family.

An absent spouse placed an extreme burden on working mothers. Amy, a middle-class Asian American, explained that her husband was always working: "He has this obsessive personality about him. So once he gets involved in something, he just zones in and just forgets about everything else." His focus on work meant that other responsibilities were ignored, even before he and Amy had their daughter: "He just, he loves his computer. I know he makes a living with it, but he also likes to read so much about technology and he also does stuff on his own, so he reads all this stuff. But I feel like he's glued to the screen and there are times I get so angry with him about that." Amy was left holding down the fort.

SARAH: Okay. Now I'm going to ask you some questions about the division of labor in the household. I'm going to read you a list . . .

AMY [INTERRUPTING]: Me, me, me.

SARAH: Exactly. I read you the list, [and] you tell me if you think you're primarily responsible, or do you think your husband is primarily responsible, or do you think . . .

AMY [INTERRUPTING AGAIN]: You're wasting your time. It's just Amy, Amy, Amy.

Amy's husband considered her solely responsible for all household and child care duties and had since they had married when she was still working full time.

Even women who did not work extreme hours could find their own work ties strained when their husbands had very long days. Janice, a white middle-class woman, grew up in a working-class family, and she met and married her middle-class Chilean husband, Eric, the foreman for a construction firm. After her marriage, Janice found a job at a national shipping company and worked her way up in the company hierarchy. When she became pregnant with her first child, she considered leaving work, but "I actually liked my job enough that I didn't want to lose it. I felt, what are the chances of finding another job like that?" Janice remained full time after the birth of her second child, again deciding not to leave work. But her husband's work schedule made it difficult for him to help at home, because he "wasn't making it home in time to watch them." Then things got worse, and "his hours changed after a whole bunch of different situations at his job," after which he found a new position that was a three-hour drive from their home. Eric's continued absence left Janice alone at home and she decided to switch to a part-time position.

The time bind came not only from resistant husbands but also from inflexible workplaces. Despite the changing nature of work-family lives, institutions continue to remain resistant to new family forms.[8] Most of the middle-class women who expected to be continual workers did not experience workforce challenges that made them contemplate leaving work until after having a child. Once a child was born, however, workforce stresses were compounded by new time demands and women's desires to spend more time at home with their family.[9] Donatella explained that while she had loved her job as a lawyer, after she had her first son, she began to despise the concept of billable hours. For lawyers, billable hours are the only hours that matter at the end of the day, and Donatella saw these hours as being in direct competition with her son for her attention:

> I just hated that every minute of my day had to be accounted for, and I just found that it always stressed me out; did I get my billable in? Did I put in enough billable for the day? Did I, oh, did I forget to document that, or, if you were out and you didn't have your billable sheets with you, and then . . . I just found it so stressful.

ATTEMPTS TO REMAIN FULL TIME

Most middle-class women expected that the workforce and their families would accommodate their desires to be full-time workers and involved parents.[10] Most had grown up in middle-class families and had faced little resistance to their life goals. They grew up in an era in which women's entrance into the labor market seemed unremarkable and unstoppable. When they faced challenges, therefore, most of the women who expected to be continual workers made changes to their workforce participation in an attempt to remain in the labor market full time.

Almost all of the white and Asian middle-class women who expected to be continual workforce participants made multiple attempts to rearrange their work and family options before they left the workforce. Before Donatella, who started this chapter, left the workforce, she left her law firm for a consulting company in an attempt to find work with better hours. She had hoped that this would allow her to reduce work-family conflict, but even though the hours were better, she still found herself torn between the two:

> [The consulting job] was closer to a nine-to-five kind of job. The difference was that it required a lot of networking and client interaction, so oftentimes I might have to go out to dinner with clients, or there would be some kind of function that I would have to attend in the evening, and that kind of, you know, took me away from my family, so it became complicated as well.

Donatella found that although she could not find flexibility, she was very reluctant to leave work.

> And my husband was very supportive to whatever I wanted to do. He's like, if you want to quit, just quit. But I couldn't quit. I don't know why—I could not quit. I think part of it was that I just didn't want to give up what I had; another part of it was that I didn't want to go into something that was unknown to me. And it was suffocating in a way.

Unable to reconcile her work-family conflict, Donatella eventually left work completely.

Institutions were often blind to women's need to spend time with their families. Right out of law school, Tracy, a white middle-class woman, took a legal position that she believed would allow her to weave her work and family life. Because the position focused on research, she wouldn't have to go to court or to do a lot of networking for a big firm. Her responsibilities included work "on the computer, research, writing and reading the reports, briefs and stuff like that. . . . You just do your job and that's it." But the job proved less flexible than she expected. When she was pregnant with her second child, she wanted to find a way to work fewer hours. She was working close to sixty hours and wanted to work forty, still full time, but not for a lawyer. She explained:

> When I was on maternity leave, I really did think I was going to go right back full time. But then . . . they said that they wanted me to take the job to be promoted and I said no, that I wanted to go less, not more.

Tracy wanted more flexibility, but instead she was offered a promotion that would demand more hours, not fewer. While Tracy attempted to negotiate with her company so she could remain full time, they told her that she needed to take the promotion or look for other work. She worked for additional firms before deciding that part-time work was the only viable solution for her family.

Rearranging schedules and depending on family members allowed some women to extend their employment. Barbara, a white middle-class woman, stayed employed after having her first child and even after her company went through a merger. The new company didn't treat its employees well and her hours dramatically increased; after the merger, "it was not a good place to work." But Barbara decided to keep going, enlisting her mother to care for her daughter. "The first four months were a blur. I mean, I don't even know how I got through it. My mother helped me tremendously." It was not until her father became ill and her mother unavailable for child care that Barbara could no longer manage the dual demands of her sixty- to seventy-hour week and her husband's eighty hours and absence from the home.

When Amy, a middle-class Asian American, became pregnant, she and her husband agreed that she would take over his full-time marketing firm and work full time from home, while he would find a position in a larger company. They hoped that his new job would provide more financial stability and her new job would give Amy the flexibility she desired when she had their daughter. "He decided to go out and work for somebody else. So I took over [the company]. So we switched." This switch didn't work out quite as anticipated, as Amy found herself home alone with a new baby and a time-consuming job, with a husband who worked very long hours and did not participate in household work. After a year, she pulled back to part-time work.

When Work Disappoints, Home Beckons the Working Class

It may seem easier to explain the pathways of the working-class women who expected to pull back; they didn't expect to be continual workers; they sought less education and job skills and left work as they had expected.[11] Yet the women who expected to be occasional workers were, like Angela, often surprised to find good work, at least in their early years of employment. The majority spent more years in the workforce than they had anticipated and many returned part time in later years. Few left the workforce when they first had a child, or even after the birth of a second child.

None of them, however, experienced long-lasting good work. Instead, they generally found what appeared to be good work, followed by a significant challenge at work or at home, after which they pulled back from the workforce. Building on Nelson and Smith, I considered a job "bad work" if it could not be full time or year round, if it was unstable, if there were no benefits, if it lacked flexibility, was rarely interesting or enjoyable, was disrespected, was poorly paid, or did not offer the opportunity for advancement.[12] Although Nelson and Smith use a more static concept of employment, I suggest that a job can turn from good work into bad work, most often during management shifts that change workers' responsibilities, benefits, level of control over their work or schedule, or their sense that their work is respected by their employers. Unlike their pulled-back contemporaries who expected to be continual workers, the pulled-back workers who expected to be occasional workers did not make multiple attempts to stay. Most of the occasionally oriented women left "bad work," as table 5.1. notes. The majority of these women experienced a change from good work to bad work, at which point they left because they held low expectations about future workforce possibilities. When they faced a roadblock, it let them know that they were correct to have expected to be occasional workers who would not find much success in the labor market.[13] For these women, challenges were a sign that it was time to pull back from work.

WHEN GOOD WORK TURNS BAD

While some of the steady workers faced surprising challenges, many of the pulled-back workers had unexpectedly positive experiences at first. Many, like Angela, successfully and happily wove full-time work and family for a period of time. It is often assumed that working-class women pull back because they find their work less interesting or less rewarding, yet most of these women enjoyed their work at first. It was only when jobs turned into bad work—with reduced flexibility, new tasks, and disrespectful managers—that women began to draw back.

When Alyssa, a white working-class woman, "got a job as a manager of a clothing store in the mall," she had finally found a job she loved. She was paid well and "liked the clothes that we sold and got a discount on them [laughter]. There really were no minuses other than the fact that the company went out of business." Alyssa's early triumphs led her to discard her expectation that she would leave work after having her children. Instead, she continued to search for work that would be as satisfying as that first position. From there, Alyssa found a position working at a gym, which she left "when [she] decided to go back to school for the medical coding":

> Actually I was going to school and working there at the same time but then I finished the medical coding and I got a job in a doctor's office. Let's see . . . why did I decide to do that? Because that is when Clinton was first becoming president and they had all those ideas about health care reform and about how the health care industry was going to be the biggest boom ever.

Although Alyssa had originally expected to stay at home, she spent many years searching for good employment and gaining better training in order to find a career

TABLE 5.1.

WORK PATHWAYS BY PRESENCE OF GOOD WORK AND FAMILY SUPPORT (n = 80)

Work Circumstances	Steady (n = 39) (%)	Pulled Back (n = 23) (%)	Interrupted (n = 18) (%)
Good work (n = 49)	90	35	33
Family support (n = 40)	69	26	39

that would be long lasting. Even when the workforce appeared to offer promise, challenges were ever present. Alyssa had expected that her work in the medical field would prove to be an important career change, but the work was less interesting than she had expected. While it had once seemed filled with potential for advancement, she began to wonder if her job was a dead end. She thought "somebody up in the management [was] stupid," because every time she applied for promotion, she was denied. Several years after the birth of her second son, Alyssa decided to pull back to part-time work.

Valerie, a white working-class woman, didn't know what she wanted to do when she graduated from high school. She worked for two different law firms as a secretary, but didn't particularly enjoy the work. "I just decided to take—I actually took the test to be a police officer. So, I guess I just thought I wanted to do it. And, I don't know why—security. My father worked for the city, I guess like that, and then from that list, the sheriff's office were looking for people, and they called me. I went on an interview. It seemed different, so I took that job." Valerie stayed at the job after the birth of her children, finding it more interesting than she had expected work could be. When she injured herself on the job, Valerie left the workforce entirely, even though her injury would not have prevented a return to work at a later date. "I worked there about two or three years, and then I fell and hurt my back, and I stopped working. I haven't worked since then." Although her injury occurred on the job, she received no worker's compensation. Valerie felt that this was just par for the course for employers and decided to stay at home with her children, rather than risk another injury at a new job or fight for benefits.

Some women never had the opportunity to experience good work. Challenges at work were particularly hard for low-wage workers to overcome. Gina, a white working-poor woman, worked as a "mail girl" at a mortgage company after she dropped out of high school. With little education and no other work experience, Gina believed there were no better options out there in the workplace (and she very well may have been right). However, she did think that marriage provided her with a better option. Discussing her decision to leave her job at the mortgage firm, Gina emphasized the role of marriage:

SARAH: Now, what made you decide to leave your job?

GINA: Because I was getting married.

SARAH: Okay, and what happened then? [Pause] Did you start working somewhere else, or did you have children, or did you do something else?

GINA: No, I just stayed at home.

SARAH: And have you been employed outside of the home since your marriage?

GINA: No.

While Gina's decision to leave the workforce when she married gave her freedom from a job she found onerous, it did not give her the financial security she had hoped for. Her husband found it difficult to find steady work and, at the time of the interview, they were living with their two children in public housing and relying on state assistance.

FAMILY CHALLENGES

While the middle-class women who pulled back faced a time bind, the working-class women were more likely to report that their spouses participated in the household chores. When working-class women faced challenges at home, it was most often from spouses and other family members who believed that their workforce participation was not worthwhile—not worth the cost of child care or the burden it placed on extended kin. Researchers have speculated that paid work buys more influence for working-class women, because these women need to work and the family is more likely to recognize the importance of their financial contribution.[14] On the other hand, middle-class women's work is more likely to be able to support the family and it may be more likely recognized as a legitimate type of work.[15] A small number of working-class women faced charges that their earnings were so insignificant that they were not worth the time spent away from the family. Working-class women, then, may not be immune to the charge that their workforce participation is selfish.

Although most working-class women found support at home, some faced claims that their work was self-indulgent; class did not protect these women from the charge that a woman's paid employment was for herself and not for her family. Jackie's husband objected to her employment after Jackie, a white working-class woman, had their first child, because he felt her income could not make up for the loss of her presence at home.

I was working in the city. My last job I worked for [a publishing company as a secretary], and then I became a mother. So I was pregnant with my first one and then I had to leave, because my husband was like, "You're not going to work. It doesn't pay." I didn't make $100,000 where I had to keep my career, where I was making big money.

She returned to work several years later, after the birth of her third son, when her mother-in-law joined the household. She hoped that this time she would be able to keep her job. Jackie enjoyed the time out of the household and the "little bit of money" that it brought her. But her husband had strong objections to her employment and at the time of our interview, she gave her two weeks' notice. "My husband wants me to stay home and raise this little guy [pointing to the toddler]. So he really feels that— my mother-in-law lives with me, but it's better that the baby knows me. Because he knows her better than he knows me, because I'm never at home." While Jackie repeatedly attempted to have her husband recognize her right to work outside of the home, he continued to challenge this belief, letting her know that he would "rather just stay an extra hour at work to make the money there [that she was] making."

When women's work was considered secondary, it made steady workforce participation difficult. Dana, a white working-class woman, explained that she did jobs that people didn't expect her to keep: "I think the jobs that I'd gone for are women's jobs, like I've never branched out to—like I went for the telephone operator, I went for the receptionist. Those are mainly women's jobs. I mean at least that's how I see it." This was how her husband saw it as well, and he expected her to be the one who pulled back from the workforce, despite their similar earnings.

Even when women held higher-status jobs than their husbands, the worthiness of their work continued to be judged. Linda, a white working-class woman, left work as a pharmacist after she discovered that she was pregnant with her second child. While she out-earned her husband three to one, they never discussed the possibility that he, a truck driver for a shipping company, might stay at home. Linda also enjoyed her work more than her husband did, explaining that her work was valued by "the customers that came in. You had their respect right from the start." While Linda and her husband did not discuss the possibility that he leave the workplace, they did discuss that Linda's job as a pharmacist "was not the same as being a doctor," not the type of career that demanded a full-time commitment. Both she and her husband felt, as she said, "The prospect of making money is great when you have a big family, but I still think your kids are young once and that's what I'm here for them." Since Linda's job as a pharmacist was not, in her words, "a real career," like a doctor's, she could sacrifice it, and the family would make financial sacrifices, so she could stay home with their children.

In addition to active challenges to their workforce participation, working-class women were also more dependent on fragile networks as they cobbled together child care for their children. The loss of a caretaker was particularly difficult for working-class women, who often could not afford paid child care and relied on extended kin for help.[16] Jill found a job through a high school job program at the age of sixteen and stayed with the same company until she was twenty-five, long after the birth of her first two children. Of that job, Jill said, "I loved it. The company closed— that is why I stopped working. Otherwise I would probably still be working." When the plant closed, Jill thought about looking for a new position, but then her father died. After her father's death, Jill's mother decided that she was no longer up to acting as the caregiver for Jill's children. Jill had earned a good salary at the plant, but after it closed, she knew she would be back to earning minimum wage, because she had few marketable skills. Between her lack of skills and the loss of the free child care, continued workforce participation seemed unattainable.

Traditional Expectations Fulfilled

Just under a quarter of the pulled-back women—about one in ten of the total group of respondents—pulled back because they held strong beliefs that only mothers could care for children. These women were both working class and middle class, and their work experiences did not appear to influence their workforce participation decisions. While work and family experiences appeared far more important than traditional gender ideologies in the lives of most of the study participants, the women in this group were the exception.[17]

Megan, a white working-class woman, spent several years working for a fashion company before she branched out to work for herself. "I enjoyed [it] because of the flexibility and it was more money and I could make my own hours. It wasn't so structured, so it worked out well for me. And then what happened was, I found out that I was expecting my daughter. I did it for as long as I could and then as close to my due date. When pregnancy came to the end that was it for me." At the time Megan left the workforce, she out-earned her husband four to one; she earned $80,000 annually to his $20,000. Megan's husband worked as a food distribution receiver for a hospital and she said that he hated his job—"If he could change tomorrow he would." Megan said:

I knew I wasn't going to leave my newborn. Unfortunately my husband's parents had passed away at a very young age—both of them—as well [as mine]. So I knew that I was going to be at home—that wasn't even a question. I couldn't afford to put them in child care, day care, and that wasn't something that we had wanted to do.

Megan's explanation did not take into consideration the possibility that her husband, who was unhappily employed and making much less than she was, might leave his job. Further questioning found that Megan and her husband never discussed the possibility that he might leave the workforce instead of her. In Megan's case, financial needs not only did not influence her work decision, they also did not influence who left work.

Isabel, a working-poor Latina, and her husband met when they were thirteen. "We were boy and girlfriend—together since we were thirteen. So we married when we were twenty." Isabel finished her high school diploma before they married, but her husband completed only middle school before he went to work. They struggled financially. "We are very financially stressed, like always, because we married too young. We have been—[in] trouble—financial problems all the time." Despite their financial challenges, Isabel decided to stay home with their son when she unexpectedly became pregnant.

> SARAH: How do you think having your son affected your life?
> ISABEL: I couldn't realize my dreams to work—and my professional dreams. But I think that was the most. Because in fact he gave me more. . . . So when I had my baby I was so happy. So I could leave anything else.
> SARAH: So, why did you decide to not work after you had your son?
> ISABEL: Because I saw my husband's uncle and aunt, they were working, and their kids, they were not like very emotional, the same way as my husband that my mother-in-law didn't work. So I put it inside and I thought it was more valuable for me to stay at home and taking care of myself—of my baby.

Isabel decided that caring for her son was very important and could be done best by her, rather than by a relative or paid caregiver.

Paula, a white working-class woman, had a job she loved when she met and married her husband, but after she became pregnant, she knew she "had to quit." She was not working, she said, "Because I have the children. . . . I think spending time with my children and the experiences: seeing them develop and the milestones that they [take]. You know, their first walking and crawling and their first words." She explained, "I think, I think it's very hard to stay home. I think people really underestimate the mother, quite frankly."

Komal, an Asian American upper-middle-class woman, expected to have a traditional family structure after she left her parents' home. It took her longer than expected to find a husband and, in the meantime, she earned a college degree and a medical degree and completed her residency training. But she always knew that her schooling and employment would not continue once she married:

> I was not expected to work, no. Just to get an education, that was the expectation. . . . Well yes, my parents only wanted me to get married. And then it's your husband's responsibility [to decide if you should work].

Komal's husband, a lawyer, was easily able to provide for the family with his six-figure salary. While Komal's husband's high earning power allowed her security in her traditional family structure, she planned to stay at home regardless of his salary. Others who indicated that staying at home was predetermined, like Megan, Paula, and Isabel, faced great economic hardship after leaving work.

The Consequences of Pulling Back

What did it mean to pull back from the workforce? The majority did not leave work entirely. They returned to part-time work within a few years or never left entirely, simply reducing their hours after they left their full-time positions. The women worked part time for a combination of reasons, including financial ones, personal fulfillment, and social interaction. Social class did not appear to influence women's part-time employment: half of those who returned to part-time work were middle class, as were half of those who remained at home. Working-class women who pulled back faced financial challenges even if they did return to work, and their husbands often worked a second job. Middle-class women's husbands did not work second jobs, but they did work increased hours at their first jobs. Across classes, the women reported husbands were less available than they would have liked. The majority of pulled-back women faced surprising financial challenges regardless of social class.

PART-TIME WORK

The majority of the women spent only a few years at home before reentering the workforce on a part-time basis. The women attributed reentrances to the family's need for money. While this was certainly a contributing factor, women returned to work for a complex set of reasons, including financial need, personal independence, and the desire to build social ties outside of the home. Once in the workforce part time, the women again struggled with work-family conflict and the demands of the workforce. While they often found this easier than they had as full-time workers, they too faced many challenges.

WHY GO BACK PART TIME?

Many women remembered both the good and the bad of their workforce experiences and returned part time in the hope of finding good work in a less demanding position that would still provide valuable income for their families. Women often found many aspects of work satisfying and were glad when they returned to part-time work. Many decided to go back to work part time because they missed the companionship and the responsibilities. Part-time work was valued for its schedule flexibility and for the opportunity to interact with people outside of the home—something that many women missed when they left work.

When asked what she liked about her part-time job as a pharmacist, Linda, a white working-class woman, provided a long list. When asked what she didn't like, she replied:

> I don't know. . . . I don't know what I don't like about it—I like everything about where I work. I guess maybe just being away from home, like think[ing] about it, if I get a chance to think about it. I can't wait to get out of this house. Just to have some time to myself. You know, just dress up and get out [chuckling]. . . . I think working gives you a higher self-esteem, like you're qualified to do something that you're good at. When you know you're good at it, it's rewarding; and that you're able to help somebody and you know what you're talking about.

While the rewards of work are generally attributed to full-time work, women who returned to work part time often spoke of recapturing self-esteem and a sense of identity or purpose. Sociologist Pamela Stone notes that these attributes are often greatly missed by women who leave employment.

Many working-class women returned to part-time jobs that were less prestigious, and they described finding both frustrations and triumphs at work. Jackie, a white working-class woman, had given notice at her part-time job at a big box store when we met. Her work was often frustrating because the company had strict rules for its employees and she often felt disrespected by the management, who didn't recognize the challenges of her job and that "dealing with the public is very difficult." But she knew that she was skilled at her job and that elderly customers always sought her out for help in the aisles. Her job validated her pride in her people skills and it also provided her with financial relief. "It gives me a sense of independence and it makes me feel good because I feel like I'm making money. But other than that, because when you're at home, and you're a mom, you depend on your husband to support you and you feel like, oh, you got to ask him for every little thing."

Like Jackie, many women experienced ups and downs in the workforce, and women who worked in low-wage jobs rarely felt only negatively about their workforce experience. Isabel, a working-class Latina, worked part time cleaning houses. She explained that she did hard work: "Sometimes I get so tired. I think it's very exhausting with the job." Despite the physical challenges, Isabel said, "It's nice because I'm alone, doing my job. So I got air conditioning in the summer and everything; it's okay. I do my job. It's hard work, but, I mean, I'm happy with what I do."

Even though Isabel told me that many people might not respect her work, she enjoyed the independence it gave her. Her work was "rewarding," as were workforce conditions that allowed her "to do whatever [she] want[ed] to do."

Women's desire to go back to work mixed with their concerns about how to care for a family. Angela, a white working-class woman, wanted to go back to work at a job that would allow her to remain at home with her children. Her mother had worked for a medical transcription service for over ten years, and she knew that this position had allowed her mother great flexibility in her schedule. She wanted to find the same type of flexibility, but it took her three years to reenter the labor market, because jobs like these were hard to come by:

> I had called [the recruiter] for about three years straight. I did actually want to get the job before I did, it just never worked out. And she finally called me and says: "I'll give you a shot." And it worked out. Thank God because it's definitely good.

The flexibility of this job allowed her to care for her children and earn some extra money.

After the birth of her second child, Margaret, a white middle-class woman, found part time work at a day care center. She enjoyed the work so much that she decided to earn a bachelor's degree and then worked toward her master's in order to become a teacher. When we met, she was the only pulled-back worker who planned to return to the workforce full time after two decades of part time or no employment. She explained that both her desire to teach and her husband's support would allow her to go back to work: "I kind of had . . . expectations that I would marry someone who, if I wanted to go to work, he would help out in the house, which my husband does. He took a vital role. I mean, if I got up for the two o'clock feeding, he got up for the four o'clock feed."

Women's expectations about what would happen when they left work after the birth of a child often did not match reality. Some women had anticipated that staying at home would be more fulfilling than they ultimately found it to be. Dana, a white working-class woman, explained that she took maternity leave and left her company after she had her first child. But she did not stay out of the workforce for long. "I was home for three weeks, then I got a job with [a local hospital] on the switchboard, a telephone operator." She hadn't expected to go back to work part time only fifteen weeks after her daughter was born. "And the minute they put her in my arms, I [said,] 'I can't leave her.' And my mother said, 'I knew it. I knew you weren't going to do it.' So that was that." Except that wasn't that, as Dana quickly grew lonely at home and asked her mother to help with child care, so she could return to work part time.

Some women did not leave work in the first place; they simply switched from full-time to part-time work. Alyssa, a white working-class woman, had a flexible schedule and her employer, a medical billing company, allowed her to switch to part-time work several years after she had her second child. "I love my hours. That's really the key thing. I'm able to work around the children's school schedule and otherwise I wouldn't be able to be there." Alyssa's family lived out of state, so she was unable to rely on them for child care, which meant that a flexible work schedule was critical for her continued employment.

Not everyone had successful transitions back to work.[18] Time out of the workforce meant that even if financial need did drive a woman to work, she might not have success finding employment. Anita, a white working-class woman, spent close to fifteen years not employed, raising her three children. When her husband found out that he had a potentially life-threatening cancer, Anita needed to go back to work, but she reported:

Nobody will hire me. I looked. I tell you, I looked, but you know. [Pause.] What [did] I want? I [didn't want] to have somebody else raising my kids. I chose to stay home with my kids. . . . So where does that leave the stay-at-home mom who has hardly any computer skills?

It had left Anita unable to find work other than part-time seasonal work during the holidays. While financial need drove Anita back toward work, she was unable to find anyone willing to hire someone with such limited work experience. She found some work one year during the holiday season in a clothing store, but nothing more permanent.

While not all women faced the challenges Anita did, most found returning to work less straightforward than they had hoped. When I met with Grace, a white working-class woman, she had had several interviews, but hadn't found a job yet. She believed it would be impossible to break back into her former career as a paralegal and law student. After ten years at home and five children, Grace continued to feel conflicted about her decision to pull back.

I definitely have lower self-esteem since I have been home. I feel that my role is devalued. When my husband comes home and he is like, "Okay, I need to unwind now," [I feel like,] "You had your chance to unwind between work and here. You had a ride home. You get to listen to the radio. I have not left work in the last seven days, so please take them and give me twenty minutes to just go for a walk." It is hard to have time for myself, and I feel just the whole world is devalued.

Attempts to return from part-time to full-time work were also constrained by family demands. Monique, a working-class Latina, recounted, "I don't know if I told you that I had gotten myself a full-time job, and that didn't work out after two days. It was like—my husband was like, "This is Saturday. I mean, you know, the kids—[he asked me,] 'Who has to go here?' And [he complained,] 'The other one is a handful.'" Her husband also proved reluctant to alter his schedule to accommodate the kids' needs: "And the kids have a dentist appointment, which I kept canceling because I couldn't take them, and then he couldn't take them, and the weekends they're not open. It was just—it was madness." In the face of these pressures, Monique decided that full-time work was unrealistic.

STRAINS OF PULLING BACK

Living in a family in which only one person is employed full time can cause financial strain, and the majority of the women I interviewed had spouses who worked long hours, either at one job, in the case of the middle-class women, or two or three jobs, in some working-class families. Both middle- and working-class women faced similar problems once they had left work: long hours for their spouses and financial challenges.

MIDDLE-CLASS HUSBANDS: LONG HOURS AND
SOMETIMES FRAGILE FINANCES

Middle-class women often expected that their husbands would work long hours. It was just part of the job—in fact, it had been part of their jobs, too, until they had pulled back from the workforce.[19] But these hours often caused husbands to be less attentive to their families than the women thought was desirable. Some of the middle-class women whose husbands worked long hours had contemplated divorce, because they felt alone. Middle-class families also were surprised to face financial challenges once an income was lost. Middle-class families were not immune to fierce financial pressures, and the loss of one income placed some families in financial distress. Events that occur in most lives—unexpected illness, rising health care costs, job loss, college expenses, and more—all contributed to making middle-class families more fragile.[20]

Long hours were part of the job for most middle-class husbands, and the husbands of women who had left work often worked even longer hours in an attempt to make up for a wife's lost wages. Barbara, a white middle-class woman, married a man who owned his own delivery business, which meant extremely long hours. She explained that her husband worked very long hours: "he will be leaving at one o'clock in the morning" typically, and return in the late afternoon, generally by 6 P.M. or so. Long hours were coupled with jobs that required travel. Janice, a white middle-class woman, was married to a foreman for a construction firm. Her husband had a college degree and often managed large-scale projects with hundreds of workers. Janice felt that he pushed himself to work ever-longer hours because, she said, "He always has this desire to go, like after a while he gets like an itch to go further. He always wants to do better and make more money. He never stays in one place too long." When large construction projects in their Connecticut town vanished, he moved on to a new company located three hours away. For the last three years, they had had a commuting relationship, in which they lived apart four days a week. Janice explained, "[My husband] is renting an apartment down here and he comes on weekends. Friday he watches [our kids], Saturday, Sunday he is at the house."

Middle-class women reckoned that husbands who worked long hours were part of the trade-off for financial stability. But when long hours did not bring lucrative salaries, women faced both a mostly absent spouse and the added stress of financial instability. Nicole, a white middle-class woman, argued with her husband, telling him:

> "You know, you are there until like seven at night, eight o'clock or nine, and what are they paying you? So I get frustrated too, Dave. You are not a banker; you are not a lawyer." But I understand him wanting to do well at his job. But there are times I am frustrated [with] just, like, the fact that it is nonprofit. I am like, "How long are you going to be there?"

Nicole felt that her husband had earned his MBA and should be earning a commensurate salary. After a period of unemployment, Dave decided to leave the business world and to become the chief financial officer of a nonprofit organization. His decision to work at a nonprofit jeopardized Nicole's decision to pull back, because the family lost first her salary and then a third of his salary, making it challenging to meet mortgage payments. Although Dave had greater responsibility and longer hours in his new job, he made less money. Nicole worried that they were no longer adequately saving for college and that both Dave's income and his time at home with their sons had decreased.

For the most part, middle-class women did not worry about unexpected scenarios that could cause the family to struggle financially.[21] But some women did worry that if their husbands lost their jobs or were injured or ill, the family would face real financial troubles. Tracy, a white middle-class woman, explained that even though her family income was over $200,000 annually, she felt financially insecure. "Like if, God forbid—and my husband does have disability insurance. But I've just seen so many people, if you get ill and stuff like that, that I would say if something happened to him. I mean he does have a lot of insurance on him, but still." The family had a significant amount of debt from their college and graduate schools and a sizable mortgage.

Before Margaret, a white middle-class woman, finished her education and returned to part-time work, her husband faced a serious illness. "He had a heart problem. . . . That kind of stressed us out." His job, as a low-level manager for the city's sanitation department, was secure, but they wondered how they would manage without his full salary if his illness forced him to leave work. He hated his job, because, Margaret said, "He feels stagnated. He's tired of doing it. It's twenty-seven years [that he's worked there]. He's had enough. . . . He's tired. He's sick to death of doing it. It was too long to do it." But when he became ill, they worried that he would not be able to keep this disliked job, because the family could not afford to lose it or to lose the health insurance it provided to him and the rest of the family.

WORKING-CLASS HUSBANDS: MULTIPLE JOBS AND FINANCIAL DISTRESS

If middle-class families struggled, how did working-class families manage to survive with only one primary earner? Workers, particularly those in the working class, face "a long-term squeeze" in which the average wages for men have dropped, health insurance has become less available, hours at work have grown, and pensions for the retired have become less accessible.[22] When working-class and working-poor women pulled back, then, their families keenly felt the loss of their income. Most families responded by sending the husband out to work a second job or to work longer hours at his current job.

Women's part-time work did not pay well enough to decrease the financial strains on the family.[23] When she returned to part-time work, Angela worked fifteen hours a week, a third of the hours she had previously worked, but she earned one-sixth of her original salary. Angela's husband, Joe, worked eight to five, five days a week as an administrative assistant for an electric company. Joe had worked as an electrician when he was younger, but an off-the-job accident made it impossible to continue doing such physically taxing work. His company moved him to an administrative position, which was lower paying and had no possibility for promotion. As a side job, Angela said, "He works—he does electrical work for—it's like a friend. He's a friend but he owns an electrical business." Although his company no longer allowed him to do this work for them, his friend paid him off the books, giving Joe an extra twenty to forty hours of work a month, depending on the season.

Despite his efforts, and Angela's return to part-time work, the family was often under financial strain:

We'll want more money [chuckling]. I don't think money could make people happy, but it has to help, obviously. And I think that's—if I had to look forward and see what would make me the happiest, is to be able to do our jobs but not to the point where we're stressed out. Because what I'm feeling now is, you work so hard and at the end of the month you're still, like, scrounging, trying to figure out, okay, wait, this came up and you've got to pay this.

Despite Angela's part-time position and her husband's second job, the family felt that they were an unexpected bill away from bankruptcy.

A second job was the most common way to increase income levels in families in which husbands were the primary breadwinners. For many spouses, this meant time spent in less desirable work. Valerie's husband, Tim, worked long hours. She said, "He probably works sixty to seventy hours a week." Tim enjoyed his full-time job as a firefighter, but not the part-time work he did as an electrician. "He loves the firefighting one. The electrician one, not so much. It's okay, but he loves the fire department." Like her husband, Valerie's father had also been a firefighter. Although he did not work a second job, Valerie, a white working-class woman, felt that her parents had been better off than she and her husband were: "I think they had more money than us." Her husband's salary did not go as far, Valerie believed, as her father's once did. She believed that they were less prepared to deal with the "little things. . . . Like something comes up and we wish we had more money."

Leaving work made some women feel like they experienced a downward class shift. Although Monique, a working-class Latina, had a bachelor's degree, the middle class moved out of reach after she left her job as a teacher to work part time as a secretary in the doctor's office where her husband worked. To make ends meet, she said, "[My husband] works from Monday to Friday in the doctor's office [as a low-level technician] and that's, I would say, forty-plus hours. Then he does the real estate [showing houses for a company], not every day. It depends whether it's a good market or not. But in a week, you know, I would say it's about twenty hours at least in the real estate."

Husbands also increased hours in their first job to compensate for the loss of the wife's income. Dana, a white working-class woman, married Bill, who worked full time for the city in the boiler room. It was a hot and dirty job, but it paid well and they hoped it would allow them to one day retire in Florida. Until that day, however, they had multiple bills to pay and numerous financial problems. Several years before our interview, they had accumulated debt on their "credit cards mounting up to about $34,000." To pay off their debt, Bill worked extended overtime at his job. The money was good, but it meant, Dana said, "He works [full time plus both days] every other weekend. He works—he'll work twelve days straight, for two days off. So he doesn't have enough [free time with his family]."

It was not uncommon for the husbands of the working-class women to work long hours in jobs that they did not enjoy. Linda, a white working-class woman, explained that her husband worked "say about maybe fifty" hours a week for UPS. Her husband worked nights, the "9:45 [P.M.] to 11 A.M. schedule." Although Linda's husband hated his job and "[couldn't] wait to retire," he worked long shifts to earn the overtime necessary so that their sons could attend parochial school. The local public schools were not highly rated by the school board, so Linda and her husband decided that their eldest should attend the local Catholic school. "My son's going into high school. And he's going into a Catholic high school . . . so he's been going through public school all the way up to this time, so now it's Catholic [school] and now, you know, another bill."

A husband's full-time employment did not prevent families from facing great financial jeopardy, particularly when the husband earned the minimum wage. Gina, a white working-class woman, and her family lived on the brink of poverty. Her husband worked "five days a week" for the "city of New York." But without a high school diploma, Arthur was only able to find minimum-wage work as a janitor for a housing project. Their family of five survived in a two-bedroom apartment in the subsidized housing projects for which he worked.²⁴ Jill's husband also worked full time and weekends. Like her father, Jill's husband drove a truck, but his earnings couldn't pay the rent—they could barely cover the other bills, and Jill, a white working-class woman, often wished "he could make more money [because] things [were] a little tough." Jill and her family relied on her parents for financial support. After she and her husband had their first child, her parents invited her family to live in the top two floors of the family's shared home, because her parents believed, as Jill said, "[We] will probably never be able to afford a house [of our own] for the kids. We live basically check to check."

Many of these families operated without a safety net and were unprepared for a husband's job loss or ill health. Isabel's husband worked as a driver. "He delivers groceries for a company." But it wasn't always easy for him to keep his job. "He was a dishwasher first. He worked for a restaurant. Then he was a cook—and then he didn't like it—and then he went to be a driver for a dealership." Because her husband disliked working for a boss, they decided to open a small business, using all of their savings. But the business failed and, Isabel explained, "Yeah, it was bad. Financially it was all our savings, they were gone. And emotionally it was hard because my husband want[ed] to do something . . . and we couldn't." Isabel reasoned that structural changes were partly responsible for the tough times her family faced:

I think I have [it] worse [than my parents], because my mother with elementary school [education], she could get a good job. Now you have to be [a] college-educated person to get a good job, a good paid job.

With a high school education for Isabel and a middle school education for her husband, there were few work opportunities. Even once she returned to work, they always worried about the next challenge, which would potentially throw the family into financial ruin. Isabel explained that she always worried about her family's health: "I mean if we get sick we have to pay very high bills."

Conclusion

Conventional wisdom suggests that financial resources are an important factor in women's workforce participation, allowing middle-class women to leave work while forcing working-class women to remain employed. Yet the lives of the pulled-back respondents show that financial resources are an unreliable predictor of whether or not women worked, because many other factors played a more important role than money did in determining women's continued workforce participation. The women in the pulled-back category were more likely to be white than their contemporaries and none of the African American women were in this category. Moreover, only white and Asian middle-class women pulled back, while only white and Latina working-class women did so. This suggests that race intersected with class in women's continued workforce participation, but further research is necessary with a larger and more racially diverse sample.

While social class did not drive women to remain in the workforce, class did play a significant role in how women pulled back from the workforce because it influenced how they perceived full-time work, their workforce experiences, and the level of resources available to navigate challenging experiences at work and at home. Unlike the steady workers, the women who pulled back trod diverse paths to similar results. Working-class and middle-class women pulled back from the workforce in equal numbers, suggesting that pulling back was not reserved for the middle class. But working-and middle-class women left work for very different reasons. The middle-class women had greater resources and finances, and they gained high levels of education, made strides in careers, and often found good work. But they faced greater time demands at work and, at times, more pressure to provide intensive caregiving to their children.[25] The working-class women, on the other hand, had fewer resources, were more dependent on unstable care networks, were more likely to experience bad work, and faced criticism that their work wasn't worth the effort of finding child care. The working-class women were often surprised by how much they liked work at first and most were employed full time longer than they had anticipated. But they often lacked the education, training, and social networks to find well-paid work.[26] Moreover, working-class women also found it more difficult to find jobs with flexibility or the hours they wanted.[27] They were also more likely to find themselves at the mercy of their employer's timetable, unable to take time off work to care for a sick child without consequences. Looking at the women's pathways, rather than their current work status, allows us to see how class influenced the process through which women left work.

6

A LIFE INTERRUPTED

Cumulative Disadvantages Disrupt Plans

LIFE IS OFTEN thought to be a predictable journey. A woman obtains an education, finds a job, gets married (more often than not), has a child (again, more often than not), makes a decision about staying in or leaving the workforce, and life goes on.[1] But what happens when life takes an unexpected turn? The lives of the interrupted workers were filled with the unanticipated. In this chapter, I explore why some women were unable to follow a stable path. These women's lives were defined by financial challenges and family instability, and their work was defined by hard choices and few options. Despite these challenges, the women did not give up their attempts to have a more stable pathway and they continued to plan and search for new and better beginnings.

In this chapter, we meet women who followed a very different pathway than the women from the other two groups. They did not weave work and family together or strain to manage work-family conflict. They did not pull back from the workforce, changing their ties to work. Instead, the women struggled to gain a foothold in one world or the other and found they could not. Given their lack of success at home or at work, they turned to the other, only to find they could not gain traction there either. This left them constantly unbalanced, searching for tenure in an unstable world. The interrupted workers often felt denied access to the decisions that the pulled-back and steady workers made. They were much more likely than the other women to have experienced a dramatic change in their family structure, such as a divorce or the death of a parent or spouse. Unlike their pulled-back and steady contemporaries, interrupted workers reported facing a lack of family support at a key moment in their lives.[2] They were also more likely to find only bad work options than the other women.[3] Sociologist Glen Elder's research suggests that disruptive events can have long-term negative effects, forever altering one's life course.[4] Just over half hoped to work continually, while the other half hoped to work only occasionally, but all found these dreams out of reach.

Bad work, caregiving responsibilities, unstable relationships, and health challenges disrupted women's work pathways. Almost all of the interrupted workers were working class and working poor.[5] When employed, they worked as line cooks, retail clerks, bartenders, administrative aides, and in other low-paying jobs. Class played an important role in these women's lives, as they often gained little education and few workforce skills before they entered the labor market and then found only jobs that were not financially rewarding. Women employed in the service sector, as the majority of the interrupted workers were, faced the greatest challenges on the job: "persistently low wages, little or no job security and few if any benefits."[6] Family emergencies caused long withdrawals from work, and the return to work that followed rarely was as lucrative as the work they had left behind.[7] Personal illness was also very disruptive, as the interrupted women had few resources on which they could depend. Their illnesses often resulted in job loss, which could cause temporary homelessness or continued economic struggle.

The experiences of the interrupted workers most directly contradict the assumption that financial needs keep working-class women employed, as most of the women had great financial needs, yet this did not keep them steadily employed. Even when women who were the sole financial supporters of themselves and their families found employment in the service sector, they rarely stayed employed for long, because the working conditions were so poor.

While the messy reality of women's lives means that neither working steadily nor pulling back is as exclusive and final a situation as the conventional wisdom implies, there remains a cultural expectation that women will make some sort of choice about whether and how to work. The interrupted women entered and left work within a broader cultural framework that expects women to choose either work or home, and they attempted to meet these expectations again and again. The interrupted workers did not hold different expectations than their steady or pulled-back counterparts: they expected to work either continually or occasionally and made repeated attempts to achieve their goals, even when they might have left work or abandoned an unsuccessful marriage. Their repeated attempts to follow their chosen path suggest that shared cultural values about the importance of work and motherhood in women's lives shape their decisions about work and home even in the face of significant structural constraints, such as poor work opportunities and a lack of family resources.

When Nothing Goes as Planned

Why were the women in the interrupted group unable to follow a steadier path? The majority of interrupted workers were working poor or working class, and they faced poorer work conditions and fewer familial resources than their steady and pulled-back counterparts. The interrupted women were more likely than other women to have family members with poor health and to experience poor working conditions, volatile relationships (including abusive spouses), and their own health strains. Regardless of an interrupted worker's early expectations, she often had very little choice about how and when to work.

Three of five interrupted workers expected to work continually when they entered the labor market. Two of five interrupted workers expected they would be occasionally employed throughout their adult lives. While both groups ended up on the same pathway, they approached the labor market quite differently, particularly at first. Those who expected to work continually found themselves pushed out of the workforce by poor job opportunities, family demands, and health concerns, while those who expected to stay at home found themselves unable to achieve and maintain a traditional family. Lacking the family resources to remain at home, they felt pushed back to work with very few workforce skills and little to no experience.

WANTING STEADY PARTICIPATION, BUT FINDING BAD WORK

The majority of the interrupted workers grew up in working-class or working-poor homes and, despite their interest in working, most never gained the skills necessary to find good work.[8] More than half of the interrupted workers desperately wanted to work, but they simply did not have the cultural or social capital necessary to gain access to educational opportunities. Education levels remain a key indicator of socioeconomic status, influencing labor force participation levels, income, occupational status, wealth, and workforce conditions.[9] Less than one-fifth had attended college, which is to be expected given that the majority grew up in working-class or working-poor families.[10] More dramatically, two-thirds of the interrupted workers had less than a high school education.[11] Americans who do not finish high school are often the poorest among us and have life chances measurably lower than their better-educated peers.[12] Women without diplomas often work in minimum-wage jobs that have few economic or social rewards.[13] The type of work available to them is often in harsh environments in which neither they nor the work that they do are respected.

The majority of the interrupted workers' concerns about the workplace stemmed not from the type of work, but from the conditions—little flexibility, low pay, and job insecurity—and the treatment—a lack of respect for their work and themselves—they received at work.[14] The interrupted workers described skillfully handling unruly customers, recalcitrant coworkers, and the overall demands of their work. But many explained that their employers had little regard for the work they did and expressed disdain for them personally, a level of disdain which the interrupted workers perceived was reserved for people like them—people who worked in jobs that weren't considered worthwhile.[15] The women described facing contempt for their jobs both at work, from employers and the public, and at home, from their spouses and friends. While half of the interrupted workers expected to be continual workers, they found themselves repeatedly disappointed by bad work opportunities. In the face of such challenges, they left full-time employment.[16]

Workforce challenges prevented women from remaining steadily employed, but it did not necessarily dissuade them from this goal. Sherri, a working-class white woman, greeted me at the train station with much excitement. She had called me upon receipt of my letter to make sure she had a chance to participate in the study. Upon meeting me, Sherri grabbed both of my hands and explained with conviction that she believed all women needed to work and she was invested in her own steady workforce participation. However, during our discussion, I learned that she often had left full-time employment for months or even a year or two. Sherri's goal of full-time steady employment was often challenged by the reality of her poor workforce opportunities. Sherri explained that at her last job, like so many of the prior ones, people acted as if she didn't know how to do her job:

> Oh my god, it was horrible. And I couldn't deal with them and their snootiness and thinking they know it all. I ran a kitchen. [When my boss gave me a hard time, I would want to ask:] "How many people do you feed? Please shut up." [My boss would tell me:] "Go downstairs and do the books like you do [for the food orders]." [I was frustrated by his involvement and would want to say to him,] "It's like, you know what, don't come up here and tell me [how] to do my job. I've been doing it a long time."

As a result of the lack of good work, she explained, "I've worked so many places." Rather than pull back from the workforce entirely, Sherri continued to search for a job after periods of unemployment. She rarely spent longer than six months in one position, finding that the low-paying jobs for which she was qualified did not offer her any self-respect.

Despite these challenges, work was often described as an integral part of a woman's identity, and the interrupted workers were not willing to give up on the possibility that good work could be found. The continual motion back and forth in the labor market was part of their search for good work. Dawn, a white working-class woman, always wanted to work and found her first job as a file clerk in a small legal office. Dawn worked hard and soon found herself promoted to administrative assistant when an employee left permanently after her maternity leave. But the firm was small and Dawn didn't receive health insurance, so after six years without health insurance, she moved on. The lack of benefits can turn otherwise good work into bad work because of the financial insecurity that a lack of health insurance brings. That six-year period was the longest period of workforce stability in Dawn's life. She had since worked in over a dozen jobs, including as a 411 operator, a drug runner, and a yoga instructor.

Women who faced financial hardships, and therefore needed to work found themselves in poor working conditions.[17] Sometimes these conditions were such that despite great financial needs, women found it impossible to remain employed for long. Oftentimes, women with no high school diploma found themselves casually employed by companies invested in minimizing their full-time and permanent employees.[18] Although these women hoped for full-time and steady employment, it was difficult to come by, and when they found employment of any kind, it disappointed. Like Sherri, Sharon, a white working-class woman, faced repeated frustrations in the workplace. Sharon spent much of her young adulthood in part-time minimum wage work. In 2006 she worked for six months at a grocery store but had left work at the time of our interview. She explained that it was common for her most recent boss to make "jokes" that "the deli girl in the back [Sharon] is a bitch." Sharon, an interrupted worker, considered staying, but decided that her son would be better off if she did not work in a demeaning job and, instead, left her position to focus on raising him.

UNEXPECTED CAREGIVING RESPONSIBILITIES CHANGE STEADY PLANS

In addition to the challenges faced in bad work, the interrupted women also found their early workforce and education plans disrupted by changes in their families. Women are more likely than men to be pulled out of the workforce to care for a child or other relative.[19] Time out of the workforce often results in lost wages and in challenges to returning to full-time work.[20] Vanessa, a working-class Latina, was an only child. When her father was forced to retire early, Vanessa and her mother knew that money would be tight, since her mother had been forced to retire early from her job as a typist in a bank. Vanessa finished college and found an entry-level job, but soon afterward, her father had a stroke and her mother reentered the labor market to help Vanessa cover the bills. But they couldn't afford to hire a caretaker and her "father just started getting worse and worse. And, unfortunately, I had to take a leave of absence. I had no other alternative. I tried to put it off as much as possible. In the end, it was the only decision I could make." After Vanessa left her entry-level job, she spent three years caring for her father full time. With a three-year gap on her résumé, Vanessa could not successfully reenter the workforce. After several unsuccessful job searches, Vanessa reluctantly took a position working at the service counter for an airline—a position that was far below her education level and which she promptly left after six months. She had not worked steadily since.[21]

Taking on the role of full-time caregiver can be costly. It can mean lost wages, certainly, but for the interrupted workers, it often meant their life course was altered permanently, partly because of the timing of their workforce exit. My findings suggest that women pay a high cost for time out of the workforce, particularly in the early stages of their careers, as time spent caring for others makes it difficult to return to a steady work pathway.[22] Maureen, a white working-class woman, had expected to work continually. But her dreams of college and steady workforce participation were diverted when her father became ill. "My father had gotten really sick and had cancer and he chose to stay at home through a hospice. So I had to move back home, I guess, to help out with the family. . . . I had a change in my life plan." Maureen quit her job to care for her father; after his death, she realized that she could not return to her formal career after so much time away. She explained, "So I started working at a car repair shop. I was bringing my car in for service. And that was it. They had a sign there that they were hiring."

A lack of family support during early years postponed some women's workforce entrance and their education, particularly when this lack of support came at critical periods of transition.[23] Erica, a white working-class woman, was fifteen when she became pregnant. While she had dreamed of becoming a veterinarian, both sets of parents insisted that Erica and her son's father marry and that Erica drop out of school. While her husband was sent to work at his family's business and to complete high school, Erica was expected to raise their son: "You know, I always thought that I wanted to work outside the home, but then when I had my son, I really never had a chance to think about it. . . . I really did not have an option, because I really did not have a chance and then he was here." Erica's family did not provide her with the opportunity to finish high school—indeed, they told her in no uncertain terms that she was expected to drop out of high school to care full time for her son. Not finishing her high school degree had a lasting effect on Erica's ability to get work and remain employed full time.

Dreams of full-time employment could also be challenged by unstable or violent relationships. Arlene, a white working-class woman, married and had two children soon after she graduated college.[24] She "had high expectations" of what she would do after college, but she "rarely worked," because her abusive spouse would not let her, demanding instead that she focus on caring for their sons. Her struggle to find independence from him was difficult and, at the time of the interview, he remained in her life, although they no longer lived together.

EXPECTING TO PULL BACK

Many of the interrupted women who expected to be occasional workers left the workforce far earlier than their pulled-back contemporaries. Almost all of the pulled-back women finished school, found a job, married, continued working after having children, and left the workforce after their children were older. In contrast, the interrupted workers who expected to work occasionally generally left the workforce at a young age immediately after childbirth or did not enter work until after they had had children.

Women who married and left work at a young age often expected that they would not reenter the workforce. Darla, a white working-class woman, explained, "I married my childhood sweetheart. We got pregnant and then married at nineteen. We were together five years at that point." Darla had always expected to be a stay-at-home mom, so when she became pregnant, leaving her job as a hairdresser seemed like the natural progression.

> To me, like, I didn't have to worry about pension and benefits and—because I was going to get married. I already had my guy. And my father kept pushing city jobs: "You're not going to get rich but it's the long run. It's still, you know, the long run." My mother wanted me to go to college. You know, "You got to go to college, got to go to college." And I never wanted to go to college. I was not—I had my job—being a mom and a wife.

Darla left her job as a hairdresser, confident that her husband would provide for her and their child.

Laura, a white woman from a working-poor background, grew up with a single mom. She said, "I was so young when [my father] left." The family faced a lot of challenges after he left: "We had a lot [of] stuff going on in my family. There was a lot of dysfunction. It was not your typical growing up with the white picket fence." As a result, she said, "[I] never got to really finish high school because I was basically taking care of my sisters and my brothers." Laura was able to earn her GED, and she enrolled in the local community college, hoping to find a way out of her situation. But during her second semester of college, Laura discovered that she was pregnant, and she dropped out of school to marry her childhood sweetheart and raise their children.

Time out of the workforce could lead to bouts of unemployment, in rare circumstances, for middle-class women. Unlike Laura and Darla, Ruth, a white middle-class woman, finished high school and earned a college degree in nursing before she got engaged to be married. When she became engaged, she explained, "I just resigned from there, because I had got engaged and then I was supposed to get married." When her impending nuptials did not materialize, Ruth found herself unable to find stable employment: "I'm not really like full time. I'm working full time but it was on a temporary basis but with the school system." Ruth experienced multiple periods of unemployment following her failed nuptials.

Marriage and childbearing often seemed like the best way to escape a difficult home environment. Carol, a white working-poor woman, explained that she grew up in a poor family that relied on public assistance. During her adolescence, her father struggled with cancer for two years before he died and during that period, her mother was so busy with her father that Carol "had to drop out of school to take care of the baby," her little sister. After his death, Carol wanted out of her family responsibilities:

Once my father died, I was very rebellious and very angry at everybody. [I] really didn't want to watch my sister anymore. I didn't want to go to school. I didn't want to work. I didn't really [want to do anything]—so I wasn't really too happy with anybody.

Carol met her husband at that time and soon after they began dating, she stopped working and dropped out of high school for good: "Then I didn't work because I was with my husband." Husbands seemed to offer an escape from unhappy lives.

Some women who hoped for a traditional family found this dream unachievable, even in the early stages of a relationship. Donna, a white working-class woman, hoped to marry her high school sweetheart and did not want full-time employment. When she became pregnant, she expected him to marry her, but he was already seeing another woman.

We were young when we got together, and I had my son, and he went off with somebody else, and had a kid with her, but it became like a triangle situation . . . and it was always me that had more of feelings, I guess, in the relationship, because again I was blinded by thinking he had to love me.

Donna moved back home to live with her parents when it became clear that her son's father would not marry her and she had no idea how to find stable employment.

When women expected that marriage would materialize soon after leaving high school, they were unprepared to go to work. Wanda, a white working-poor woman, had expected to find a husband and marry early, but she did not. Instead, she had to enter the workforce and spent ten years employed after high school:

> My first real job was at [a] supermarket. I was there for a while, like for a year or so . . . and then my job after that, I worked in the city in the Trade Center for [a phone company]. I was a receptionist there, so that was like my first, like, real—business kind of job. I was there about six months. . . . So after that I got another job—another temp job—and again, Trade Center. Oh, then I worked for a brokerage house for like [a couple] years, which I loved. It was a great place. Then I worked at [a car dealership] uptown. Then I worked at [another company] downtown. They did all the television transcripts.

Wanda explained that she had cycled in and out of the workforce many times. "I had periods of unemployment, like, in between, like six months unemployment [every year or so]." When Wanda finally met and married her husband and they had a son, she was excited to stay home and raise her child. "I wasn't interested in coming back [to work] for a long time. At least until when he started school. I didn't want to go back when he was [not in] school." Although Wanda eventually managed to pull back (but only for a short time, as we'll see next), she was not prepared to work as a young adult, having expected to marry, and she spent many years moving in and out of work.

WHEN PULLING BACK IS DISRUPTED BY VOLATILE RELATIONSHIPS

But these marriages did not last. Divorce is often an emotionally and financially painful process, even when it is necessary.[25] This was particularly true for the inter-rupted women who had always expected to be stay-at-home moms. When faced with divorce, these women had few job skills and few resources on which to depend. Laura, a white working-class woman, returned to work full time when she and her husband separated. Although he agreed to remain married to her to maintain every-one's health benefits, his child support payments could not provide for the family; he gave less than $10,000 annually. While this was more than most women received from child support, it was not enough to sustain an adult and three children living in New York City. Laura had to return to the labor market:

> I started working in a diner doing the register. And then from the diner, I actu-ally learned how to bartend. And this I started because this was the easiest

thing for me to do with children. While they're sleeping, [a good job] is cocktail waitressing and bartending. And then basically I started getting sick of that and went back to doing my bookkeeping.

After Laura reentered the workforce, she worked part time doing "bookkeeping and accounting because I always was good in the accounting fields," but found it challenging to find full-time work that would allow her to care for her children. She was fired from her last job after missing work for child care issues. While she had found full-time work again as a bookkeeper for a yacht club several months before our interview, Laura worried that she would not last long in the position. She explained about the new manager: "He's just not giving me the respect or leaving me certain things when he should, like notes to let me know who's coming." In the face of this lack of respect, Laura expected that it was quite possible that she was "going to be fired by the next board meeting."

Remaining at home full time stopped being an option when a relationship came to a halt. Some women found themselves in abusive relationships and realized the only way out was to find work that would give them the independence they needed, but this work was hard to find. At twenty-one, Darla, a white working-class woman, was living with a drug-addicted husband and an eighteen-month-old toddler.

You know, when you're teenagers, you experiment with drugs, you drink, you do different things. Now when I got pregnant, of course, everything stopped for me. He continued down that path. Then after the baby's born, you can't get drunk and do a three o'clock morning feeding. So I stayed completely sober and he continued to party on. . . . Because he was doing drugs, so it leads to financial problems. It leads to paranoia, the emotional problems, and all sorts of shit. So he lost his job because he never woke up on Saturday mornings. He got his paycheck on Friday—Saturday he never woke up and went to work. So we had a one-and-a-half-year-old in the house. We have an apartment and there's no work.

Darla might have stayed after her husband lost his job because she hoped he would straighten his life up. "And I gave him six months to [get straight]—because you can't deal with every issue. If he just drank, if he just did drugs, if he just didn't have a job but everything combines, then you can't do it. You know, it's six months, let's go." But she knew the six months were up early when her husband became physically abusive: "I got up and I called the cops and I called my father."

After Darla and her husband separated, she felt as if her whole life plan "blew up in [her] face." She had been "working part time at the hairdressing" and wasn't prepared to be in charge. She explained, "I'm now supporting [us]—being a single mother raising a son." After their separation, Darla's financial situation became extremely unstable. She depended on a combination of seasonal work at the post office and hairdressing to pay her bills. With few discernible skills, Darla spent the following fifteen years moving in and out of the workforce, searching for work. After several years, she moved back in with her parents, because she could not find steady work.

Not working was dangerous when women were married to an abusive spouse, as they struggled to find independence. Carol, a white working-class woman who had married to escape her father's illness, discovered that she had married an abusive husband. She had to move to a different state for several years, she said, "Because I started having problems with my husband. I had problems with my husband—[not] the first time, that time I told you I took pills or whatever [to escape the abuse]. And I was trying to straighten out and just wanted to get away [from] him, and I moved." After she left her husband, Carol found different types of minimum wage work. "I worked for [a bar] for like two and a half [years] and then I went up to the deli, which was closer to my house. And actually, believe it or not, [I made] more money and [it was] off the books, so I took that." Personal problems combined with a lack of resources made it difficult for women to remain employed. Carol left her husband after years of abuse and had to leave her community behind, because she feared for her life. After she and her husband separated, she moved back to New York City to get some physical distance from him. But she found it practically impossible to find steady work:

> When I first moved back here, I wasn't working right away. I was really having, that was when I had a really bad nervous breakdown . . . but eventually I got on my feet—uh, not quite on my feet—but I was better. I worked for Davis Electric, which is a small electrical company, and I did the billing and phone calls and stuff like that.

Carol didn't stay at that position long. "I left there and I started working at a nursing home doing private duty for a friend and a couple of old people; I was cleaning for them and helping them shop and stuff. So I was making money off the books and that worked out. Then I applied for the postal job. So that's been about, now, about a year or year and a half." Carol had left the post office and was, once again, unemployed shortly before our interview.

When her boyfriend left her after the birth of her son, Donna, a white working-class woman, had no high school degree and few skills. She lived with her parents for several years, but eventually needed to find her own place:

Before that I was living in at my dad's house, and I was supporting myself in the sense that I had some money coming in [by working at a bar two nights a week], but I was living at home, so it wasn't until actually my son was a year old that I moved here, that I had to be like, okay, now I really have to support myself.

Donna's new responsibilities led her to look for new work. She worried that at the bar she would not be able to stabilize her finances.

[Working at a bar] was always good because it was cash money, you know. And then it's like you filed a tax [return] and yourself, no big deal. And you could always rely on money for that day, but then it's also unstable because when you're getting a paycheck, a nine-to-five paycheck, you can balance your life a little more knowing [where the money is coming from].

While she came to realize it was unlikely she would ever be a stay-at-home mom, Donna found it "impossible" to break into a nine-to-five field, because she had no history of being a steady worker. She continued to work sporadically at different bars for the next fifteen years. At the time of our interview, Donna was unsteadily employed in the entertainment industry, working two of the previous five months. Prior to this job, Donna had worked in "dozens" of bars over the last fifteen years. When asked about full-time employment, Donna laughingly queried, "Have I ever had a full-time job?" Answering her own question, she explained, "I was a bartender for years. That's been the most consistent, but I've never had a nine-to-five type of job, not ever. I did a mail-in hair thing for a while, but that was it." Donna reluctantly identified as working poor and was dependent on food stamps and considering applying for additional state aid.

Wanda, a white working-class woman, found temporary stability when she married her husband and had her son. But after her son's birth, her relationship with her husband deteriorated.

After I had my son, things got worse. It was like [my husband] never really wanted to do anything, and then he never even wanted to stay awake to watch a movie with me. He fell asleep and I was like, "I feel so alone." There's nothing worse than feeling lonely when you're with someone. So that's how I'm here right now.

Wanda divorced her husband and returned to the workforce, finding only part-time work. Divorce not only forced women unexpectedly back into the workforce, it also created strong feelings of financial insecurity. Wanda explained:

I [would like] to be financially secure so I could give my son to have every opportunity in life that he could have and just to, just feel secure where I live. Like
right now I don't feel so secure living here because this house is for sale. It's in
foreclosure, so I feel like the rug could be pulled out from under me at any time.
So I guess what I'd like is just to have a stable place to live where I don't feel like
I have to leave, if they have [to] kick me out or whatever, and just so my son
could have every opportunity.

Wanda's financial insecurity meant that she needed to work, but her erratic work
history and lack of job skills meant that it was difficult to find a stable position.

An article in the *New York Times* lamented that while "in the past, less educated
women often married up," this is less possible today.[26] The *Times* noted that, according to sociologist David Popenoe, while men used to marry "way down the line,"
today they are more likely to marry their demographic peers. The article concluded
that this trend left middle-class women much better off than their working-class
peers, because of the likelihood that they would marry other similarly situated men
and combine their incomes. Yet the *Times* article did not consider the consequences
of failed marriages. Many of the women in the interrupted group who expected to
be occasional workers thought that economic security would be found through marriage, but when marriages dissolved or did not appear, these women struggled to
find steady work, having failed to gain the necessary skills and experience for full-
time work.

PERSONAL ILLNESS

A small number of interrupted women faced health problems or dealt with sub-
stance abuse, as did similar numbers in the other two groups. Unlike their contemporaries, the interrupted women lacked the resources to respond to these problems.
Where physical or mental health problems, or even drug abuse, were challenging
speed bumps in the lives of women in the other two groups, they forced the interrupted workers off their pathways, forever altering their workforce participation.[27]
Middle-class and more stably employed working-class women sought treatment,
took a leave of absence from work, and then returned to employment or to full-time
caregiving for their children. Some of the interrupted women did not have access to
these options, because their resources were too limited.[28]

Some of the poorest women began their history of erratic workforce participation
at a young age. When no one in their family worked steadily, it was hard to gain
access to the skills and resources necessary to finish high school or to find steady
work. Mohmun's mother was drug addicted and living on welfare when she gave

birth to Mohmun, a black working-class woman, and gave her to a family friend to raise. This woman, Mohmun's godmother, raised her until she was twelve, when her mother demanded to have her daughter returned to her. Mohmun explained that growing up, "I wanted to be either a lawyer or an accountant and I'm neither of the two, nowhere near it. But, yeah, I would say as a child I had high dreams. But somewhere along the line I think . . . it just seemed like it all vanished."

Mohmun lived with her mother for a year or two and then ran away from home when the relationship became strained. At fourteen, she started working part time, living on relatives' couches until they found her extra mouth an expense that could not be managed and she was once again asked to leave her household. By sixteen, Mohmun was addicted to cocaine and by eighteen she was addicted to heroin. Her workforce participation became erratic and remained so until the year before I met her.

Jean-Louise, a working-poor black woman, wanted a better life than her parents had had. She grew up with parents who struggled to put food on the table for their eight children: "Money was never enough. We never had enough to eat, enough to buy anything, because we were so many. . . . Financially it was very tight." When she was in high school, Jean-Louise's parents decided to concentrate their resources on her continued success.[29] She went to college on a scholarship, earning a nursing degree. Soon after her graduation, Jean-Louise found work as a nurse and rented a large house for herself, her daughter, and, she said, "[My] mother, my father, my sister with [her] three children, my [older] sister, and another brother." As the primary provider for six adults and four children, Jean-Louise would likely have struggled financially for much of her life. But when she was diagnosed with schizophrenia at twenty-eight, her family lost its sole source of financial support. Although there were numerous adults in the household, Jean-Louise was the only one with schooling beyond ninth grade. In the ensuing fifteen years, Jean-Louise spent several periods in a mental hospital. When she found medication to manage her disease, she found occasional work, although none as lucrative or stable as nursing, nor was she able to stay steadily employed for long. Although an extreme example, Jean-Louise's experiences illustrate how a lack of financial and familial resources can both push women into the workforce and yet also keep them from managing challenges that might pull them out of work.

Mona, a white working-poor woman, grew up in a working-class family. Mona hated high school and dropped out, earning her GED instead. Although she hoped to go to college, she had a "nervous breakdown" soon after she started taking classes at a local community college. After multiple hospitalizations, Mona was diagnosed with a mental illness. She found it difficult to find full-time employment:

I would work. I was working part time from when I was sixteen, and then, sometimes—I had a full-time job when I was eighteen for a little while. Then I worked, you know, part time on and off, when I could find it. . . . For a while I did some work as a receptionist, and then I had another nervous breakdown, a very serious one, and I ended up going on disability, which I'm still on, and I am on disability now. So I have mostly just [been] temping as a receptionist, trying to find a job.

When I met her, Mona had held over two dozen jobs over the past fifteen years. Although she was on disability, she wanted to be able to work full time and recently had had two different full-time jobs. Like Jean-Louise, Mona found that her illness made it difficult to hold a steady job. Also like Jean-Louise, Mona had few resources to turn to when faced with these challenges. She lived in public housing on $7,500 a year, which is what she received from disability.

While it might be tempting to suggest that the women with mental or physical health problems were simply anomalies, research by the U.S. surgeon general suggests that they are a significant part of the larger U.S. population, with over 25 percent of the population living with mental illness in a given year, although far fewer struggle with the severe illnesses described in this section.[30] Furthermore, it is impossible to know if problems such as drug addiction or mental illness led to interrupted work. Steady and pulled-back women with similar problems, including Miranda, Janice, Grace, and Gina, managed to find access to pulled-back or even steady pathways, because they had greater resources than the interrupted workers. While the debate over the causal arrow between mental and physical health and wealth continues to rage,[31] it is clear that the interrupted workers in my study who suffered from these serious health challenges both found it impossible to find steady work and had few resources on which they could depend.[32]

Consequences of Interrupted Work: Cycling In and Out

Once women had left work or entered work, why did they either move back into the labor market or retreat again? Why did the women then not stay the course in their new positions? Unlike the interrupted workers, the pulled-back workers in chapter 5 who experienced bad work either left the workforce entirely or returned to part-time work. Yet the interrupted workers repeatedly sought full-time employment, despite their multiple challenges. While money clearly motivated women's pursuit of full-time work, it was not the only factor in their repeated returns. The women returned to work searching for good jobs, and most continued to believe that better employment could be found. Women went back to work because work was an important part of their lives, because they desired financial independence, and because they felt they had few other options. They left work once again when they found themselves in bad jobs.

FINANCIAL INDEPENDENCE

As we have seen throughout the book, the financial benefits of paid employment are important aspects of women's lives. Money is important because of the benefits to the women and their families. It also is about the financial independence that making your own money provides. Women's commitment to work often stemmed from their desire for financial independence. This trait was also seen in many of the steady workers, but those women most often had greater labor market skills on which to trade. The interrupted workers described a fierce desire for financial independence along with few skills for realizing that dream. Dawn, a working-class white woman, explained that after her first workforce experience: "I never wanted to want for any-thing...so I started working full time. So as soon as I started making my own money and stuff, it was, I'm like, 'I'm not going to want for anything.' I'd buy, like, shampoo and stuff for myself."

Dawn's struggle to remain in the workforce was connected to her financial needs, but also to her desire not to want in the way that her divorced mom had. When we met, she had been stably employed as a yoga teacher for almost a year—her longest stretch of employment in over a decade. She hoped that this would bring financial stability too. "I have one credit card that's—I'm so close to paying off. I have $1,500 left on it, and as soon as I pay that off, then I'm going to buy the health insurance, that Healthy New York, the health insurance. But that's the only thing that worries me is not having health insurance," she explained.

Workforce participation could also bring financial independence from an abusive or domineering spouse. Arlene, a white working-class woman, had worked on and off throughout her early adulthood. When she first attempted to leave her abusive spouse, "I got unemployment for a while and I went to school, and unemployment paid while I went to school; and then I got accepted to another special program and graduated." Arlene saw full-time work as her opportunity to get away from her hus-band. She explained that while many people waited until finishing the program to find work, "I actually planned to work ahead of it. I was not waiting until then to find a job."

Although stable employment could bring financial security, it also could tie women to work that they did not necessarily enjoy. In her late thirties, Erica, a white working-class woman, finally earned a paralegal certificate and started work at a law firm. Her son graduated from high school, and she felt financially secure for the first time in her life. But she did not love her work, and she missed the interaction with clients that she had had as a hairdresser. One of her coworkers suggested that she go back to school to earn an associate's degree in nursing.

> I had some money saved. I cashed in my profit sharing, which was [my] retirement plan, and basically that is how I was able to go back to school, so by [the] time I graduate, I am going to have no money in the bank, so it is just timing, just perfect. There is no failure here because if I fail, then I have no money left.

She hoped that this bet would pay off and lead to stable and enjoyable work that would be financially rewarding.

Not all women aspired to steady work after they faced repeated challenges in the workforce. But many of them could not afford to remain out of the workforce for long. They cycled back when financial needs forced them and then left again when these needs eased or they could no longer bear their working conditions. Sharon, a white working-class woman, explained that her workforce participation was often due to her inability to pay her rent. She managed to go several months without paying rent, but once the landlord caught on that the rent money wasn't coming in, Sharon was out on the street and in need of work:

SHARON: [When I went back to work], I was a wreck. I was still into drugs, just different ones at this point and quit.

SARAH: Quit working?

SHARON: Quit working and stayed there for about until I got evicted.

SARAH: Okay.

SHARON: Until I got evicted from my apartment, so about six months, seven months [I was out of work].

SARAH: And you got evicted because you were not able to pay the rent?

SHARON: Yeah, was not able to keep up the rent. My mother had paid it here and there, but there was only five and change [months left unpaid].

After Sharon's eviction, she went back to work for a period of time because her mother was unable to cover her rent, and she decided she and her son couldn't move back in with her mother again. Although her financial need pushed her into the workforce, her next job at the grocery store did not last long, and she was unemployed again by the time we met.

Although money was often a motivation for workforce participation, it was balanced by women's desire to find good work. Donna, a white working-class woman, sometimes worked for television and movie production companies when she wasn't tending bar. She helped organize the street traffic when the companies were shooting on public streets and enjoyed the work more than bartending. She particularly enjoyed working on productions for ads, because while they were low paying, they treated their employees well: "It's great because it's kind of, like, you know what, you still would like to get more money, but at least [you] have a little more dignity for yourself, and you don't get treated like shit [like you might at other companies.]" Donna's work at the production companies remained sporadic as she sought work where she would be respected.

THE IMPORTANCE OF WORK

The majority of women who had expected to be continual workers did not lightly accept their decision to leave work. Some were reluctant to let go of childhood dreams of full-time workforce participation.[33] Many had deeply held fears about financial dependence on a spouse and when they had a challenging experience at work, it did not lessen their fears about homemaking. Others simply had no one at home to support them, so if they left the workforce, they knew that it was only a matter of time before their finances forced them to reenter. For the interrupted workers, this cyclical pattern involved returning to the workforce when they thought they had found good work only to be fired or disappointed and retreat again. Unlike their pulled-back contemporaries, like Gina or Jill, who left the workforce when they faced disappointments, the interrupted workers returned, again and again, searching for better employment. If the labor market pushed them out, their desire to work, fears of dependence, and family circumstances pushed them back in (but often not in the way that we might expect). Many strongly identified as workers, despite their struggles, although research on working-class men and women suggests that identification with the workforce is most often a white middle-class male experience.[34] Working-class men (and women, although this research often focuses on men) are thought to hold an "instrumental" perspective on work, in which work is a means to an end and not, in and of itself, the end.[35]

While certainly not all of the working-class or working-poor women identified strongly with the workforce, many did, suggesting that identification with work is not necessarily a middle-class attribute. Gender played an important role in this identification process, as many interrupted workers felt that they had chosen continual work. Making the decision to work strengthened women's identification with paid work. As with the steady workers, women interested in working or who feared the dependence of homemaking continued to search for better opportunities, even when the workforce proved less than kind in returning their interest.

Identification with work often stemmed from an interest in a particular line of work or an expectation that work would provide interesting challenges. Sherri, a white working-class woman, said, "[I] always wanted to do what I do."

I was responsible for feeding [my siblings]. We didn't have a lot of money; we just had what we had. Whatever was in the refrigerator, that's what I would come up with, and that's when we would eat at night. I always loved cooking... and that's what really got me into it. And I was young. I would go to work and sleep for two hours, go out with my friends, and then go back to work [at her training program at Burger King].

Sherri felt like this would be a good job and envisioned her success: "I could be running the place. That's all I want[ed] to do is run the place 'cause I knew what I was doing. I knew everything about it." That job, like so many others, did not turn out as Sherri had planned, but Sherri remained committed to her ideal of being a worker. She also remained hopeful that her employment would prove to be a change of tides in her favor. Of her current job, Sherri said, "But this job is stress free. I go there, then I do my work, and that's it. People there are so nice. It's a nice place to work."

To an outside observer, harsh economic living conditions could explain women's continual efforts to find employment. But, as we saw in chapter 5, many women stopped looking for work despite facing severe financial challenges. Some interrupted workers continued looking for work, even when working could hurt their overall finances. Mona, a white working-poor woman, explained that for women receiving government benefits, "It's like not enough money to justify [working] because by the time you lose food stamps or SSI, or a portion of it, by the time they take away your benefits, you get like half the money." Mona explained that although there would be no financial benefit for her, she would still "like to be able to work," which is why she continued to go to a work program for people with disabilities: "I'm in a program now where I do work. I do. They give me work to do, they give me a number of work to do."

Full-time workforce participation also signaled an entrance into the broader community. For many women, this kind of labor market participation meant they were becoming like everyone else. Mohmun, a black working-class woman, had spent years struggling with drug dependency, and she explained that trying to find work was the first sign that she was finally better. "For some of us—to just want to have a normal life. My life didn't become normal until twenty-eight, and I don't even know if that was still normal at that time." At twenty-eight, she put her children in foster care and started a drug treatment program. When she completed the program, Child Services returned her children and she began a series of temporary jobs. But she found the work unfulfilling and looked for something more meaningful. After working for different social service organizations, Mohmun found full-time employment the year before our interview and hoped that it was the first step toward a new life.

Identification with paid work was sometimes a rejection of a homemaker position. One of the driving factors behind women's lasting commitment to continual work was their fear of dependence. For others, it was less fear than disinterest in being a homemaker. Identification with work was seen in opposition to the dependence that they attributed to homemaking women. When her daughter was twelve, Bridget, a middle-class Latina, married for the second time. Despite her abysmal work history and her husband's successful job as a pharmaceutical representative, Bridget worried about being dependent on him forever:

> Well, I've always felt, since seeing my mom, as she didn't work and my father had to always support us and everything. Even though we didn't struggle, I always resented the fact that my mom always had to depend on him. And I've always said that I would never, ever depend on a man. I don't care if he's loaded; I will always work just to have my own stuff, my own money. Where if I want to just get up and go, I just leave.

Although Bridget's husband earned enough to allow her to leave work, Bridget's fear of financial dependence kept her employed (albeit always temporarily) and always searching for better employment. Similarly, Sherri, a white working-class woman, explained, "[When my mother's] marriage broke up, she lost her house, you know what I mean? She lost it all."

Some women found that they could not leave work simply because they did not fit a culturally acceptable model of who does this—mothers. Without children, it was harder to justify pulling back from the workforce. Maureen, a white working-class woman, worked when she had a job, but left when she wasn't enjoying the work. She explained that when she left one of her many secretarial jobs, she just decided that she needed a change: "I liked the job. I did not like the industry at all. My little office, the people that I worked with, were very nice. My work duties were very nice. But the industry in itself is very cutthroat. Nothing that I really cared for."

She then reentered the workforce because she got "bored" at home. She had never had children: "I don't like kids. I don't like little kids. I just never had that maternal instinct. And I've known that from childhood. I would never even babysit as a child." Without children, Maureen lacked a socially acceptable reason to leave the workforce entirely, and her partner and their friends and family members would not have understood such a movement. At the time of our interview, Maureen held two part-time jobs—one a secretarial job for a small firm that she did from home, and the other a receptionist position at a local gym.

Although "a job" may "not be a career,"[36] the promises that it extends may cement women's commitment to the labor market. Research on working-class women's lack of identification with their employment may overemphasize the difference between working- and middle-class women's attachment to the labor market, minimizing the struggles that working-class and working-poor women face to remain employed. This is, in part, because working-class women's continued employment is often attributed to family needs, assuming both men and women need to labor in these families. But as the lives of the steady, interrupted, and pulled-back women show, family finances mask other reasons that women continue to return to the labor market.

Conclusion

Just under one-fifth of participants followed interrupted work pathways. Although the media remains focused on whether women are opting out of work, my research suggests that a sizable group of women can neither opt in nor opt out. All of the women expected to work either continually or occasionally, yet none were able to meet their goals. The lives of the interrupted participants were defined by their inability to follow a stable path. They faced unstable families, little money, and unreliable social networks and had few resources to rely upon to face the challenges life presented them.

Among my respondents, the most striking difference was between those in the interrupted group and everyone else. These women worked for companies that expected them not to be long-term employees, and this created work environments in which long-term work became untenable. The women who worked steadily and those who pulled back found both successes and frustrations in their work. In many ways, they followed fairly similar paths up to their mid to late twenties. The interrupted workers, on the other hand, followed a very different path, and almost all of these women were in the poorest group. This suggests that the differences in workforce participation may be starkest not between the working class and middle class, but between the working poor and everyone else.

Over half of the interrupted workers expected to follow steady pathways. Most wanted to work, and many held deep ideological convictions that work was important in women's lives. These women were also less well educated than the other study participants. In contrast to scholars who argue that these working-class women's work options are undesirable and explain women's withdrawal from the workforce,[37] my research suggests that even the interrupted workers enjoyed many aspects of their work, as long as their work was respected. Dissatisfaction with the workforce most often stemmed from the respect given (or not) to them and their work, not the type of work they did or the conditions of their work. This can help us to understand why women continued to return: they enjoyed working—they were simply searching for a workplace that would respect the work they did.

The remaining 40 percent of interrupted workers had expected to participate occasionally in the workplace. Most married young and had little to no experience in the workforce when they pulled back to care for young children. They believed that economic security would be found in their marriages and were unprepared to enter the labor market when these marriages dissolved. Once back in the labor market, they faced many of the same challenges as their continually oriented interrupted peers. They entered, left, and reentered the labor market in the hopes that better work and economic security would be around the corner.

Financial need could demand employment but not necessarily produce it.[38] Furthermore, the type of employment women found was not always the full-time work they hoped for. Needing to work, then, may lead to workforce participation, but it might not lead to full-time or long-term work. Women with the greatest financial need to work were almost always also the women with the least rewarding workforce opportunities. Women employed in the service sector faced what economist Jacob Hacker calls "the rising specter of workplace insecurity" and, more often than not, found themselves unemployed within a short period of time.[39] Companies that did not want or need long-term employees hired the women in the study who worked in low-wage jobs. As a result, the women reported poor treatment at work; they found not only a lack of flexibility, but also a general lack of respect for their work and for themselves personally. Women whose only workforce options were low-wage service industry work rarely remained employed for longer than six months at a time.

Negotiating Expectations

7

FOR THE FAMILY

How Women Account for Work Decisions

PAULA, A WORKING-CLASS white woman, was satisfied with her decision to stay at home with her children. "You know, my one sister put it well: 'You get one chance to raise your kids and why not be there the whole time?'" Despite her satisfaction with her situation, Paula reported receiving conflicting feedback from the people in her life.

> People look down on you if you do work; people look down upon you if you don't work. So this, you know, in a way I think it's harder now because I think you get judged so much and everybody has a very strong opinion. So, you know, for me this is the best situation. And somebody else . . . might look down upon it.

Like many of her female peers, Paula felt caught in the center of the cultural maelstrom that followed the rapid entrance of women into the labor market. Not only are more women working, but women have also increased the amount of their adult lives spent in the labor market.[1] Women are following divergent work and family patterns, creating new family forms, and delaying or forgoing childbearing altogether.[2] Regardless of a woman's work trajectory, there remains what sociologist Sharon Hays calls "a no-win situation for women of childbearing years."[3] In her research, Hays finds that women who work too hard are accused of neglecting their children; women who have no children are depicted as cold; mothers who work are "mommy-tracked"; and women who don't work are called unproductive or worse. Researchers find that, like Paula, most women are left feeling that their decisions will be criticized, regardless of what pathway they choose.[4]

In this chapter, I consider how women described their decisions about work in the previous chapters and compare this to their responses when I asked them why they had left or remained at work. How do women justify these choices in a world in which their decisions about work are closely scrutinized? While the previous chapters show that class, race, work experiences, and family support contributed to women's decisions to pursue different work pathways, most women accounted for their work-family decisions by pointing to "family needs." When asked to explain decisions to leave the workforce, women said that their family needed them to be home. When asked to explain decisions to stay in or return to the workforce, women replied that their family needed them to work. This shared framework actually allowed them to remake gendered expectations of caregiving to fit divergent work pathways. By using a frame that stressed obligations to their families rather than the fulfillment of their own needs or desires, both employed and nonemployed women affirmed cultural expectations about women's selflessness.

Accounting for Women's Work

In mid-twentieth-century America, labor in the home was divided by gender. Women were expected to care for others through personal attention, while men were encouraged to provide for others through breadwinning as they simultaneously sought personal fulfillment.[5] During this period, individual achievements became the purview of men, while family attachments increasingly fell under women's domain.[6] Sociologists played no small part in the dissemination of this worldview, as they, most prominently Talcott Parsons, argued that women's role was in the home and that men belonged in the public sphere. These historical gender divides have long been judged as more nostalgic ideals than actual practices for many men and women, but they continue to hold significant cultural meaning in modern America.[7]

More recently, women's entrance into the labor market has reshaped the boundaries that allocated the private sphere to women and the public sphere to men. While women's moral obligations were historically filled primarily by intensive caregiving in the home, women now have multiple means through which to fulfill their familial devotion.[8] Yet expectations about motherhood have increased, not decreased, since women moved into the workforce, even though employment creates differences in the intensity and form of women's caretaking.[9] The cultural idealization of mother-hood continues to shape expectations about women's work and their employment opportunities. Mothers face the brunt of gender discrimination in the workforce, as their commitment to the workforce is questioned, their abilities are doubted, their salaries are diminished, and their opportunities for advancement are curtailed, all because of expectations about mothers' employment.[10] Sociologist Mary Blair-Loy notes that the cultural values attached to the term *family* demand selflessness from women: "women's devotion to the family trumps all other commitments."[11] The historical moral connotations of women's paid work remain salient—staying at home continues to suggest altruism, while working suggests selfishness, particularly for well-off women.

Today women practice more intensive levels of mothering than in previous eras, and these changes demand not only more time but also more emotional work as both employed and nonemployed mothers accept an overall goal of being an attentive mother.[12] Working mothers have not given up the ideology of intensive mothering, and instead spend a significant amount of energy making up for time spent away from their children.[13] Women without children are not left out of these debates, as they, too, find themselves the subject of much scrutiny about their childbearing decisions.[14] Wendy, a white middle-class woman, believed that she was not hired right out of law school because of the possibility that she would have children one day:

> One of the judges was interviewing me. I had just gotten married. And he said to me, "Oh do you think you'll be having children soon?" And I said, "Oh, I really haven't thought about it yet. I don't know." I did not get that job. He gave it to this ridiculously unqualified man who did not work out well at all.

In fact, all women face obstacles to their continued workforce participation, because of the possibility that they could be mothers.[15] Even as demands about motherhood have increased, so have expectations that women will participate in the labor market. But just as motherhood comes with a set of cultural dilemmas, so, too, does women's paid work. Countless news stories promote the myth that working mothers are not happy, lamenting the physical and emotional toll paid work takes. The popular media continues to lead with stories headlined, for example, "Stretched to [the] Limit, Women Stall March to Work," despite copious research finding that women's employment enhances their quality of life.[16] Women also face skepticism in the workforce, as the cultural ideals of intensive mothering are not always compatible with the demands of the business world.[17] In male-dominated fields, discrimination against intensive parenting again leaves women disadvantaged.[18] Within this framework, cultural fears about the cost to children of women's paid work abound, despite a substantial amount of research that finds children are not harmed by women's paid labor.[19] These fears undermine the legitimacy of women's workforce participation and increase expectations about the benefits of intensive mothering. But despite the increasing pressures of motherhood, women's work in the home (and paid work that resembles this type of care work) remains devalued.[20] So while women face intensifying cultural demands about mothering, the economic and emotional costs of this task remain underacknowledged and underrewarded.

The media has dubbed the fallout from these conflicting messages the "mommy wars." In recent years, a book with just such a title hit the bestseller list, while books about "loving and loathing your inner housewife" and the "feminine mistake" received extensive media coverage. In a conservative spin on these issues, Caitlin Flanagan sharply criticized working women, portraying these women as selfishly missing their children's lives or (of those without children) being too busy to perform their "wifely duty." At the other end of the political spectrum lies Leslie Bennetts's polemic about women who have left the workforce. Bennetts contends that stay-at-home mothers do not understand the financial peril in which they have placed themselves, lamenting, "'having it all' has become a discredited goal. It's too hard—too stressful, too exhausting, too frenetic."[21] Regardless of the authors' political orientations, women are pitted against each other in a titillating media frenzy over women not living up to society's expectations.

Yet the frenzy may tend to exaggerate the singularity of motherhood in women's lives. Women often experience a deep ambivalence about intensive mothering ideologies.[22] Authors Susan Douglas and Meredith Michaels argue that there is a "chasm between the ridiculous, honey-hued ideals of perfect motherhood in the mass media and the reality of mothers' everyday lives."[23] Women are also following divergent work and family pathways, creating new family forms, pursuing increased work commitments, and delaying or forgoing childbearing altogether.[24]

Women's identities—as workers and as mothers—continue to be in conflict, leaving them with few work or family choices that will not be subject to scrutiny.[25] At a time when no one decision can be seen as a cultural mandate or a secure social position, women are likely to be uncomfortable with their own choices and, perhaps, critical of those who have followed other paths.[26] The women I studied certainly felt torn. Donatella, a white middle-class woman, noted, "It kept me up at nights. I just couldn't deal with the guilt of giving up the career, or the guilt of not being a good mother." Given the likelihood that women will follow diverse work pathways, all of which may be subject to moral judgment, how do women negotiate the cultural maelstrom surrounding women and work?

Creating Accounts

To answer this question, I developed a theoretical framework for understanding how women negotiate the tension between their increased work-family options and the ideology of intensive mothering. Sociologists Marvin Scott and Stanford Lyman propose that people create "accounts" to explain behavior that will be "subjected to valuative inquiry."[27] In other words, when people expect that their behavior will be judged critically, they attempt to explain their behavior in a way that makes it more socially acceptable. I expand this concept, arguing that people's accounts of their actions provide a way to negotiate between actions and prevailing cultural schemas. Because women's actions as they relate to work and family are almost always subject to evaluation from the outside, they may develop strategies to protect themselves from criticism.

Family scholars have long noted the disjuncture between women's explanations of their actions and the underlying factors behind these actions. For example, working-class women refer to their work as a job, rather than a career, to distance themselves from ambitions that could be perceived as selfish.[28] Middle-class women, on the other hand, call a decision to leave the workforce a choice, to reclaim a sense that they had options even when their choices may have been quite limited.[29]

In the tradition of these family scholars, I suggest an active use of rhetoric in which accounts can be understood as the product of the negotiation between actions taken and the cultural meanings attached to these actions. While the accounts may not give women control over their work-family lives, they may allow them to amend their narrative to appear selfless, a key component of the family schema as described above.[30] Accounts allow women to emphasize behavior they believe will be more socially acceptable, such as decisions made to care for family and to minimize behavior that might be seen in a negative light, such as decisions made for themselves.[31] If women are judged regardless of their work-family trajectory, accounts may provide them with the ability to recreate cultural schemas to fit their own circumstances.

Similar Accounts

How, then did respondents explain their labor market decisions? As we saw in chapters 4–6, when asked to discuss their workforce participation, the women gave remarkably complex narratives that highlighted the importance of work opportunities, class, race, and family support. However, when asked why they had decided to leave work or stay at work, the women's stories became considerably less complex.[32] Despite the salience of class, race, work experiences, and family support, when asked to justify their work decisions, my respondents emphasized the role of family needs in their work decisions. Their strikingly similar accounts about the importance of families stood in sharp contrast to their divergent work patterns and varying job and family experiences, suggesting that the women constructed "for the family" explanations to negotiate the cultural schemas that frame women's paid work as selfish.[33]

The women had different accounts about why they left, but the underlying message was very similar: work decisions were made according to family needs. Women who worked steadily and women who pulled back to part-time work explained that labor market participation fulfilled their families' financial needs, as Cynthia, the white middle-class woman from chapter 1, did when she stayed at work, she said, "so I could make all the extras and everything . . . for them." Those who had pulled back explained that time spent in the home fulfilled children's personal needs, as Virginia, the white working-class woman from chapter 1, did when she said that she left work to "be home for the kids." Moreover, the majority of women accounted for their work decisions by emphasizing that their decisions fulfilled both financial and personal needs. Women who worked focused on how their work fulfilled their family's financial needs, but they also pointed to how this decision fulfilled their family's personal needs. Women who stayed home focused on how this fulfilled children's personal needs, but they, too, added that it fulfilled financial needs. The unanimity of women's explanations about work decisions suggests that women feel most comfortable attributing work decisions to the need to care for others, rather than to an individual pursuit. Although women discussed both their satisfaction and dissatisfaction at work in their narratives, when specifically asked to justify their work decisions, they pointed to their family experiences, not their experiences at work, to account for their actions. I should note that I did not intend this question to put women on the spot (nor did I anticipate this singular response), but the fact that most discussed their family needs, rather than other factors, suggests that questions about women's work decisions bring forth cultural ambiguities about the validity of women's paid workforce participation.

THE EXCEPTIONS

While the vast majority of women used some form of the "for the family" language, just under 8 percent of the women did not provide such accounts when asked to justify work decisions. Of these six women, half were working class and half middle class. Half of this group reiterated details from their work narratives, explaining that job opportunities and family support explained their work decisions. Vivian, a white middle-class woman, flatly said no, she had never considered not working. "I have to do work. I love it. . . . I know that I am needed; and people, basically, like the advice that I might give; and it's practical; and knowing that I can help—that means a lot to me. That's why I'm here today." This forthright discussion of the importance of work in her life was not particularly common in women's accounts—although Vivian had spent more time in school than most women, earning a graduate degree, perhaps explaining why she differed from her contemporaries.

Yet some women who did not use a "for the family" account still clearly connected a desire for paid work with selfishness. These women provided what I call a modified version of the "for the family" account. They did not say that they had made their decisions for their families, but that they had deliberately made decisions not to have any children, so that they could make work decisions for themselves rather than for others. When asked about her work decisions, Lindsey, a white working-class woman, explained that raising kids was a "a really important job. And if you're not going to [stay home], then you don't have kids"; otherwise "the children are suffering." Lindsey's worldview, in which working moms shortchange their children, made it difficult for her to imagine that she could do both. "I don't have children. I tell you I don't have children because I'm kind of selfish. . . . I love what I do. I enjoy it and the money is really good. . . . I am used to working and having a certain income," she said. Work, with its personal and professional rewards, was incompatible with motherhood, a selfless pursuit, according to Lindsey.

These accounts emphasized the incompatibility of work and child rearing. Emily, a white middle-class woman in pursuit of her PhD, gave a similar explanation:

> I wouldn't say I'm, like, extremely ambitious, but I want to be able to get a good position and I want to be, you know, respected in my field. I think that in general, you know if you have a child, you're going to have . . . be less able to . . . you're going to have less time to spend on your career.

While these women did not say that they had made career choices to aid their families, they did say that because they had work-centered goals, they had decided to forgo having children. This suggests that the overall cultural logic that intensive mothering is incompatible with the desire to participate in paid work was shared by these women as well.

ACCOUNTS OF FINANCIAL NEEDS

Both women who remained employed steadily and those who pulled back to part-time work explained that their work decisions fulfilled their families' financial needs. Many of the work narratives described in the previous chapters are reconsidered here, as the women often presented accounts that diverged from their work narratives, sometimes even contradicting them. I discuss them here to highlight the emphasis women placed on familial reasons to leave work. Since she entered the workforce at eighteen, Cynthia, a white middle-class woman, who described her work as "fascinating" in her work narrative, had never taken more time off work than her paid twelve weeks of maternity leave. But when asked why she had decided to remain employed steadily, Cynthia explained that when she first became pregnant:

> I kind of wanted to quit, but then since I had my mother and she kind of encouraged me, "Oh stay at work," . . . so I could make all the extras and everything. Because we could have managed on my husband's salary, but you know she was just encouraging me to stay at work, so I could do better for them.

Cynthia justified her decision by explaining that her work helped fulfill her family's financial needs, and therefore her familial obligations. She also emphasized that her mother encouraged this decision—her family felt that she was doing the right thing.

By arguing that financial needs mandated steady employment, women demonstrated their altruism in two ways. They showed how they would prefer to care for their children full time if that were possible, and they decried the pursuit of personal achievement. Lucille, a white upper middle-class woman, declared she had to remain in the workforce:

> With me having the job, or the better job, I needed to continue to work. . . . I was planning to stay another year and a half to get vested in certain economics—and then I planned to leave. I think if my husband would've been earning a little bit more financially, I may have considered something part time.

Lucille's account focused on her husband's inability to find a higher-paying job. But Lucille had spent years working her way up the ranks, being heavily recruited by multiple companies, and earning her position as a chief financial officer for a major corporation. Yet her work narrative about her amazing work success (she was the highest-paid woman in the study, earning over $400,000 annually plus extensive benefits and stock options) was absent from her account of why she remained.

In many ways, white women borrowed a language historically employed by black women. Although African American women experienced very different realities than their white contemporaries—even middle-class blacks had fewer social resources and lower-earning spouses than their white counterparts—white and black women similarly discussed the need for their paid work. African American women unanimously described growing up in communities in which it was expected that women needed to work for their families. When Tina, an African

American working-class woman, was growing up, she said, "Everyone around me, their parents worked; so it wasn't like there were people who had stay-home moms." In fact, scholars have long noted that African American women are expected to work. Author Lonnae O'Neal Parker notes that for black middle-class women, not working "was not an option at all."[34] As we saw in chapter 3, black women were more likely to take workforce participation for granted.

While not all black women worked steadily, they did all say that women needed to work for their families. Gabra, a middle-class African American, explained that her continued employment as a program analyst at a law firm was never in doubt. When Gabra and her husband had their first child, she said, "I made four times what [my husband] made, so it wasn't even a consideration. We couldn't live off his salary." Looking back at chapter 4, we remember that Gabra also found her share of work success and enjoyment. After she started working as a computer technician for a major law firm, she said, "It just started going up from there. I went from writing code to doing software applications to analyst work, and from that I became a project manager." Although Gabra had explained in her work narrative that she greatly enjoyed her work, she emphasized her familial obligations when asked why she remained employed. Even in African American households in which both spouses made salaries over $100,000 a year, women explained that they continued to work "for the family." I asked Tonya, an upper-middle-class African American, why she had remained employed full time.

> TONYA: [Leaving work] was never a question.
> SARAH: It was not a question because you wanted to go back or because of other reasons?
> TONYA: Financial reasons. . . . I am on this good track, careerwise, and [my husband] is not.

Tonya earned $300,000 annually, and her husband's job with a city agency paid $100,000. Although Tonya out-earned her husband, she also enjoyed her work more than he did and was more committed to her career. In earlier parts of the interview, she explained that she found her work "rewarding": "It is an entrepreneurial type of environment. So, I can pretty much do a lot of things and you also get a recognition for doing things and making a contribution." But she pointed to the financial necessity of her work, not its other rewards, when explaining her work decisions.

Even women who did not have children used future family obligations to explain their steady workforce participation. They deflected the possibility that ambition fueled work decisions by pointing to a future altruistic motive. At forty, Lila, an upper-middle-class Asian American, had never married and had no children. Having spent her twenties earning her podiatry degree and her thirties building a successful practice, she explained that she needed to remain committed to building her practice so that she could get to the point, she said, "When I can feel financially secure that I say, okay, I can take care of myself, now let me take care of another human being." At thirty-two, Parul, a married upper-middle-class Asian American, explained that she, too, worked to put herself in a secure financial position before she had children. Although Parul had termed her work "fun" (see chapter 4) and enjoyed great success, she explained that the need to provide for her future children was most important: "It was always about getting a job, doing education, get a good job to be financially secure for them." That women without children emphasized how their work could benefit future children tells us how strong ideals of intensive mothering are in women's lives.

Similarly, the women who had pulled back to part-time work or followed interrupted pathways also stressed how their work decisions financially benefited their families. Women who worked part-time emphasized that they returned to part-time work to fulfill financial needs. They did not discuss the other reasons, highlighted in chapter 5, that women might return to part-time work. Virginia, a working-class white woman, explained, "A mother should be home with their kids," but this isn't possible today, because "financially, [women] have to actually work in order to make it possible for their kids to have more." While Virginia's account focused on her altruism, she left a full-time job that she disliked when her family was in financial straits and returned to a part-time job she loved in a period of growing family financial stability.

After three years at home, Angela, a white working-class woman, started working part time, and then she and her husband made the decision for her to go back to work because, she said, "We decided we definitely could use the money." By returning to work part time from home, Angela explained that she fulfilled her children's needs through both financial provision and personal attention: "I feel like I can participate, give something to my family, and still be there for my kids. You know I'm there for their school, to bring them and pick them up. . . . So yeah, I definitely feel like I'm giving something toward it—toward the family." Angela defined her decision-making process as being driven by her ability to fulfill these familial obligations. Like many of the women who had remained employed full time, in her account she did not discuss her work experiences, such as the company buyout that led to her demotion.

Other financial accounts compared the benefits of part-time work to nonemployment, emphasizing the financial benefits of working part time for families. Tracy, a white middle-class lawyer, explained that her part-time work was a huge financial asset to her family, particularly in comparison to her sister's decision not to work: "My twin sister, she's staying at home, so she's not making any money." Tracy felt better off than her sister, who had "a harder financial time." But Tracy earned an eighth of her full-time salary, while working half the hours. By presenting an account of the financial benefits of part-time work, however, Tracy emphasized the benefits of her work decisions for her family and occluded the loss of income that the family faced when she changed from full-time to part-time work and the time bind challenges she had faced that led her to leave.

The women's emphasis on the financial benefits of their decisions, even when not employed, suggests that women felt a strong obligation to share in the household financial burdens. Some women stressed that not working meant not having work-related costs. Barbara, a white middle-class woman, left a job at which she had earned close to $100,000, approximately half of the family's annual earnings. She, too, pointed to the financial benefits of leaving work: "You save a lot of money because you don't have to buy work clothes; there's the commuting, the lunch. You do save a lot of money." While Barbara focused on the real savings of remaining at home, this calculation ignored the loss of her current or future wages and her work narrative in which she described the challenges caused by the time bind. And while she pointed to the benefits to her family, we saw in chapter 5 that Barbara had stayed at work even after having twins, leaving only after a corporate takeover created longer hours and a less flexible workplace, and her father's illness left her without a caregiver for her children.

Some women's accounts included discussions of how early workforce experiences proved their financial responsibility to their families and paved the way for them to leave work to be at home. Jill, a working-class white woman, explained that early workforce participation showed "just that I would always be able to take care of them. To be always able to give them things that they wanted." Women who left work acknowledged, as Jill did, that not working did mean fewer "material things." She continued, "But they are not important as long as I have what my kids need. That is what is more important to me." For Jill, her family's need was for her to be home with them, not away from them to provide for them financially. Jill's account focused on the benefits of her work decisions for her family and even the financial responsibilities she had once taken on for them but did not acknowledge that Jill left work only when she lost her job.

ACCOUNTS OF FAMILIAL NEEDS

Accounts of financial need paint a picture of the changing moral landscape for American women. It is no longer enough, these accounts suggest, for women to be merely responsible for the family through their homemaking and caregiving efforts.

They also need to demonstrate that their workforce decisions are financially responsible. The accounts of familial needs, on the other hand, suggest a return to earlier twentieth-century American gender divides in which women were the guardians of caretaking and caregiving.

Not surprisingly, all of the women who pulled back because they wanted a traditional family form gave accounts about how they made their work decisions for their families. These women emphasized that their children needed them to be at home with them. Even though several left lucrative jobs when their husbands had poor work opportunities, these women did not discuss the family's financial needs, unlike the women in the prior section. Instead, they focused on the benefits to their children of being home. Megan, a white working-class woman who left a job at which she made $80,000 annually while her husband made only $20,000, said, "I knew I wasn't going to leave my newborn. . . . It's not about what you want to do anymore, that's like out the window; everything revolves around them." While Paula, a white working-class woman, did not leave as prestigious a position as Megan, she, too, explained that once she became pregnant, she did feel that her leaving work put additional financial strains on her husband: "I think the stress of being the only one to support the family is a lot less [when the wife works]." Yet she said, "When I had my son I never, I couldn't leave him. You know I felt like I wanted to be there. I felt like nobody could love him unconditionally like I do."

Like Paula and Megan, almost all of the women who had pulled back focused on how not working full-time fulfilled their children's personal needs. But the majority of the pulled-back women did not leave work right after having a child, as Paula and Megan did. Instead, the majority left work in the face of workforce disappointments or a time crunch between work and home. It is important to note that these women valued their time at home with their children, and this analysis does not minimize its importance or intend to indicate otherwise. Instead, my analysis shows how the women's accounts placed great emphasis on a culturally acceptable factor for leaving work—their children—and minimized the importance of other factors, such as poor work opportunities or lack of family support, which might suggest a more self-interested motive.

Jill, a married working-class white woman, remained in the workforce after the birth of her first two children, but she decided not to look for a new job after her employer closed unexpectedly. With only a high school degree and few marketable skills, Jill felt ill prepared to find work. Despite these factors, she focused on the familial benefits of leaving work: "I just felt like I needed to be there for them. It was important to be home for my kids and be involved in their full lives. It is still very important. It is good to know that somebody is there to help them out if they need it." Although Jill experienced both a desire to be home with her children and a difficult job situation, her account minimized the importance of her job loss and focused on her ability to be at home with her children.

Like Jill, most of the women who pulled back from the workforce focused on the importance of their presence at home. Angela, the white working-class woman whose new employers treated her like a "dingbat," introduced herself by saying, "I work part time from home so I can take care of my children." With this introduction, Angela immediately linked her personal identity to caregiving and downplayed the fact that she didn't leave work after having her children, but only after her new employers had demoted her to the secretarial pool. After dropping out of high school, Gina, a white working-class woman, worked as a "mail girl" at a mortgage company in a job that she "really disliked." After she married, Gina left her job, saying, "I'd rather raise my kids and then maybe find a job."

Similarly, Wendy, a white middle-class woman, pointed in her account to the changes in her life after she had children and her child's need for her attention, rather than work-family conflict that she experienced. "It's just everything changes when you have a child I guess. You have to, like, to take care of that person all the time. And, then, that's your whole entire life is that, instead of what you had before." Although Wendy had changed jobs multiple times to remain employed full time, when asked about her work decisions, her account emphasized that it was her responsibility to her children that led her to pull back to part-time work, not her inflexible workplace or her husband's absence from household and child care chores.

Interrupted workers, too, pointed to the benefits of their bouts of unemployment. In their accounts, these times were often framed as periods to spend additional time with families, rather than as a retreat from paid work. Sherri, a married, working-class white woman who had cycled in and out of the workforce for over twenty years, described finding a job, spending a year or less in a position, and then moving on. She told of employers who looked down on her, noting "their snootiness and thinking that they know it all." But like the others, Sherri's account emphasized the benefits to her son of staying home, rather than the personal reasons she might have for leaving work:

> I couldn't count on [my parents]. And that was a big thing. My kids would never have that. My son, I pick him up everywhere and my stepson too. But that's just the one thing I wanted to be sure. To have time for every one of them—I think it's very important.

While Sherri clearly wanted to be a better parent for her son, she also had problems at work, yet her account of her workforce decisions only focused on the benefits for her son. By focusing on the altruistic factors, Sherri distanced herself from "bad mothers," who continued to work full time: "[Working mothers] have these children to appease their husbands and they don't like their kids and they don't want to take care of them. I think that's just a horrible, horrible thing." Similarly, Anita, a white working-class woman who had been unable to find good work, explained:

> Seeing your kids grow up, you know, from taking their first step to bringing home their first, you know, gold star. You are there. You are there for your kids, you know, instead of them coming home to nobody, you know, or a sitter or having somebody else.... I chose to stay at home. But, yeah, it was definitely a major benefit to that. You know, not worrying, too, of who is watching my kid, who is there for my kid.

Like most women, Sherri and Anita felt drawn into the "no-win situation" of the "mommy wars"; they used their accounts to draw a distinction between themselves and other mothers, giving themselves the higher moral ground by focusing on the altruistic reasons that led them to leave the workforce.

Sherri, Angela, Anita, and Gina were all dissatisfied at work, yet they did not mention bad jobs in their accounts of why they left work. While the women were clearly aware of their dissatisfaction, they did not highlight this experience, instead stressing the benefits to their children of their being home. In a *New York Times* article, economist Heather Boushey noted: "A woman gets laid off and she stays home for six months with her kids. She doesn't admit that she is staying home because she could not get another acceptable job."[35] Nor does she admit that the time crunch was not solvable nor that her husband was less supportive of her career than she had hoped he would be. While the women's work narratives acknowledged these circumstances, their accounts drew attention to how leaving the labor market benefited their families. An account of pulling back for the family provided safe standing, in a way that discussions of job closings, new bosses, or reduced flexibility might not have.

Women who worked steadily were not immune to cultural pressures that demanded they personally fulfill their families' caregiving needs. In fact, most women who work spend a significant amount of time on caregiving activities.[36] Most of the steady workers who emphasized the financial benefits to their families of their work, also included in their accounts discussions of how they continued to personally care for their families. Steadily employed women also discussed the personal sacrifices they made by remaining employed, a language that stressed that they were the ones who absorbed the costs of full-time work. Lucille, a white middle-class woman, recounted that she had no time for herself in the evenings:

Yes, I work full time. The minute I come home it's—the child is mine. I play with the child. I make some lame-type dinner because I don't have time to clean the kitchen—cook, clean the kitchen, and put him to bed. I like putting him to bed because I get to see him.

While Lucille worked an eleven- to twelve-hour day, she sacrificed her own personal time so her job did not prevent her from providing her son with personal attention.

Claudia, a working-class Latina, similarly emphasized how even though she worked full time, she had made sacrifices to her career so that her son would come first:

You know what, I have always made David my priority. I always do take the time off for him. So, even if my job [pause] I had to quit one of my jobs, because I didn't spend enough time with David. . . . Sometime last year, I tried [a new position in the same organization] out for six months. But because you had to work holidays, and they didn't give you the work schedule you wanted, and I need a daytime job, and you would have to work Saturdays. I had to let it go, because I wasn't spending enough time with David.

Claudia went back to her lower-paying position and forwent the possible promotion, because she worried that it interfered with her relationship with her son.

Women who worked steadily discussed not only the personal sacrifices that they made for their children but also the benefits of their paid work for their mothers. Cynthia pointed to how her mother was able to provide the personal attention that her children needed, saying, "She wanted to watch the baby." Cynthia fulfilled her obligation as a mother and also as a daughter, because caring for children was "exactly what [my mother] wanted to do." Cynthia gave her mother a task that kept her fulfilled when she no longer had her own children to care for and gave her children the caretaker who had taken care of her for so many years. Although Cynthia also benefited from her mother's caregiving, which provided her with the support needed to continue to work, she highlighted the benefits of this arrangement to her mother, not to herself.

Similarly, Gabra explained that her decision helped her mother, who had lost her job after 9/11:

My mom was coming to the end of her unemployment, so instead of looking— we made the decision as a family, instead of looking for a one family [house], we looked for a two family [house]. And in exchange for child care [my mom and stepfather] could live in the other portion of the house, which is what we did. It really works out.

A growing number of families are now faced with caring for both children and aging parents, and women continue to bear the brunt of the caregiving load.[37] While these accounts may underemphasize the benefits that the women received from their mothers' caregiving efforts for their children, they certainly reflect a changed family structure in which families are now caring for aging parents as well as rearing children.

Expanding economic and social opportunities provided women with new opportunities outside the home, but these new opportunities may not have led personal fulfillment to supplant women's moral obligations to their families. When asked why they made workforce participation decisions, they provided accounts of decisions made for the family that often did not acknowledge (or even match) their work-family circumstances. While the majority of employed women described themselves as "satisfied" with their work and over three-quarters went on to say that given the choice, they would prefer to work, the majority also said their family obligations explained their continued workforce participation. While the majority of pulled-back and interrupted workers left work when faced with bad work and little family support, they, too, said that they left work for the family. Using family needs to account for continued workforce participation allowed these women to negotiate the "no-win" cultural dilemma by connecting work to family rather than to an independent life.

Conclusion

Gender is a system of linking in which social practices become linked to different groups of people.[38] These links can be strong or weak and they can change over time. While traditional gender divides linked women to the practice of caring for others and men to personal fulfillment through work, recent social changes have suggested that these links have weakened in recent years. Men are increasingly participating in the rearing of children, while women have expanded opportunities to find autonomy outside the home.[39] However, not only have the links to these practices altered over time, but the ways in which these social practices can be fulfilled has also changed. Women's obligatory caregiving has expanded in recent years to include work in both the public and the private spheres. It is no longer unquestionable for women only to pursue work inside the home, but neither is it culturally acceptable for women solely to pursue individual fulfillment through paid work. While women have broken away from traditional models of caregiving, they continue to bear responsibility for a gendered ideal of moral selflessness. Familial care work is now being performed in more arenas and the women in the study indicated that they felt obligated to perform care for others and to minimize the personal benefits of work. Just as women's opportunities have expanded, so too have their moral quandaries. As women negotiate these competing demands of work and family, they present remarkably similar accounts of very different actions. Gendered practices linking women to caregiving are being recreated on a daily basis, in numerous new ways, as women struggle to reconcile personal actions with moral expectations.

This chapter provides a theoretical frame through which to understand how women negotiated these changing moral ambiguities through rhetoric. Building from research on women's use of language, I tease out important distinctions in how language is deployed—as part of a larger narrative or in response to a particular question that evokes larger moral questions and cultural schemas.[40] Identifying the women's use of accounts allows for a broader theorization about the larger cultural significance of their responses, as their responses help us to develop a better picture of the moral ideologies tied to work and family practices. Although chapters 4 through 6 show that class, race, workforce experiences, and family support all contributed to women's work decisions, my investigation of accounts finds that despite work narratives that vary greatly according to class and race, women provide similar accounts for their work decisions. My use of accounts allows us both to see how women negotiate moral dilemmas that they faced and what they perceived these moral dilemmas to be. By distinguishing between narratives (the stories told in chapters 4 through 6) and accounts (the stories told in this chapter, when women were directly asked why they had left or remained at work), I find that women feel comfortable stating that they enjoy or dislike their jobs in their work narratives, but find it less acceptable to point to their work experiences when explaining their work decisions, instead deploying a "for the family" explanation for paid work.

By studying accounts provided across race and class, my research expands on earlier findings to suggest that the moral connotations of women's paid work are far reaching and not confined by class or race. Both employed and nonemployed women and middle- and working-class women strategically deployed "for the family" language when asked about their work decisions. While more middle-class than working-class women remained steadily employed, and middle-class and working-class women described very different reasons for leaving work, they presented remarkably similar accounts when asked to justify their work decisions. Although African American women historically described working for their families, today this language is shared with their white, Asian, and Latina contemporaries. Moreover, even African American women living in households with six-figure incomes deployed this language, in much the same way as their white upper-middle-class contemporaries did.

While the women's accounts suggest gender as an unyielding institution, their actions suggest a world in which caregiving practices linked to gender are being transformed. There remains, however, a gendered division of moral labor. While the accounts provide women expanded ways to fulfill caregiving and to pursue individual goals, they do not overturn moral gender ideologies that connect women's workforce participation with selfishness. In fact, the remarkable staying power of traditional culture divides is reflected in the discrepancies between women's work narratives and their accounts, which suggests women felt obligated to respond to traditional gender schemas. The extraordinary entrance of women into the labor market need not undermine cultural expectations that women's work should be connected to family obligations, because ideals of caregiving have expanded to include financial provision. Part of the resilience of the cultural schemas, then, comes from people's ability to modify gender schemas, while not challenging their overall authority.

By investigating women's accounts of family obligation, I find that women do not experience gendered social practices as static, but instead develop strategies to navigate current gender schemas, redefining their moral obligations in terms that better fit their current circumstances. The identification of these processes contributes to our understanding of how traditional gender divides remain culturally relevant, how people expand cultural schemas to fit their own social location, and how the process of expanding the framework of a schema through this negotiation process can allow traditional gender schemas to remain salient even while different actions are incorporated.

Women negotiated gendered cultural constraints through accounts of their workforce participation, and while these accounts allowed women to follow different paths, it did not give them access to better jobs or to institutions that were family friendly. The work narratives of the women with participation gaps provide ample evidence of the constraints faced by both working- and middle-class women. Accounts can provide moral high ground but cannot provide women with access to social or structural equality. The "for the family" language masked the importance of class, race, work experiences, and family support in women's workforce decision making, minimizing the reality that decisions reflect personal alongside familial needs, as well as structural opportunities and constraints.

8

HAVING IT ALL

Egalitarian Dreams Deferred

THE WOMEN IN this study faced daunting challenges. Where their mothers began adulthood at the precipice of revolutionary change, these women grew up in the aftermath of change, in a world filled with new opportunities but many of the same constraints. They faced the illness of spouses and lovers, parents and children. Some faced job loss, often more than once. Others had painful divorces, while still others celebrated theirs. Some had unexpected pregnancies, and others faced challenges in the search for a partner or decided to have fewer children, forgo childbirth, or leave the workforce. Unlike their mothers, they entered the workforce in unprecedented numbers, and the majority spent much of their young adulthood employed. Yet more like their mothers than they may have hoped or expected, the women faced repeated obstacles to their continued employment, including inflexible workplaces, a burdensome second shift at home, and, in the worst cases, poor pay, few opportunities, and a workplace that treated them as disposable. Despite these challenges, they formed families, forged work ties, and fashioned creative strategies for managing the demands made upon them as women, as workers, as mothers.

Looking across women's lives, we saw that women took not two common work pathways (working or not working), but three: some women worked steadily, others pulled back from paid jobs, and still others repeatedly moved in and out of the labor force. By identifying these three pathways, I found that the largest difference between the working and middle class is in the steady and interrupted pathways, not in the pulled-back pathways to which so much attention has been given. In fact, the majority of the middle-class women worked steadily, while less than one-third of the working-class women did so. Working-class women were much more likely to follow interrupted work pathways than their middle-class peers; 40 percent of working-class women did so compared to only 5 percent of middle-class women. While middle- and working-class women pulled back from work for different reasons, they pulled back at similar rates. Finally, the last section of the book investigated the continued focus on need as an explanatory factor for women's work, finding that most women, regardless of class, pointed to their families' needs when asked why they had followed various work pathways. Both employed and nonemployed women portrayed their employment decisions as based on family need, selflessly tied to others rather than driven by personal ambitions and failures or structural opportunities and constraints. The cultural expectations about selfless motherhood that lead women to say that they make work decisions for their family most likely continue to drive the public discourse about need.

Yet the women's narratives about their workforce experiences were much more complicated than their accounts of family needs. The women did consider their family needs when making work decisions, but, more important, these decisions were shaped by structural opportunities and constraints. All women in the study weighed the costs and benefits of working, and, for the most part, the metrics they used were similar. Most women demonstrated some level of choice in this decision-making process, but all of them also experienced constraints. Overall, those with the fewest constraints followed steady work pathways while the others took either pulled-back or interrupted pathways. The cases of the pulled-back and interrupted women suggest that the working-class women had fewer opportunities to stay in the workforce than their middle-class counterparts. Ultimately, the frames of need and choice constrain our public consciousness, pigeonholing women's work as selfishly chosen or unrewardingly forced. Instead, women examined the possibilities that lay before them and made decisions that they believed would be best for themselves and their families. We must move beyond the need and choice frameworks to create new ways of understanding women's labor that better reflect the realities of women's work: the structural and cultural obstacles and the personal and familial rewards. Until we do so, it is unlikely that women will be able to "have it all"—to have both a full family life and a full work life.[1]

Which Way to Look?

How could the women in this study come closer to their dreams of having it all? Many conservative pundits and institutions have suggested that we should look to the past for answers. In 2009, *New York Times* columnist Ross Douthat wrote that despite the fact that "American women are wealthier, healthier and better educated than they were 30 years ago, ... the achievements of the feminist era may have delivered women to greater unhappiness." Conservative institutions, such as the Family Research Council and the Heritage Foundation, sprang up in the wake of the civil rights and women's movements, and these groups claim that the changes brought by women's entrance into the labor market have not been positive ones: more families headed by single mothers, increased divorces, and increased abortion rates. But the lives of the women in this study suggest that we will not find answers to today's problems by looking to the past. Work has become an important component of women's lives, and, as Virginia explained in chapter 1, gives many women a reason to get out of bed in the morning. Moreover, the economy, both in America and elsewhere, has become dependent on the participation of female workers. If we cannot look back for answers, we must look forward, taking a page from Virginia, who continued to believe in new possibilities despite her share of disappointments at work.

Looking Forward

Working in America today means spending more time on the job, more economic instability, and less job security, especially for the working class.[2] The lack of affordable day care or paid family leave means that many families rely on a patchwork system to provide care for their children while they are at work or in emergencies. Simply put, the American workforce is not structured to make having it all a viable possibility for most families. Both men and women are left wanting more: "American parents—90% of American mothers and 95% of American fathers—say that they wish they had more time with their children."[3] Squeezed at work and at home, families need real solutions to these problems.

As we look forward, we must suggest ways to develop new institutional responses—both workplace and federal policies—to work-family conflict and to think about what cultural shifts may be necessary to build a more egalitarian society. These responses need to take into account the sizable class differences among women and the changing needs of families when all adults in a household work. There is no easy solution for these problems, as there were important class differences among the respondents. Remembering that working- and middle-class women left work for very different reasons, policy suggestions must address the different challenges across classes that women might face at work and at home. We must also address the ways that cultural beliefs about intensive motherhood undermine women's long-term workforce participation for both middle- and working-class women.

Class Matters: Making Work More Equitable

Since the 1970s, women have made great strides in the labor market, and the women I spoke with benefited from an economic and social revolution. But these changes have been incomplete, leaving many working-class and working-poor women on the margins of the labor market and in some of the most vulnerable social positions.[4] Policies focusing on educational attainment and the creation of more good jobs for the working class and working poor could improve the lives of the greatest number of women. While women are more likely to gain high school and college degrees than men, there are large discrepancies among women both across class and race, with higher high school and college graduation rates for middle-class and white women.[5]

Increased wages may be the best way to create more egalitarian opportunities for women at work. Over the last thirty years, low-income families experienced a huge drop in their income—an average of a 29 percent decrease, while families in the middle third of the income bracket saw a 13 percent decline.[6] In other words, when adjusted for inflation, two-thirds of American families are now making less than they did thirty years ago. Only families in the upper third experienced an overall gain of seven percent.[7] Raising the wages of working-poor and working-class women would go a long way toward reducing the wage and work gap between working-class and middle-class women. Since women continue to make less than men, and this gap is particularly apparent among nonprofessional women (approximately 80 percent of all women), they may have less incentive to remain employed when they receive low pay—particularly when they are faced with high child care costs.[8]

The lives of the women who followed interrupted pathways suggest that the problem for workers is not simply a problem of declining wages, but also a decline in good jobs.[9] Sociologists Phyllis Moen and Patricia Roehling note that the current labor market depends on two workforces: the primary workforce of full-time steady work and the "secondary workforce" that is composed primarily of women and that "does not require the wages, benefits or security associated with jobs in the primary sector."[10] This secondary labor market is primarily made up of bad jobs, positions that are considered easily replaceable and temporary and are often in the service sector, which hires more women than men.[11] Many of the interrupted workers found themselves employed by companies that had no real investment in maintaining their continued employment.

When companies can rely on the availability of an underemployed short-term workforce, they have no incentive to treat workers better. The women who worked in these sectors were the least successful and most unhappy. Because women are more likely to take time off from work and bear the subsequent costs of the difficulty in returning to the labor market, women make up a sector of the workforce that is most vulnerable to this type of exploitation. If we are to gain a more equitable workforce, we must consider how to increase the value of long-term employees, by giving employers incentives to treat low-skilled workers better.

These changes require not only policy changes but also a shift in our cultural understanding of whose work is valued and how we reward people's paid work. The distinctions made between blue-collar and white-collar work often devalue the work done by the working class. While it may be poorly paid or overly routinized or vigorously demeaned, the work that women do, both in the home and in poorly paid sectors of our economy, is important and necessary to keep our society functioning. Most interrupted women left their jobs not when they found out that they were paid poorly (they already knew that) but when they were demeaned or their contributions belittled. Structural changes that bring greater financial rewards to working-class work may do the most toward changing minds about the value of women's work.

Families Matter: Reducing Work-Family Conflict

It has been more than thirty years since the economist Heidi Hartmann wrote that our economic system relies on the presence of an unpaid worker in the home.[12] In the ensuing years, the doors of boardrooms, courtrooms, and hospitals have opened to female workers, but institutions have not changed further to accommodate a workforce that no longer can rely on the support of an unpaid worker at home. As women entered the workforce in increasing numbers, the demands on parents, particularly mothers, increased, not decreased, placing additional burdens on women and men already strained by the loss of a full-time caregiver. For the over 80 percent of my respondents who were employed, at least part time, these burdens were experienced in different ways—middle-class women were more likely to face extremely long work hours, while working-class women were more likely to face inadequate child care provisions and a lack of resources to afford paid child care.

While companies have come a long way in incorporating women into the paid labor market, little has been done systematically or nationally to address the loss of the unpaid worker in the home in the wake of women's entrance to the labor market. Although fathers are participating more in housework and child care, their increased participation cannot replace a full-time caregiver in the home, particularly when all adults in a household work full time.[13] As a result, families are often left struggling to provide care for their children, facing additional challenges when children are sick or need additional care.[14] Working-class women are particularly vulnerable, because they rely on a network cobbled together from family members, friends, and paid caregivers.[15] Reliance on multiple caregivers makes women's workforce participation tenuous, because women are more likely to be the primary caregivers and are more likely to leave work if child care needs cannot be met.[16] Broader access to a free, or heavily subsidized, day care system would be an important step toward building a more equitable society.

Between 90 and 99 percent of children aged three to five years in Italy, Belgium, and France have access to publicly run day care, unlike the United States where day care is only universally available when children enter kindergarten.[17] Furthermore, since families in the United States must rely on a jerry-rigged system of private care facilities, poorly paid home care workers, and family members, the overall quality of day care in the United States is poor.[18] Not only is access to publicly supported child care less available and often of poorer quality in the United States, child care costs have become yet another source of inequality. In France, families from all classes spend approximately 7 to 8 percent of their income for day care for children under the age of three.[19] In America, low-income families spend up to 22 percent of their annual income on child care, while higher-income families spend 6 percent.[20] Ironically, the women whose work is the least remunerative must pay the greatest proportion of their income toward child care. Child care costs may outweigh the benefits of work, particularly in low-income families. A national day care system would go a long way toward addressing this challenge.

Paid parental leave, including longer maternity leaves, should be another priority. As most parents attest, having a child dramatically changes lives, from bihourly feedings to new sleeping patterns. Yet only 10 percent of working mothers have access to paid maternity leaves.[21] The majority of women who spoke to me about their pregnancies reported having, at best, six to eight weeks of state-required disability leave after giving birth. Most felt that this did not provide them with enough time to acclimate to the new demands on their time. Virginia explained, "There needs to be some kind of more maternal leave. Definitely. [There needs to be] some sort of leniency [for when] the mother would go back to work." Virginia then suggested that America should emulate some of the more progressive European plans: "Europe, I think they have, like, at least a year [of maternity leave]."

While it is hard to imagine generous family leaves being incorporated into American public policy, Sweden has recently introduced policies that allow for both maternity and paternity leaves that pay 80 percent of the parent's salary and allow for 480 total days of leave (that can be taken by either mother or father), provided that the father take a minimum of sixty days leave.[22] By adding incentives to encourage both mothers and fathers to take these leaves, the government has also attempted to address concerns of discriminatory penalties at work that occur when only women take these leaves.[23] Longer maternity leaves might also pave the way for companies to do a better job of retaining well-trained employees, because women who are unable to go back after three months (when most day cares charge high rates for infant care) could go back after a year (when child care costs drop). More generous paid parental leaves would be critically important to working-class and working-poor women, who are more likely to need to take time off from work than women from other classes and who pay a higher wage price for motherhood.[24] Paid leaves or even more generous unpaid leaves could allow these women to return to the workforce without penalties, such as loss of wages and being "mommy-tracked."

When I first invited women to participate in this project, I opened our phone conversation by saying, "I realize that you are likely quite busy, but if I only speak to women who aren't busy, then I will have little understanding of what women's life is like today."[25] Most of the women laughed at this, and some, like Cynthia, said that they agreed to participate because the statement so aptly summarized their lives. Cynthia, whose story is found in chapter 1, explained, "I always feel so frazzled and hurrying about things." But she wished that she could "spend more time with [her kids] and less time worrying about cleaning and work stuff." In fact, research suggests that women's and men's lives are becoming more rushed, and the majority of women report that they often feel overburdened by the twin time demands of work and home.[26]

Middle-class families are most likely to face extreme hours of overwork, but, as we saw in chapter 5, working-class fathers can work two or even three jobs to support a family, and, in families when both parents work, there is less time to spend on the work that used to be done by a stay-at-home caregiver.[27] Middle-class workers are more likely to work extremely long hours, but they also have greater access to flexible hours.[28] More than two out of three American workers report that they have little to no control over their work hours, and almost 90 percent of American workers have less than two weeks of vacation and sick days per year.[29] And single mothers work more total hours (including paid labor and work done at home) than married mothers and married fathers do.[30] It could not be more plain that the way that we work isn't working for most American families. Work-family researchers suggest that it will be necessary to restructure organizations to provide more flexibility in the hours and the manner in which people work.[31] This may mean reducing the emphasis on visibility at work for professional workers, allowing them to take advantage of the flexibility built into their work days. This may also mean providing additional paid sick days and paid parental leaves for lower-income workers. These types of policy changes require an understanding of how work-family challenges are experienced differently across classes, so that the policies created can respond to a diverse workforce.

Gender Matters: Building an Equitable Future

I am often asked what I think I would have found had I interviewed men instead of women. I think, and current research would support, that many of my findings would be similar if I investigated men's work patterns. I would have found evidence of all three pathways—steady, interrupted, and pulled back—although I suspect few men would be in the pulled-back category, as men who act as stay-at-home care-givers remain a decided minority.[32] I likely would have found that job conditions matter for men, too, and that they also leave work when they find it unrewarding or when they feel unappreciated or belittled, but men may be more constrained in how they leave work. There would have been class and race differences for men, too, although Leslie McCall's *Complex Inequality* suggests that it is necessary to investigate specific workforce circumstances to understand how race, class, and gender intersect in people's work lives.[33]

Despite the likelihood that men's and women's work pathways have many similarities, the lives of the eighty women I interviewed suggest that gender continues to play a significant role in women's workforce participation. Gender is a socially constructed framework that influences how people do things big and small: dress, walk, parent, find jobs, and live their lives. Yet multiple gender ideologies operate at the same time; women can wear dresses or suits to work and they can work steadily throughout their adult lives or leave work to care for children and be primarily responsible for household chores.[34] But cultural expectations about what is appropriate gender-specific behavior can limit the range of options available and how people can negotiate those options.

It may not be enough to enact policies that provide better jobs, access to affordable child care, paid maternity and paternity leaves, and increased workplace flexibility. As long as "ideal-worker norms,"[35] that is, who is considered the best worker, remain tied to gender, reducing work-family conflict may remain out of reach for most women. Gender continues to influence social norms about why women work. The women's accounts of their workforce decisions suggest that those decisions are connected to family needs. Although men likely also feel a burden to participate in the workforce and support a family, they are less likely to think that society construes their decisions about work as selfish if they are not immediately tied to family needs.[36] Women, on the other hand, described an overwhelming cultural mandate to connect their work decisions to their families' needs. Changing expectations about women's roles as mothers has demanded more intensive participation from mothers in their children's lives. My findings suggest that an important component of women's changing workforce participation is the ideal of the selfless woman. Decisions to work steadily are acceptable, as long as women explain that these decisions are related to family needs. Similarly, decisions to leave work were also explained as fulfilling family needs. Even when work decisions reflected women's own desires to keep a well-paying and interesting job or to leave one that paid poorly and was disrespected, women explained that they worked for their families. Most of the women felt torn between their desires to pursue work strategies that considered their job satisfaction and family support and the expectation that they would pursue choices that were best for their families.

But what if there was a way for women to express a desire to work that could incorporate both the familial reasons and the personal ones? Over the last thirty years, women have entered the workforce in large numbers and have made considerable progress in the public sphere, and men have made strides at home, steadily increasing their participation in child care and household chores. Yet women remain obligated to legitimize their work decisions, using accounts of need to defend actions that led either to employment or nonemployment. We must move beyond these accounts, recognizing that women's work decisions incorporate the personal and familial benefits of work and the disappointments that women face at work and at home.

Few of the women felt that they "had it all" when I met with them. Although many led satisfying lives, they imagined a golden era in the future, a time at which the demands of their and their partners' paid work would be less and their children would not need constant care. Asked to think about her future, Virginia speculated, "I would like to work.... How old am I? Thirty-five. Maybe ten more years and then I would like to retire." But how would she attain that goal? Virginia gave her easy laugh. "I'm going to win the Lotto.... But [sighs] I don't know. I think I'll be where I am now. Work, home, kids." Like Virginia, most women in the study expected that having it all was as improbable as winning the lottery.

The media is filled with examples of writers who gleefully emphasize that women can't really have it all. In fact, the phrase "having it all" often is used to reproach women for wanting too much. In this demoralizing framework, women may want to have it all, to have both work and family, but they will learn that they can't. Writing in 2002 for *USA Today*, Karen Peterson says that successful women are "having it all— except children." In a 2005 op-ed column for the *New York Times*, Maureen Dowd writes that the problem for professional women is finding a husband willing to accept an educated wife, because high-powered men are more likely to want "the young women whose job it was to tend to them and care for them in some way: their secretaries, assistants, nannies, caterers, flight attendants, researchers and fact-checkers." These authors write that women may want to have it all, but they cannot. Women may have a career, but they cannot also have children or attract the attention of a man.

While having it all is sometimes appropriated in these antifeminist ways (suggesting that women are asking for too much), I use it here to suggest that having it all, too often, is out of the reach of both men and women, and that, as a society, we might aspire to the goal of achieving equality at home and at work for both men and women. Achieving this goal will require attention to the needs of working class and middle class, to the needs of women and men, and to the needs of people of all races. These goals require a new political commitment to reduce work-family conflict, to create a changed work environment, to develop family-friendly policies, to promote good jobs for all, to raise the minimum wage, and to ensure equal opportunities across race, class, and gender in the workforce.

There is no one solution that will make having it all within our reach. But Virginia's words suggest a path forward: "We all work and strive, because every parent wants the best for their kids." If we are to take her words to heart, then we must all work and strive to find solutions to create a more egalitarian world for our next generation.

Appendix

I began this project with three goals: to investigate women's work pathways, to understand why some left work while others stayed, and to find out how women themselves described their work decisions. While there have been larger studies that have shown that working-class women are less likely to be employed than middle-class women, there are few well-developed theories for why this is the case. I chose to use in-depth interviews because a qualitative study design would allow me to study women's perceptions of their work choices, the motivations behind their work choices, and the meanings that they attach to these choices. Interviewing women, then, would allow me to develop better theories about women and the meaning of their work in the twenty-first century.

Different research methods can help us understand different aspects of women's workforce participation. Quantitative research is particularly useful for showing national trends in women's labor market participation but is less able to explain the process through which labor market decisions are made. Qualitative research is better suited to meet this goal, but it often relies on snowball or network sampling—methods of finding people that do not rely on the principle of randomness. The potential for self-selection bias is quite high in such studies, and nonmeasurable bias is often built into the sample. These methods can result in overly homogenous samples that may exaggerate the differences between classes.

In an attempt to address these challenges, I devised a strategy that would draw from both qualitative and quantitative methods. I conducted in-depth interviews—to examine process—and I used a random sample of eighty women—to ensure a diverse population. Although this is a small group, the random sampling process can give us confidence in the generalizations made here. In the social sciences, it has long been accepted that the data from qualitative interviews—that is, the answers given by respondents—can be systematically compared to develop "analytic generalizations" that provide insights into the topic—in our case, women and work.[1] These insights, when developed through careful study design and analysis, can give us a deeper understanding of the processes through which women enter and leave work and how they understand this process.

Selecting a Sample

As life history analysis offers the possibility to examine the intersection of people's personal choices and the time period during which these decisions are made, it is important to choose people who are at similar life stages. Since the variation in women's work decisions could stem from structural changes due to social change, examining one cohort allows for an analysis of how social transformations influence women. For the purposes of this study, I examined the generation of women who were born between 1966 and 1976, targeting women between the ages of thirty-two and forty-two at the time of the study. These women followed the first big wave of women into the workforce and were influenced by the feminist revolution of the 1970s but not part of it. They were also old enough to establish themselves separately from their parents and to have made decisions about work and motherhood or anticipated such decisions.

I decided to include both women who had married and those who had not, and those who had children and those who did not. I wanted to include all women in this age category, because women's work and family choices are closely tied together. Interviewing women who had decided not to marry or not to have children might help us better understand cultural and social norms about women's work.

And how would I find the women in New York City? I had chosen New York because I lived there at the time of the interviews and knew that I could find a diverse group of women there. It would be impractical and too costly for me to try to find women across the country. I knew that I wanted to find people through random sampling, but knocking on doors in neighborhoods would have had several difficulties. First, it would be hard to know if women in the age bracket I wanted to study lived in the household. Second, many apartment buildings in New York City have doormen or other barriers that would have made it impossible to knock on doors.

Third, it was unlikely that New Yorkers would open their doors to a stranger. And fourth, it would have been incredibly time consuming to knock on people's doors.

The New York City Voter Registration Database solved these problems. The New York City Board of Elections collects data on every registered voter and the information is publicly accessible—anyone can either look through their paper records or request a digital copy. The New York City Voter Registration Database is updated several times a year and includes demographic information, including name, address, age, sex, and race. This meant that I, with the gracious and much-appreciated help of Dr. John Mollenkopf, a professor of political science at the Graduate School of the City University of New York, could identify people who would fit the criteria—those who were listed as female and between the ages of thirty-two and forty-two—and then use a statistical program, SPSS, to randomly select participants. This database is one of the largest available on New York City residents, because according to the Current Population Survey from the U.S. Census, over 87 percent of eligible citizens are registered to vote in New York City. Using this data also had a time-saving component through the easy identification of subjects and provision of accurate contact information, as it is updated several times a year.

But there was still another problem with finding these women in New York City. One advantage of drawing a sample from the metropolitan area is the diversity of possible respondents. One of the drawbacks is that many city neighborhoods contain either the very wealthy or the very poor. Neither group would particularly well represent the average American. Because one of the primary goals of this study was to understand the role of class in women's workforce participation, it was crucial that I find a diverse sample. Using data from the 2000 U.S. Census, I identified tracts—areas that were slightly larger than neighborhoods—that were most similar to the national population in terms of several key factors including race, gender, and women's workforce participation. I then devised a stratified sample, using a combined ranking of income and education level to identify the tracts by class quartile, selecting one tract per quartile. Finally, I randomly selected twenty subjects from the Voter Registration Database lists of women aged thirty-two to forty-two living in each of the neighborhoods.

Conducting Interviews

In 2006 and 2007, I conducted in-depth qualitative interviews with eighty women randomly selected in New York City. I sent each participant a letter describing the study and then followed this letter with a phone call, which screened for ineligible participants and made appointments with those who agreed to participate. There was a 70 percent response rate. This is an unusually high response rate for a study with a random sample, but I think this occurred for several reasons. This topic was personally important to many of the respondents, who felt that they had inside information that they wanted to share with me. As I mentioned in chapter 8, I devised a strategy in which I explained to participants that if only nonbusy women participated in the study, then I would have no understanding of what women's lives are really like. I hoped that this statement would help potential volunteers see the value of participating in my study, by demonstrating that I had an understanding of what women's busy lives were like, and showing that I was truly interested in their experiences. Finally, respondents received $50 for their participation, thanks to the generosity of my graduate school dissertation chair, Dr. Kathleen Gerson of New York University.

The interviews lasted, on average, two to three hours and the vast majority of the interviews were conducted in the women's homes, allowing me to gain a further glimpse into their lives. The longest interview lasted close to six hours and the shortest lasted just over one hour. I took detailed notes on every interview subject, including their features, their clothing, their homes, their neighborhoods, and anyone I met while with them. When women could not meet me in their homes, we met at Starbucks and offices (theirs and mine), and I took detailed notes on these interactions, as well. Three participants had had recently moved before the interviews and had not updated their voter registration, so we met over the phone.

I carefully constructed the interview to facilitate systematic comparisons among the subjects. The interview contained questions on topics including family history, educational background, work history, current work circumstances, dating and marriage, childbearing and rearing, gender and family ideologies, a class mobility assessment, work-family conflict, household responsibilities, and future plans. It was important to not influence women's responses, so all questions were framed in the most value-neutral way possible. All opinion questions were given at the end of the interviews, so that respondents did not feel that they had to match their actions to their opinions. I asked detailed questions about what had taken place in the women's lives and then I asked them to interpret these events, asking why certain actions or events had been taken. This was an important part of the process, as once people attempt to explain why they have taken an action, they may be more likely to attempt to match actions taken to explanations about these actions. Therefore, I asked "why" questions only at the end of each section.

Interviews rely on the responses that the interviewee shares, which might be problematic given the fact that she may provide a "socially desirable response." While it is not possible to rule out the possibility of the socially desirable response, I formatted the interview guide to present the most value-neutral starting questions, so as to not lead the interview subject toward one particular answer. During the course of the interviews, many women said things that surprised me, challenged my presumptions, and, occasionally, made me feel uncomfortable. These varying responses suggested that the majority were being as forthright as possible with me. This forthrightness came, perhaps, because so many of the respondents felt that this research was about their lives. Over a dozen respondents called me in advance of my announced upcoming call (I sent letters notifying women that I would contact them in a week or two) because they wanted to let me know that I needed to talk to them personally about these issues.[2] It would be naive to imagine that the women did not attempt to present themselves in the best light possible, but this too can be valuable, as we learn what women perceive to be the best responses.

By formulating and using an open-ended interview schedule, I was able to allow the interview subject to drive the content of her response while also ensuring that I had similar data on each subject. This meant that I allowed every woman to answer each question in her own way. For some women, I asked a question and they answered both that question and the next ten on my list, which I then skipped over. For other women, I asked each and every question, because they gave short and direct answers. While this approach demanded careful attention to their words as well as to my interview questions, I believe it gave them the opportunity to more fully express themselves in the interviews. When I asked a question and a woman responded in a manner other than I was expecting, I did not interrupt or change the course of her response. When women provided unexpected information that seemed incomplete, I probed further to better understand their responses.

Sample Diversity

The sampling strategy yielded great class diversity. But there were some drawbacks, including a limited number of women from different races and of nonheterosexual participants. While I did not control for race, I did not oversample, leaving me with a majority of respondents who were white. While this decision allows me to explore a range of issues surrounding class, the small sample size in each racial group makes it inadvisable to draw strong conclusions about the role of race in women's workforce trajectories. When possible (and applicable), I do discuss the issues of race that were most prominent in my findings. However, I believe that further research is warranted to better substantiate my findings about the intersection of class, gender, and race. The small sample size of each racial group limits my ability to thoroughly investigate this line of inquiry.

The exclusion of noncitizens and those who are not registered voters may have depressed the inclusion of some of the most disadvantaged members of our society. Although the sampling strategy may mitigate this problem, it cannot eliminate it. Additionally, since the women ranged in age from thirty-two to forty-two with an average age of thirty-eight, their work trajectories were clearly unfinished and do not represent the entirety of their work-family experiences. They do, however, capture the first twenty years or so of adulthood, an ample time period to study. Finally, since only one participant identified as gay, it is impossible to identify whether heterosexuality privileges or constrains a woman's workforce participation.

Confidentiality

Confidentiality is an important aspect of qualitative social science. It allows people to participate in interviews for a book such as this without fearing that there could be consequences for what they share. Many women shared very private information with me, some of which was not included in this book at their request, and it is important to make sure that their participation remain confidential. I take these concerns seriously and have done my best to conceal the identity of participants. All names have been changed—including the names of the participants, their spouses, their children, and their workplaces. I used pseudonyms that reflected the nature of the women's names, as many had names that were important reflections of their ethnic, religious, or racial heritage. The Social Security Administration database provides detailed information on names given to babies in the years that the women were born, and I primarily used pseudonyms that were common in those years. I made exceptions for those cases where women's names were not common and searched for similar pseudonyms that reflected specific ethnic or religious origin.

Direct quotes are used whenever possible. At times, I used brackets to indicate that I am filling in a sentence with my own words. I tried to limit this practice, so that the women's words were not filtered, but it was necessary in some cases, such as when the women used a specific name that could identify them, when the audiotape recording of a word was inaudible, and when the phrasing of a sentence might be confusing to a reader without several pages of transcription. I tried to avoid the last as often as possible, but I did not want their voices to be left unheard simply because of a lack of context.

Analysis

Once the interviewing process was over, all of the interviews were transcribed and entered into the Atlas TI software package. I coded field notes, interview transcripts, and other pieces of data according to categories such as entrance into the workforce, the wage gap, unpaid labor, marital status, presence of dependents, and gender ideology. When unexpected patterns emerged, I developed new analytic categories, such as workforce ties. To better understand women's labor market participation, I also traced women's employment history, charting their entrances and exits from the workforce. This process led me to develop the three different pathway categories.

Life-history interviews invite subjects to create narratives about their life events, which tell us which events the subjects perceive to be important in their lives.[3] In this tradition, I created a work history section in my interview schedule, which included descriptive questions about the women's workforce participation.[4] I coded the answers to the questions from this section, such as stories about a new boss or newly inflexible work schedule, as work narratives. At the end of the work section, I asked respondents to explain their work decisions. Depending on their work history, I asked, "Why did you decide to leave work?" or "Did you ever consider leaving work? Why or why not?" This section preceded the family history section, and I asked these series of questions before I introduced any questions about work-family conflict. While it is possible that respondents anticipated that I was asking about work-family balance here, this was not, in fact, my original intent, and I did not introduce families into the interview until later. In fact, it is very interesting that women interpreted a question about work as a question about work and family. The responses to these questions were coded as accounts, because they were justifications that came specifically when prompted by an interview question. The only exception to this was participants' spontaneous introduction of themselves to me, in which they evaluated their work decisions, as in "I'm a stay-at-home mom, so I can care for my kids."[5]

There was no evidence that the accounts were false consciousness; in fact, it seems entirely likely that both family needs and the details of their work experiences found in their narratives were important factors in their decision making. Instead, we can see how accounts can be agentic, allowing social actors to negotiate cultural norms through their explanations of their behavior and deflecting potentially negative judgments about their actions.

In-depth interviews rely on people's memories of their lives, which are undoubtedly clouded by age and distance. While I take these qualifications seriously, I feel that they did not compromise the integrity of the research. Despite concerns over the limitations of women's recollections, life history analysis remains the best method for collecting longitudinal qualitative data, as many scholars in this area have demonstrated, including Mary Blair-Loy, Anita Garey, Kathleen Gerson, and Pamela Stone. Other methods, such as those that follow a panel of subjects over the long term, would be prohibitively expensive and would contain other problems, such as participants leaving the study. By constructing the interviews in a chronological manner, asking first about their parents, then their school experiences, their work, their dating, and so on, I worked to reduce errors in women's recollection. Women also recalled feeling differently about work and family as young adults than they did at the time of the interview. This can also increase our confidence in the findings, as women did not attempt to create a coherent narrative about their lives. The very subject of this study is women's own understanding of their lived experiences and their perceptions of their work trajectories—and we must assume that these understandings are shaped by time, as well. Recollections of the past may be limited, but it is women's current understanding of those past events that shape their lives today.

Notes

1. Throughout the book, I discuss the decisions that women make about work. It should be noted here that I always consider these decisions to be constrained in some (and sometimes many) ways. As Reskin and Maroto have recently argued, "job seekers choose jobs for which to apply or turn down. But it does not follow from the fact that some people train for or seek certain kinds of work that most workers choose their occupations. Treating workers' distributions across occupations as reflecting workers' choices does not square with how labor markets operate" (2011: 83). Labor markets operate in such a way that some women have better options on the table from which to make their work decisions than do other women.

2. Crittenden 2001; Garey 1999; Ginsburg 1989; Rosen 1987; Stone 2007; Williams 1991.

3. The gender divide in moral labor is often thought to remain salient today, even as there have been changes in these divides (Folbre 2001; Gerson 2002; Kimmel 1996; Moen 1992; Bernard 1981).

4. Blair-Loy 2003: 4–15. I build from Mary Blair-Loy's premise that work and family are cultural schemas—packages of beliefs and understanding—that have been "institutionalized and partially internalized models for cognition, morality and emotion" (2003: 175). Moreover, Blair-Loy contends, we must also consider how "culture provides powerful moral evaluations and evokes intense emotions" (2003: 176).

5. As men were not interviewed in this study, it is impossible to know if men would give similar explanations for their workforce participation. In fact, the women's responses do suggest a considerable shift in traditional expectations about caregiving. However, although men likely also feel a burden to participate in the workforce and support a family, they are less likely to think that society would construe their decisions about work as selfish if they are not immediately tied to family needs (Coltrane 1996; Kimmel 1996). Scholars have long noted that men have more access

to free time and self-interested tasks than women (see Cancian 1987; Hochschild 1989, 1997). This suggests that this particular way of framing workforce participation as "for the family" (and its use across class, race, and employment level) may be particular to women.

6. See Levy 1995; Collins 1991; Garey 1999; Johnson 2002; Blair-Loy 2003: 89; Hacker 2006: 88. Please note that I use "work," "paid work," and "workforce participation" interchangeably here. A long line of noted scholars have clearly demonstrated that unpaid labor done in the home should also be considered work (see Hartmann 1976), and I acknowledge the labor done inside the home throughout the book. I use the term *work* loosely to include all paid labor, even if the work is done in the informal economy.

7. Researchers have long argued that men's declining workforce participation and sinking wages forced women into the workforce (Glenn et al. 1994; Sidel 1990; Weiner 1985). Over the last several decades, critics of early feminist scholarship have shown that the focus on the women who entered the workforce in the 1970s obscured the fact that historically, working-class women and women of color were more likely to participate in paid work than their middle-class, white contemporaries (Collins 1991; Higginbotham and Romero 1997; Garey 1999). The increase in women's workforce participation in the 1970s was primarily a middle-class phenomenon, because working-class and minority women were already at work (Landry 2000; Rubin 1994).

8. See figure 1.1; England 2010. Husbands making six-figure salaries often work in high-status jobs with long hours, factors that increase the likelihood that women will leave work (Cha 2010; Schieman et al. 2009). Recent research by Shafer (2011) suggests a slightly different picture in which it is women's relative income compared to their husband's that influences their continued employment.

9. U.S. Bureau of Labor Statistics 2008; see also Percheski 2008; Cohen and Bianchi 1999.

10. Juhn and Murphy 1997.

11. In 2007, 63 percent of all women with children under age six were employed, as were 78 percent of mothers with children ages six to seventeen (U.S. Bureau of Labor Statistics 2008).

12. St. George 2009.

13. Goldin 1990; Blau and Kahn 2006; Percheski 2008; Juhn and Murphy 1997; Cohen and Bianchi 1999; England et al. 2004; Cotter et al. 2008; Goldstein and Kenny 2001.

14. See Williams 2000: 150–161; Blair-Loy 2003: 89; Stone 2007: 66–67, for example. In fact, Joan Williams notes that, in an attempt to gain support for the women's movement and women's entrance into the labor market, feminists "have changed [Betty] Friedan's argument that women *want* to work to achieve self-development into an argument that women *need* to work to help support their families" (2000: 153).

15. See Collins (1991) and Higginbotham and Romero (1997) for discussions of working-class women's historic labor force participation rates. See also Johnson (2002), Garey (1999), and Ferree (1984).

16. Goldin 1990; Coontz 1992.

17. Chao and Rhones 2007.

18. Bianchi et al. 2006.

19. Jacobs and Gerson 2004.

20. Levy and Michel 1991; Rubin 1994.

21. Women from working-class and working-poor backgrounds, in particular, may place a higher value on their time at home than on their potential earning power, which is likely low. This calculation places a "shadow price" on women's earnings ability versus their time spent in the home (Heckman 1974).

22. England 2010; England et al. 2004; Shafer 2011. Shafer (2011) notes that the husband's hours at work also play an important role.

23. The emphasis on financial needs diminishes the social and psychological reasons that women might want to work (Ferree 1984; Garey 1999). Work-family scholars often explain the difference in women's workforce participation across class as stemming from the differential rewards of this work. Yet, viewing working-class jobs as less rewarding may be an elitist understanding of whose work and what work could be valuable or rewarding. Historically, work done by the working class has been culturally devalued in the United States (Rose 2004). But working-class men and women often receive great satisfaction from their paid work, benefiting financially, socially, and psychologically (Komarovsky 1964; Ferree 1976, 1987; Segura 1994; Garey 1999; Rosen 1987). This satisfaction may stem from the greater autonomy that comes with a paycheck, but it also stems from the relationships established at work, the tasks accomplished, and a sense of pride in their work (Johnson 2002; Newman 1999). But still, this line of inquiry generally does not challenge the idea that working-class women need to work.

24. Stone 2007. Work-family scholars have found that a number of factors other than financial need influence a woman's workforce participation decisions. Marital insecurity and career opportunities can lead women to increase their commitment to work, while constrained work opportunities and a lack of child care support can send women toward full- or part-time domesticity (Blair-Loy 2003; Gerson 1985). Women who experience positive opportunities at work, such as promotions, may find themselves more committed to the labor market, but women who experience roadblocks, such as being denied promotions when they become mothers or being denied a flexible schedule, may turn toward the home (Roth 2006; Stone 2007).

25. White-collar professional jobs tend to be more time demanding than blue-collar or service industry work (Jacobs and Gerson 2004). Because marriages are increasingly made up of couples from the same class with high levels of education and class homogamy (Blackwell and Lichter 2004; Arum et al. 2008), middle-class couples may face a greater time crunch than working-class partners.

26. See also Boushey 2007; Williams 2010; Stone and Lovejoy 2002. Moreover, Lynne Haney (2002) finds that states define "needs" differently, constructing who constitutes the "needy" and therefore is deserving of state welfare. Just as states construct needs, so, too, do women make sense of their own needs based on their current standards of living and their social status (England 1992). As we will see, need is not simply an expression of economic concerns but is often used to encompass a wide range of demands, including familial responsibilities and personal interests.

27. It is important to note that working-class women may find caregiving and work done in the home both personally rewarding and protective—a safe haven from an unwelcoming labor market (Webber and Williams 2008; Williams 2000; Rubin 1994; Garey 1999; Howe 1977).

28. Martin 2009.

29. Hays 1996. Nonmothers are also subject to these pressures (Hays 1996).

30. The one woman who did not spend any significant amount of time in the workforce was diagnosed with lupus at a young age, and doctors warned that working could be dangerous to her health.

31. Kathleen Gerson (1985) notes that this kind of life history analysis provides an ideal method for examining what C. Wright Mills called the "problems of biography, of history, and of their intersections within social structures" (1959: 143).

32. U.S. Census Bureau 2010.

33. Sociologist Annette Lareau (2003) notes that classical debates about the study of social class demand a level of differentiation between classes that is difficult, if not impossible, to approximate with a small qualitative sample size. Instead, she proposes that occupation can serve as a measure of social class, by measuring the level of education required for the job and its authority level.

34. In two cases, I diverged slightly from this strategy: two families that included a nurse with a two-year degree instead of a four-year degree and a husband in a blue-collar job. I considered the family working class because of my discussion with the respondents, which led me to believe that they had resources (of both income and status) that were more similar to their working-class peers than to their middle-class peers.

35. This seems somewhat straightforward, but sociologists have had a hard time translating measures of social class to women, as they wonder if a woman's occupation can be used to measure social class or if it is necessary to use her husband's occupation. The "conventional approach" to stratification research assumes the family is the unit of interest in social class research and that the man, as the head of the household, determines the family's class position (Goldthorpe 1984; Sørensen 1994). There have been two primary challenges to the conventional view that measured only men's class position. One calls for a focus on the individual as the unit of analysis for class position, rather than the family (Acker 1989; Delphy 1984). The second challenge argues that it is necessary to consider the family as the unit of analysis in stratification research and that it is possible to consider women's workforce participation by examining the joint classification of both the husband's and wife's occupational class (Heath and Britten 1984; Beller 2009). Recently, there has been growing evidence that class background is located in a family and that all adult family members contribute to that position (Beller 2009). My research suggests that both wife's and husband's occupational status contribute to a family's class status. Therefore, I considered the occupation of both spouses to determine social class. If one spouse has a higher occupational status than the other, the highest status was used to determine class position.

36. U.S. Census Bureau 2007 (accessed April 28, 2009). Data on marital status is for all women over the age of fifteen, and in all other cases, for men and women over the age of fifteen. Data on divorce and remarriage is not available in this data set. Education levels are used to estimate class percentages. Race and ethnicity numbers do not add up to 100 percent because Latinos may be included in both Latino and white categories. Data for the statistic on childbearing rates are drawn from Jane Dye (2006), *Fertility of American Women: 2006*. Data describe women ages forty to forty-four; the number is slightly lower than the number of childless women in my study, but some of the women in the study were younger and may still have children. Data on employment statistics are drawn from Chao and Rhones (2007).

37. Friedan 1963: 95.

38. Gornick and Meyers 2003.

CHAPTER 2

1. Elder 1998; Moen 2001; Elder et al. 2003. Gender shapes workforce participation and family life across the life course (Moen and Chermack 2005), and women's occupational choices across young adulthood are shaped by a series of gendered transitions: entrance into work, into unions, and into motherhood (Moen and Han 2001; Williams and Han 2003). Women's paid workforce participation, often characterized by work stoppages, time out of work, and time spent

caring for children, is best understood from a life course perspective (Moen 2001; Altucher and Williams 2003).

2. Much of the research on women's workforce participation decisions remains focused on cross-sectional data, rather than longitudinal employment trends (see Boushey 2008; Cohen and Bianchi 1999; England et al. 2004; Cotter et al. 2008). Although this research provides important challenges to the choice and need frameworks, it depends on a fairly static picture of women's workforce participation.

3. Spain and Bianchi 1996.

4. Milgrom and Petersen 2006: 183. There may be important class differences that can be discovered by looking at longitudinal work pathways. Although research on working-class women has suggested that the distinction between full-time and part-time work reflects an elitist understanding of what kind of workforce participation counts as committed work (Garey 1999; Zavella 1987; Ferree 1984), the costs of part-time work have been documented (McGrath et al. 2005; Spivey 2005), and working-class women may face the highest cost (Budig and Hodges 2010; England et al. 1999). Women of color and those from working-class or working-poor backgrounds are more likely to take time off and pay a penalty in their inability to earn higher wages or even find a position comparable to the one they held before leaving work (Gerstel and McGonagle 1999). Because part-time and full-time work are rewarded differently, and these rewards can continue for decades after work disruption, it is necessary to understand why some women continue to work full time while some pull back to part-time or no employment. While these data suggest there may be important class differences in women's employment that can be discovered by looking at longitudinal work pathways, the majority of life course research focuses on middle-class women (see Altucher and Williams 2003; Hostetler et al. 2006; Williams and Han 2003).

5. Hacker 2006.

6. The orderly progression of participation in a particular field has long been characterized as a characteristic of middle-class employment. Historically, working-class men and women have had less access to stable work patterns than their middle-class contemporaries (Wilensky 1960; Moen 2003; Pavalko 1997). As a result of their dual responsibilities to work and home, women's work patterns are often more "disorderly," i.e., characterized by more disruption, than men's (Hostetler et al. 2006: 85).

7. The career mystique is wearing off as companies demonstrate that they will no longer exhibit loyalty to their employees (Moen and Roehling 2005; DiPrete and Krecker 1991). Men and women across classes are facing increasingly unstable employment—an employment characteristic that was only found among the poorest workers several decades ago (Hacker 2006). Working hours are increasingly nonstandard; two-fifths of all American workers are employed outside a nine-to-five schedule, generally in service-sector jobs that offer low remuneration and little chance of promotion (Presser 2003). Changes in how employers structure their workers' time have brought an increase in hours for men and women in professional positions and a decrease in hours for those in the service sector (Jacobs and Gerson 2004). On the one hand, long working hours can create a strain, particularly on dual-earner families, as work intrudes on family responsibilities and time spent with loved ones. On the other end of the spectrum, working-class and working-poor women are increasingly likely to be employed part time, yet report a preference for full-time work; underemployment also strains the family, as families struggle financially.

8. For a detailed discussion of these three pathways see Pavalko and Smith (1999). This differs from some research of other life course and work-family scholars, who have suggested somewhere

from four to six possible work pathways for men and women (Moen and Han 2001; Williams and Han 2003). The anthropological terms *etic* and *emic* are useful in teasing out these differing findings. The majority of work-family life course research can be thought of as etic, asking what observational data tell us about men's and women's occupational pathways. My approach borrows from the emic approach, asking what is the culturally meaningful significance of different occupational pathways. In contrast to Moen and Han (2001) and others, I broaden the steady and pulled-back categories and add a third, fully separate category, the interrupted workers.

9. Life course researchers provide an excellent conceptual approach to understanding men's and women's workforce patterns (Williams and Han 2003). Changes to the economic structure and to gendered workforce participation must result in new ways to think about long-term employment (Moen and Han 2001; Williams and Han 2003). Gender must be seen as a crucial component in career formation, and research on women's workforce participation must incorporate gender into the heart of the analysis (Moen 2001; Moen and Han 2001). They suggest that women's workforce participation trajectories should be termed "work-family pathways" to fully incorporate a gender lens into the analysis of women's workforce participation. While I am cognizant of their concerns, I think that it would be misleading to use "work-family pathways" to describe the focus of this study, as I am not attempting to analyze differences in women's family formations, only differences in their workforce patterns. Moreover, this line of research often uses the terms "work pathways" or "career pathways" to describe the different work patterns they find. I use "work" pathway, as "career" is often thought to refer primarily to middle-class work.

10. I do not use the term *employed* for this category, because many of the women in the other two groups were also employed. The distinctive feature for this category is continuous full-time employment.

11. I consider thirty hours a week of employment to indicate a commitment to full-time work. Although this differs slightly from the Bureau of Labor Statistics guidelines of thirty-five or more hours a week, there was a clear difference among my participants between those who worked thirty hours or more and those who worked less. Most averaged between thirty-five and forty hours a week, but, as women often have additional caretaking responsibilities at home, women who maintained at least thirty hours per week had work loads and child care responsibilities that were more like those of their peers working thirty-five to forty hours than of those who worked twenty. Using thirty hours per week as the standard for full-time work also suggests my commitment to new ways of thinking about full-time work that could help to reduce work-family conflict.

12. Although it is important to note that they will likely face financial penalties for their time out of the workforce (Budig and Hodges 2010; Spivey 2005).

13. Maria considered her mother and her stepfather (her mother's third husband) her parents. She called her stepfather "Dad" and her biological father "my father." I use her terminology here.

14. Arlie Hochschild (1997) found evidence that job sharing or part-time work solutions often came under fire when facing new management.

15. Howell 1973.

16. Like Maria, Erica distinguished between her stepfather, whom she called "Dad," and her biological father, whom she called her father. I use this distinction.

17. Many studies have found that divorce rates are higher among couples that marry at a young age (for a more recent study, see Teachman 2002).

CHAPTER 3

1. Gerson 2010.

2. See Hochschild's (1989) descriptions of images of working women in the 1980s.

3. Smith 2001; Kuperberg and Stone 2008.

4. Johnston and Swanson 2003; Smith 2001; Collins 1991.

5. Baird 2007; Gerson 1985; Moen et al. 1997; Risman et al. 1999. Expectations about future work are often considered part of a person's "gender ideology," which refers to sets of beliefs that guide marital decisions, workforce participation and family formation (Hochschild 1989; Risman 1998; Risman et al. 1999; Spenner and Rosenfeld 1990). Gender ideologies are not static, but flexible and responsive to life changes, such as job opportunities and marital and parenthood status (Davis 2007; Fan and Marini 2000; Vespa 2009). Under this framework, gender ideologies are at once internalized expectations about socially appropriate gendered behavior and social artifacts that must be negotiated when exposed to new situations. Since gender ideologies change across the life course, there is particular benefit in investigating gender ideologies at crucial transitional periods, as they may shape the way women negotiate these turning points (Moen et al. 1997; see also Moen 2001 for a discussion of the gendered life course). The transition to young adulthood is one such pivotal moment during which young adults make decisions (or anticipate making decisions) about a host of factors, including "continuation of education, movement into and out of the labor force, entry into marriage, and becoming a parent" (Elder 1995; Fan and Marini 2000: 258).

6. Risman et al. 1999: 322. Prevailing gender schemas can bias expectations about women's ability to participate in paid work and can negatively influence a woman's expectations about her own abilities (Ridgeway and Correll 2004: 518). These expectations may accurately anticipate the barriers that women may face; the lack of women in certain professions may impede women's ability to gain higher-status professions (Kanter 1977).

7. Gerson 2010.

8. Moen et al. 1997; Vespa 2009; Bettie 2003. Adolescent girls who hold more egalitarian gender ideologies are more likely to aspire to higher levels of education and employment (Davis and Pearce 2007). Furthermore, women's gender ideologies may influence their earnings: women with more egalitarian beliefs have higher earnings than those who hold traditional beliefs (Stickney and Konrad 2007).

9. Pierce 1995.

10. Hansen 2005; Townsend 2002; Williams 2010.

11. Garey 1999; Collins 1991.

12. Landry 2000.

13. Hansen 2005.

14. Empirical studies support my supposition that there are intersectional differences in the construction of gender ideologies. African Americans tend to hold more egalitarian gender ideologies than whites (Harris and Firestone 1998; Fan and Marini 2000), although this may be particular to working-class African Americans, as middle-class African Americans may hold more traditional gender ideologies than their working-class counterparts (Hill 2002). Hispanics may hold more traditional gender ideologies than non-Hispanic whites, particularly when it comes to the division between home and work (Ciabattari 2001; Kane 2000). While working-class women may have lower expectations about the opportunities available in the workforce, middle-class

women, particularly white women, may have higher expectations about the opportunities available to them in the paid workforce and raised occupational aspirations as a result (Baird 2007; Bettie 2003; Ferree 1987; Johnson 2002).

15. Williams and Han 2003; Elder 1995; Goldin 1990.

16. Goldin 2006b.

17. There are lifelong economic consequences to full-time versus part-time work (Spivey 2005), and working-class women and women of color have greater work gaps than do their white middle-class counterparts, particularly at crucial early workforce stages (Alon and Haberfeld 2007; England et al. 1999).

18. Scholars have tended to label women as either work or family focused (see Garey 1999 and Ferree 1987 for excellent critiques of this schema). Working-class women who need to work are seen as family focused because they could not possibly want to work in the conditions in which many of them find themselves (Ferree 1987). Middle-class women, on the other hand, choose to work and, therefore, are in pursuit of careers—a work-focused strategy. This type of differentiation privileges the work that middle-class women do and diminishes the struggles of working-class women to enter and remain in the workforce (Garey 1999; Ferree 1987; Johnson 2002; also see Ratcliff and Bogdan 1988 for discussion of the denial of the importance of work for women). It also privileges the type of work that most resembles the traditionally male form of workforce participation rather than approaches to work that incorporate commitments to both a job and family. The terms suggest that family-focused women will not have a role in the workforce, while work-focused women will not prioritize their families. Both implications are inaccurate. As we know, most women with children under the age of eighteen do work. Moreover, as the majority of my respondents were eager to point out, regardless of their workforce participation level, families were a central part of life. But this suggests a problem with the terminology we use to distinguish early ideas about work and does not imply that there are no differences in women's expectations. Indeed, there was a significant difference between Lila's expectation that she would "always" work and Angela's expectation that her workforce participation would be sporadic and done when necessary to "help out" her family.

I did not differentiate between job types when coding expectations about work. A woman who expected to work as a hairdresser and who expected to be steadily employed as a hairdresser throughout her adult life was coded as having the same type of continual workforce expectation as a woman who expected to spend the entirety of her life as a lawyer. By investigating women's expectations about workforce participation levels and not expectations about types of employment, I can better understand how working-class women come to hold expectations of steady employment.

19. Even those expecting a traditional breadwinner/homemaker division of labor expected to spend some time in the labor market before forming such a union.

20. Garey 1999.

21. It is important to note that this chapter investigates the women's class of origin, that is to say, their family's class position when they were making these decisions about workforce participation at the cusp of adulthood. The majority of participants, 75 percent, grew up in working-class families. Just over one-third of participants experienced a change in class position over their lifetimes. All of the chapters other than this one refer to a woman's class position at the time of our interview.

22. Middle-class women are delaying decisions about work and family (Furstenberg et al. 2005; Fussell and Furstenberg 2005). American women continue to follow a traditional sequence of

leaving home and marriage, followed by childbirth, but this pattern has been delayed in women's lives (Fussell and Gauthier 2005).

23. See Moen and Roehling (2005) for a discussion of this phenomenon.

24. Lareau 2003.

25. Stone 2007. See also Bettie (2003: 110), who finds that middle-class girls hold high expectations about future labor market participation—a "postfeminist" position for many of them, as they expect to balance work and family without acknowledging the feminist struggles that brought them these opportunities nor the struggles that remain.

26. Sociologists West and Zimmerman argue that people "do gender," by actively assigning girls tasks that are traditionally done by women or by dressing in appropriately feminine or masculine ways, for example. According to this social constructionist approach, gender is not a static biological difference but a social difference that is constantly achieved and maintained through attitudes, dress, and behaviors that may vary according to different situations (West and Zimmerman 1987; Lorber 1994). But Francine Deutsch (2007) notes that if gender is constantly "done," it can be undone. There is, she notes, possibility in the performative nature of gender for gender to not matter in certain situations (Deutsch 2007). Risman suggests that as women and men became comfortable with moving between different gender performances, they may be "destabilizing the taken-for-granted personae that were in the past assumed essentially to match sex category" (2009: 82). A key component of West and Zimmerman's conceptualization of doing gender is its contextual dependence. If doing gender is contextually dependent, we might assume that undoing gender may only occur in certain situations and circumstances and that it may be dependent (at least in part) on a class or race privilege. The middle-class parents' expectation that their daughters excel in the classroom was situational and allowed them to transcend traditional gender divisions and to destabilize gender categories about achievement and success.

27. This mixed approach to child rearing—high achievement at school coupled with sizable homemaking chores—that the middle-class girls described may hint at the tensions to be found later in life.

28. Author's emphasis.

29. Grodsky and Riegle-Crumb 2010.

30. For the working poor, steady employment can translate into continued participation in the education system (Newman 1999). This suggests a strong connection between continual workforce participation and education.

31. Dill 1988.

32. African American women often expect that they will not have the opportunity to withdraw from the workforce (Collins 1991; Parker 2005; Landry 2000).

33. Julie Bettie's (2003) research on gender, race, and class can help us understand how working-class families adopted this "middle-class" devotion to education and workforce participation for their daughters, as well as their sons. Bettie notes that class is multidimensional, meaning that material differences between the middle class and working class are part of someone's class origins, but class differences also have a cultural dimension in which women negotiate their inherited class with their social location and peers. This negotiation produces a performance of class in which some may adopt practices from other classes.

34. Goldin 2006b.

35. While there was less variation among Asian American women, it did exist in the middle class, but since there were so few Asian Americans in the study, it is necessary to look to future research to further explore this issue for that group of women.

36. While this finding supports other research (Collins 1991; Landry 2000), due to the small sample size, it is necessary to be cautious about this finding. However, while there were significant differences in expectations about a spouse's breadwinning among whites and Latinas, there was total unanimity among black women in expecting a nonbreadwinning spouse. This suggests that it is worth exploring these findings, as long as we keep in mind their preliminary nature.

37. Life experiences must be examined along with intersectional differences to investigate the development of gender ideologies (Vespa 2009). I focus on the importance of high school, and not college, here because I am looking at women's decision making on the cusp of adulthood, when high school ended. While college experiences also play an important role in women's future workforce participation (see Jacobs 1989), here I am interested in the processes that occurred before this pivotal transitional moment.

38. Lareau 2003; Damaske 2009; Newman 1999. Success in the classroom often equates with participation in higher education and continued workforce participation (Newman 1999; Grodsky and Riegle-Crumb 2010).

39. Howe 1977. Vocational schooling can improve the transition from school to work for students (Arum and Shavit 1995).

40. Transitions to work are made easier when schools (college, high school, or vocational) have ties to the local labor market (see Arum and Shavit 1995; Rosenbaum 2001; Deil-Amen and Rosenbaum 2004).

41. This supports Jacobs et al.'s (1991) findings that low aspirations may be attributed not to the recognition by lower-status adolescents of the constraints that they may face, but to the very real presence of those barriers in their lives. I expand on this research by suggesting that for women, expectations of occasional work may lead to fewer investments in job skills.

42. Garey 1999.

43. Rosen 1987; Rubin 1976.

44. Hoschchild 1987; Garey 1999; Rosen 1987.

45. Webber and Williams 2008.

46. Building on Annette Lareau's (2003) findings about the "natural approach" to child rearing, in which working-class parents are less involved in the daily activities of their children's lives, this finding suggests that there may be both classed and gendered differences in this child-rearing strategy.

47. This is supported by Ruth Sidel's (1990) research on women across classes.

48. This supports findings that poor women often decide to become mothers at a young age in response to what they see as the lack of other opportunities for them (see Edin and Kefalas 2005).

49. Edin and Kefalas (2005) have similar findings.

50. Moen et al. 1997.

51. This may be particularly true in middle-class homes. See Stone 2007; Lareau 2003.

52. Lareau 2003.

53. Lareau 2003.

54. Recent research suggests that while early expectations about work do not predict workforce participation, they do influence future paid workforce participation and potential earnings as well as educational attainment and workforce skills gained (Corrigal and Konrad 2007; Goldin 2006b; Risman et al. 1999; Stickney and Konrad 2007).

55. See Gerson (1985) and Jacobs (1989) for additional research on how life experiences can force women to alter earlier plans.

CHAPTER 4

1. Goldin 1990.

2. Reskin and Roos 1990.

3. Garey 1999: 44.

4. Myra Marx Ferree (1976) suggests that the involuntary nature of working-class women's work benefits their family status. Working-class women receive recognition for their work as necessary and beneficial to the family. This recognition increases their power within their families. In contrast, it is presumed that these benefits would be less available to middle-class women, whose work is perceived to be more voluntary and, as a result, less necessary and beneficial to the family.

5. This line of thinking contends that because working-class women need to work (and work in fields that require less time commitment), their identities are less tied to the workforce and allow for less work-family conflict than middle-class women experience (Johnson 2002; Garey 1999; Rosen 1987). As working-class women do not identify with paid work in the way that middle-class women do, they do not experience paid labor market participation as "intrinsically meaningful" (Johnson 2002: 66).

6. Komarovsky 1964: 57.

7. Blair-Loy 2003: 22.

8. Nelson and Smith 1999. While Nelson and Smith find that higher levels of bureaucratization also are a component of good work, this measure was not included in my interviews and is omitted here.

9. See Stone 2007.

10. This attachment to paid work is distinct from the idea of a devotion to the workforce.

11. See Collins 1991; Landry 2000; Dill 1988; Higginbotham 2001.

12. Warren and Tyagi 2003; Hacker 2006.

13. Mishel et al. 2007. Men with high school educations now earn approximately 17 percent less per year than they did in 1973 (DiPrete and Buchman 2006).

14. Greenhouse 2008: 5.

15. Research suggests that young women, particularly those living in urban areas, out-earn their male counterparts (Beveridge 2007). This trend stops when women and men reach the age when they have children, a time when women often face a "wage penalty" for motherhood, and men, particularly white men, receive a boost in their own earning potential (Budig and England 2001; Waldfogel 1997; Glauber 2008). While there remains a long-term earnings gap between men and women (Rose and Hartmann 2004), some women who remain employed steadily may retain an underexplored status advantage over their spouses. As many women have overtaken men in educational attainment, both middle-class and working-class women may experience access to better networks through their jobs.

16. U.S. Bureau of Labor Statistics 2009.

17. Wilcox and Nock 2006.

18. It is actually fairly common for low-wage workers, particularly those with illegal work documents, to find themselves unprotected by minimum wage laws (see Greenhouse 2008).

19. The women's belief that there would be opportunities does not mean barriers did not exist, but the women did assume that these barriers could be successfully navigated and approached them with this certainty. They were not always successful in these attempts, but this confidence guided their workforce participation decisions.

20. I use both *balance* and *weave* to describe women's combination of work and family. While for many women this was more of a weaving process, as Anita Garey (1999) describes, for others it was the "balancing act" Spain and Bianchi (1999) depict.

21. Split parenting shifts are increasingly common (Presser 2003).

22. Bittman et al. 2003; Brines 1994; Greenstein 2000. Gupta (2007) suggests the relationship may be more complicated.

23. Hertz (2006) discusses the multiple ways single mothers rely on an extended network of kin to help raise a child. Carol Stack (1974) also discusses the importance of relying on kin for both financial and familial support, particularly for African American families. Although Aisha's family had greater resources than those described in Stack's research, she also came from a family with close ties to their local African American communities and their traditions.

24. Moen and Roehling 2005.

25. Warren and Tyagi 2003.

26. Warren and Tyagi 2003.

27. Warren and Tyagi 2003.

28. This includes Sallie, who had a commitment ceremony with her long-time girlfriend and considered herself married, even though the state of New York did not recognize her marriage at the time of our interview.

29. See Sarkisian and Gerstel 2006. In fact, recent scholarship suggests that poor women experience few of the positive benefits of marriage that well-off women receive (Wells and Zinn 2004). White middle-class women may be most likely to reap the benefits of marriage (McCall 2011).

30. Juliet Schor called attention to Americans' feelings of overwork in 1991.

31. Gerstel 2000.

32. Spain and Bianchi 1996.

33. Spain and Bianchi (1996) find that married women's participation in the labor market has increased steadily since the 1920s, despite cultural images that purport a drop in their employment in the 1950s and 1960s.

34. Williams 2000.

35. My research cannot speculate on men's attachment to the labor market. However, a large body of literature suggests that working-class men do have more mixed feelings about their workforce participation than their middle-class counterparts (Levitan and Johnson 1982).

36. Hansen 2005; Lareau 2003.

37. Hansen 2005.

38. Stack 1974.

CHAPTER 5

1. See Mary Blair-Loy (2003) for a discussion of the cultural schemas demanding a devotion to work or a devotion to family.

2. Stone 2007: 66–67.

3. Although Stone (2007) and Blair-Loy (2003) suggests that middle-class women's path to leaving work can help us understand why working-class women leave work, my research suggests just the opposite: working-class women left work for vastly different reasons than their middle-class counterparts.

4. Women's opportunities in the workforce continue to diverge. Although 80 percent of women still earn less than the median male worker, women's earnings polarized during the 1980s when some women, particularly white, well-educated women, were able to move into high-end, traditionally male, professional jobs (Bernhardt et al. 1995). The women who pulled back, yet expected to be continual workers, typically fell into the latter category.

5. These hours are typical of highly educated professionals (see Jacobs and Gerson 2004).

6. An exhaustive amount of research has been done on the time bind experienced by middle-class, particularly upper-middle-class, women, as they work in institutions that demand long hours and remain responsible for the work done at home. For excellent examples of this research, see Hochschild (1989, 1997); Roth (2006); Moen (1992); Stone (2007); Blair-Loy (2003).

7. Stone (2007) had similar findings.

8. Gerson 2010.

9. See Stone 2007.

10. Other researchers have found young middle-class women to be particularly confident about their abilities to navigate the workforce (see Stone 2007).

11. Women often work in "occupational ghettoes," shunted into "feminine" sectors of the labor market that offer lower pay, prestige, and autonomy, and less flexible scheduling (Charles and Grusky 2004; Jacobs and Gerson 2004; Bielby and Baron 1986; Reskin and Roos 1990; Kilbourne et al. 1994).

12. This builds on Nelson and Smith's (1999) concept of good work, which is a more static concept of employment. Instead, I suggest that a job can turn from good work into bad work, most often during management shifts that change workers' responsibilities, their benefits, and their level of control over their work or schedule.

13. And they very well may have been correct in making this judgment. It is not my intent to judge this expectation or to attempt to predict what their workforce participation options may have been had they remained in the labor market.

14. Myra Marx Ferree (1987) argues that middle-class women's work can be criticized as self-indulgent (there is often no financial need for their workforce participation), while working-class women's work benefits the family more directly and is therefore protected from such claims.

15. Hertz 1986; Ratcliff and Bogdan 1988.

16. Working-class and working-poor women often rely on extended kin for aid (Hansen 2005; Stack 1974).

17. The fact that so few pulled back in this manner is, perhaps, more evidence of how changing social norms may be contributing to "undoing gender" (see discussion of Deutsch 2007 in chapter 3).

18. Pulling back from the workforce can result in lost wages and difficulties in returning to work (Williams 2007; Goldin 1990).

19. This supports Pamela Stone's (2007) findings about expectations about husbands' hours.

20. Middle-class families often are at greater financial risk than they realize; middle-class families file the majority of bankruptcies in the United States (Warren and Tyagi 2003).

21. Louise Roth (2006) found that women who left high-paying business positions also did not consider the economic consequences of their decisions.

22. Greenhouse 2008: 5. Additionally, men's average wages have declined over the last thirty years (Mishel et al. 2007). Men with high school educations now earn significantly less per year than they did in 1973 (DiPrete and Buchman 2006).

23. Time out of the workforce can lead to sharp reductions in pay (Hewlett 2007). Additionally, part-time work is largely less well compensated than full-time work (England 2005).

24. Gina did not know her husband's exact salary, although she believed it was around the minimum wage.

25. Schieman et al. (2009) show that work is more likely to interfere with nonwork activities for people employed in high-status positions. Moreover, intensive parenting practices have been shown to be most predominant among professional-managerial families (Ramey and Ramey 2009, as cited in Williams 2010; Lareau 2003).

26. Drentea (1998) shows that women who use informal networks to find jobs are more likely to end up in jobs that are low paying and predominantly female than their contemporaries who use more formal institutional ties to find work.

27. People employed in pink-collar work—in occupations chosen for their presumed flexibility—actually have less flexibility in their schedules than men and women in professional positions, which provide more flexible schedules, unsupervised breaks, and paid sick and vacation leaves (Glass 1990).

CHAPTER 6

1. Sociologists often study work entrances and attainment from a linear perspective. For perhaps the most famous sociological example of this, see Blau and Duncan's (1967) occupational status model (although this model is based on men's education and workforce participation).

2. Life course research suggests that such changes, particularly when they occur at pivotal moments in a person's life, may have lasting repercussions (Elder 1998: 6–7).

3. Nelson and Smith 1999.

4. Elder 1998. With Johnson and Crosnoe, Elder writes that there are "cumulative advantages and disadvantages" across the life course (2003: 12).

5. Research on social stress suggests that these disadvantaged women might be most vulnerable to social stressors (Thoits 1995: 4).

6. Hacker 2006: 63.

7. England and Folbre 1999.

8. Claudia Goldin (1990) finds differences in skill levels between women who work full time and those who do not and hypothesizes that they have gained these different skill levels because of their differing interests in long-term workforce participation (see also Goldin 2006a). But my research suggests that some women anticipate continual work but do not know how to gain the skills necessary to achieve this goal.

9. Pallas 2000.

10. Individuals from family backgrounds with low socioeconomic status remain much less likely to continue on to higher education than their middle-class counterparts (see Roksa et al. 2007).

11. Although some eventually earned their GED, this certificate is often not the equivalent of a high school diploma (see Rumberger and Lamb 2003; Murnane et al. 2000). In my study, those with a GED certainly found opportunities more similar to those of women without high school diplomas than to those of women who had graduated from high school.

12. Pallas 2000; Kingston et al. 2003.

13. Johnson 2002.

14. This supports recent findings that women in gray-collar jobs, similar to those of the interrupted workers, were satisfied with their employment as long as they had good working relationships with their bosses and their coworkers (Johnson 2002: 48–49). Women's satisfaction in gray-collar jobs, work that is often dismissed as an occupational ghetto, is supported by Mike Rose's research in *The Mind at Work*. Rose (2004) finds that many working-class jobs—work that is often dismissed—are both stimulating and rewarding and often require specific skill sets to be done well.

15. The categories used to differentiate between types of work—blue collar, manual, and so on—often "reaffirm longstanding biases about particular occupations" (Rose 2004: xviii; Vallas 1990).

16. Although Johnson (2002) paints an excellent portrait of the challenges faced by women with little education and of the rewards these women find in the workplace, she does not ask how these factors influence their continued workforce participation. Instead, she contends that working-class women remain employed because of their need to work. But as we see in this chapter, many women left work when they were deeply unhappy with it despite the financial pressure to remain.

17. Barbara Ehrenreich (2001) similarly found it difficult when she attempted to get by on a minimum-wage job.

18. Undereducated women, particularly mothers, form a group of workers whose employment value is, in some ways, similar to that of Marx's lumpen-proletariat, a reserve labor force that is easily replaceable and that can be employed on a part-time or temporary basis and paid minimal wages with no benefits (Marx and Engels 1978).

19. Moen 2001.

20. Alon and Haberfeld 2007; England et al. 1999; Spivey 2005.

21. Sociologists who study the life course note that people do not live solitary existences. Instead, they live "linked lives" in which changes to one member of a family may affect both that individual and those around them, as it did in Vanessa's case (Elder et al. 2003). Caregiving for parents and partners is more often performed by women and can have negative effects on the caregivers' well-being (Pavalko and Woodbury 2000).

22. Alon and Haberfeld (2007) find that this penalty is paid disproportionately by working-class women and women of color.

23. Life course research suggests that periods of transition have cumulative effects across the life course and that the timing of transitional periods is particularly important (Elder et al. 2003). Early transitions to adulthood (such as childbearing, leaving home, or entering marriage) can have deleterious effects (Harley and Mortimer 2000 as cited in Elder et al. 2003).

24. Arlene requested that details of her life be considerably changed to further protect her identity due to her fears about her abusive spouse. Therefore, details about her life have been altered. This was not done in the case of the other respondents.

25. Ahrons 2004; Amato and Hohmann-Marriott 2007; McLanahan 2002.

26. Zernike 2007.

27. As income falls, exposure to stressful events rises (Turner and Lloyd 1999). People from low-status backgrounds may be both more likely to experience stressful events and more likely to lack the resources to deal with them (Turner and Lloyd 1999). Negative experiences, such as stressful events, may have cumulative disadvantages across a person's life course (Elder et al. 2003).

28. Karen Hansen (2005) found that networks act as a safety net for people when money is short. The interrupted workers were short on money and on reliable networks.

29. See Conley (2004) for examples of this pooling of family resources for one child.

30. National Institute of Mental Health 2008.

31. Booth and Amato 1991.

32. People from low-SES backgrounds may be more vulnerable to social stressors and may be more likely to face the resulting health disadvantages (Pearlin 1989; Thoits 1995; Turner and Lloyd 1999).

33. Work remains a crucial part of people's identities and sociologists have found that even those who work in low-wage jobs want to work and get a great deal of satisfaction from their workforce participation (Hughes 1958; Hodson 1989; Ferree 1976; Komarovsky 1964).

34. Johnson 2002; Rosen 1987; Ferree 1984; Kornhauser 1965; Loscocco 1990.

35. See Goldthorpe et al. (1968) for one of the first studies on working-class men's instrumental approach to the workforce.

36. From Ferree 1987: 291.

37. Williams 2000; England et al. 2004.

38. Structural unemployment, in which workers are unable to find suitable employment opportunities, often involves long-term joblessness; this occurs because of underqualifications, geographical constraints, or lack of knowledge about the local labor market. Nationally, one-third of all employed women would like to work additional hours and earn additional money but say they cannot find the opportunity to do so (Kalleberg 2007).

39. Hacker 2006: 63.

CHAPTER 7

1. Bianchi et al. 2006.

2. Hertz 2006; Stacey 1990.

3. Hays 1996: 133.

4. Williams 2000. The cultural ambivalence about paid work leaves working and nonworking women on opposite sides, each feeling as if their decisions about work are under attack and needing to justify their decisions (Luker 1984; Williams 1991).

5. Bernard 1981; Ryan 1981; Skolnick 1979.

6. Cancian 1987.

7. Coontz 1992, 1997; Hays 2003; Blair-Loy 2003; Collins 1991.

8. Gerson 2002.

9. Gerstel 2000.

10. Correll et al. 2007.

11. Blair-Loy 2003: 52.

12. Hays 1996; Lareau 2003; Milkie and Peltola 1999; Perälä-Littunen 2008.

13. Hays 1996; Bianchi et al. 2006. In fact, the total time children spend with their parents may have increased, as fathers spend more time with their offspring and mothers devote more time to their children than in the past (Bianchi 2000).

14. Hewlett 2002.

15. Folbre 2001; Williams 2000.

16. The headline is from an article for the *New York Times* (Porter 2006). Research suggests that paid workforce participation can increase women's self-confidence, combat depression, and also benefit their children (Barnett and Rivers 1996; Deutsch 1999; Hochschild 1997; Moen and Roehling 2005).

17. Folbre 2001; Harrington 1999.

18. Roth 2006.

19. Galinsky 1999; Hoffman et al. 1999.

20. England and Folbre 1999; England 2005.

21. Bennetts 2007: 9; Flanagan 2006. See also Hirshman 2006.

22. Noted psychologists Rosalind Barnett and Caryl Rivers argue that "motherhood is not the critical issue on which [women's] emotional well-being depends, nor the event that so over-shadows all others that nothing else is important to her emotional and psychological well-being" (1996: 116).

23. Douglas and Michaels 2004: 2.

24. Hertz 2006; Stacey 1990; Altucher and Williams 2003; Koropeckyj-Cox and Pendall 2007.

25. Cultural expectations about work and family may differ across race and class. Working-class women often do not identify with paid work in the way that middle-class women do, and might not experience paid labor market participation as "intrinsically meaningful" (Johnson 2002: 66). Additionally, middle-class women are more likely than their working-class contemporaries to experience work and family as oppositional (Garey 1999). Additional lines of variation are found across race. Historically, black women have had fewer opportunities to withdraw from the workforce than their contemporaries, and African American women have long connected mothering with paid work (Collins 1991; Dill 1988; Landry 2000). Although there is compelling research that the cultural meaning of women's paid work differs across race and class, some gendered expectations about work and family may be shared across classes and races (Hays 1996: 86).

26. Ginsburg 1989; Luker 1984.

27. Scott and Lyman 1968: 46. This work builds off of C. Wright Mills's (1940) discussion of "vocabularies of motive," in which motives are the ways people explain their actions (and are not necessarily the reasons certain actions are taken). Accounts are a subset of narratives. *Narrative* is a term applied to a story a person tells about past life events that is usually recounted temporally and that tells us both about the individual's perceptions of life experiences and about the social structure in which she or he has lived (Ewick and Silbey 2003; Mills 1959). *Accounts*, on the other hand, refer to specific explanations of "decision-making behavior," in which an individual attempts to provide either an excuse or a justification for behavior that she or he expects will be criticized (Artis 2004: 772; Scott and Lyman 1968). While people likely manage their narratives so that they will be socially acceptable (see Garfinkel 1967), accounts are provided under specific conditions when respondents attempt to "negotiate public norms when morally evaluating their own lives" (May 2008: 473). More specifically, people weave narratives when asked about the events in their lives and provide accounts when asked to specifically justify "untoward behavior" (Scott and Lyman 1968: 46). Research on race finds that when prompted by interview questions to discuss behavior that could be considered morally suspect, subjects tend to return to morally firm ground even when this results in contradictions with their prior statements (Malat et al. 2010).

28. Garey 1999; Rosen 1987.

29. Stone 2007.

30. Blair-Loy 2003.

31. Emphasizing the benefits to others above benefits to self is a crucial component of accounts, as conceived of by Scott and Lyman (1968). Doing so may allow someone to "assert that his [or her] action was permissible or even right since it served the interests of another to whom he [or she] owes an unbreakable allegiance or affection" (Scott and Lyman 1968: 51).

32. We see here the emphasis women placed on accounts of their family when asked to explain their work decisions and the diminishment of other factors that such an explanation creates.

33. Accounts can provide us with insight into "culturally embedded normative explanations," as they let us know what actors see as the ideal response or action in a certain situation (Orbuch 1997: 460).

34. Parker 2005.

35. Uchitelle 2006.

36. Bianchi 2000; Hays 1998.

37. Pavalko and Woodbury 2000.

38. Connell 1987.

39. Spain and Bianchi 1996; Coltrane 1996; Deutsch 1999.

40. Garey 1999; Stone 2007.

CHAPTER 8

1. Deutsch 1999.

2. Jacobs and Gerson 2004; Moen and Roehling 2005; Hacker 2006.

3. Williams 2010: 2.

4. Leslie McCall (2001) finds that inequalities between women are even greater than inequalities between men and women.

5. Corbett et al. 2008.

6. Williams and Boushey 2010.

7. Williams and Boushey 2010.

8. Bernhardt et al. 1995.

9. Nelson and Smith (1999) argue that there has been a "decline in the quality of employment" as they find that many families now depend on workers participating in bad jobs, which are generally located in the service sector, which has been the largest site of job growth in America in the last thirty years.

10. Moen and Roehling 2005: 194.

11. Presser 2003.

12. Hartmann 1976.

13. Fathers in the United States have increased their time spent with children, giving up personal time (and sometimes even time at work) for time with children, although they report that they still do not spend enough time with their children (Bianchi et al. 2006).

14. In fact, over half of all workers report that they "cannot take time off to care for sick children" (Williams 2010: 45).

15. Hansen 2005.

16. England and Folbre 1999; England 2005.

17. Jacobs and Gerson 2004. The authors provide a convincing argument in support of public day care that also discusses some of the leading misperceptions and concerns about such programs.

18. Gornick and Meyers 2003.

19. Gornick and Meyers 2003.

20. Gornick and Meyers 2003. Recent studies confirm these disparities, finding that low-income families spend close to 15 percent of their household income on child care costs for children under the age of six, while families in the middle third of the income bracket spend somewhere from 6 to 9 percent of the household income (Williams and Boushey 2010).

21. Williams 2010.

22. This information is taken from a *New York Times* article by Kattrin Bennhold (2010). The source for the article is the Swedish Social Security Office. Additional information can be found at the U.S. State Department's Web site for Sweden: http://www.state.gov/r/pa/ei/bgn/2880.htm.

23. See Gerson 2010.

24. Gerstel and McGonagle 1999; Budig and Hodges 2010.

25. To encourage participation in the study, I wanted to demonstrate to the potential participants that I understood something about what their lives might be like, which I hoped would show that I was truly interested in their experiences. Research suggests that most women (and men) feel pressed for time, so this statement may have helped me make this connection.

26. Bianchi et al. 2006; Stone 2007.

27. Jacobs and Gerson 2004.

28. Blair-Loy and Wharton 2002.

29. Williams 2010.

30. Bianchi et al. 2006.

31. Kelly et al. 2010. Detailed descriptions of way to increase flexibility at work can be found in the work of Jacobs and Gerson (2004); Kelly et al. (2010); Gornick and Meyers (2003).

32. Research on men's and women's workforce participation rates and patterns supports my assumptions (see Bianchi et al. 2006; Spain and Bianchi 1996). I would also need to consider how to include incarcerated men, as they are likely the largest group of male pulled-back workers, but these men leave work under much different circumstances than the women who leave to be mothers.

33. McCall 2001.

34. Risman 1998.

35. Williams 2000.

36. Scholars have long noted that men have more access to free time and self-interested tasks than women (see Hochschild 1989; Gerson 2002; Cancian 1987).

APPENDIX

1. As cited in Stone (2007: 248).

2. I am indebted to these women (and to all the others who participated for a variety of reasons) for showing me how deeply important this issue was to them.

3. Mills 1959.

4. The interview schedule on work history contained many detailed questions. The following is a sampling of questions from the first of fifteen pages of questions about work experiences:

Have you always worked, sometimes worked, rarely worked, never worked? *If had worked:* When did you start the first job you had after you finished your schooling? What kind of work was it? Why did you decide on this kind of work? What were your most important activities or duties there? Did you hold different positions while there? While you were there, did you develop any meaningful relationships with people who you could consider a mentor?

5. Because my presence, as a sociologist studying work and family, could in itself be seen as a prompt to justify a work decision, these introductions were also coded as accounts.

References

Acker, Joan. 1989. *Doing Comparable Worth: Gender, Class, and Pay Equity.* Philadelphia: Temple University Press.

Ahrons, Constance R. 2004. *We're Still Family: What Grown Children Have to Say About Their Parents' Divorce.* New York: HarperCollins.

Alon, Sigal, and Yitchak Haberfeld. 2007. "Labor Force Attachment and the Evolving Wage Gap Between White, Black, and Hispanic Young Women." *Work and Occupations* 34: 369–398.

Altucher, Kristine A., and Lindy B. Williams. 2003. "Family Clocks: Timing Parenthood." Pp. 49–59 in *It's About Time: Couples and Careers,* edited by P. Moen. Ithaca, NY: ILR Press.

Amato, Paul R., and Bryndl Hohmann-Marriott. 2007. "A Comparison of High- and Low-Distress Marriages That End in Divorce." *Journal of Marriage and Family* 69(3): 621–638.

Artis, Julie E. 2004. "Judging the Best Interests of the Child." *Law and Society Review* 38: 769–806.

Arum, Richard, Josipa Roksa, and Michelle Budig. 2008. "The Romance of College Attendance: Higher Education, Stratification and Mate Selection." *Research in Social Stratification and Mobility* 26(2): 107–121.

Arum, Richard, and Yossi Shavit. 1995. "Secondary Vocational Education and the Transition from School to Work." *Sociology of Education* 68: 187–204.

Baird, Chardie. 2007. "The Importance of Community Context for Young Women's Occupational Aspirations." *Sex Roles* 58: 208–221.

Barnett, Rosalind C., and Caryl Rivers. 1996. *She Works/He Works: How Two-Income Families Are Happier, Healthier, and Better Off.* San Francisco, CA: Harper.

Beller, Emily. 2009. "Bringing Intergenerational Social Mobility Research into the Twenty-first Century: Why Mothers Matter." *American Sociological Review* 74(4): 507.

Bennetts, Leslie. 2007. *The Feminine Mistake: Are We Giving Up Too Much?* New York: Voice/Hyperion.

Bennhold, Kattrin. 2010. "The Female Factor: Paternity Leave Law Helps to Redefine Masculinity in Sweden." *New York Times*, July 15.

Bernard, Jesse. 1981. "The Good-Provider Role: Its Rise and Fall." *American Psychologist* 36: 1–12.

Bernhardt, Annette, Martina Morris, and Mark S. Handcock. 1995. "Women's Gains or Men's Losses? A Closer Look at the Shrinking Gender Gap in Earnings." *American Journal of Sociology* 101(2): 302–328.

Bettie, Julie. 2003. *Women Without Class: Girls, Race, and Identity.* Berkeley: University of California Press.

Beveridge, Andrew. 2007. "Women of New York City." *Gotham Gazette*, March.

Bianchi, Suzanne M. 2000. "Maternal Employment and Time with Children: Dramatic Change or Surprising Continuity?" *Demography* 37: 401–414.

Bianchi, Suzanne M., John P. Robinson, and Melissa A. Milkie. 2006. *Changing Rhythms of American Family Life.* New York: Russell Sage Foundation.

Bielby, William T., and James N. Baron. 1986. "Men and Women at Work: Sex Segregation and Statistical Discrimination." *American Journal of Sociology* 91: 759–799.

Bittman, Michael, Paula England, Liana Sayer, Nancy Folbre, and George Matheson. 2003. "When Does Gender Trump Money? Bargaining and Time in Household Work." *American Journal of Sociology* 109(1): 186–214.

Blackwell, Debra, and Daniel Lichter. 2004. "Homogamy Among Dating, Cohabiting, and Married Couples." *Sociological Quarterly* 45(4): 719–737.

Blair-Loy, Mary. 2003. *Competing Devotions: Career and Family Among Women Executives.* Cambridge, MA: Harvard University Press.

Blair-Loy, Mary, and Amy S. Wharton. 2002. "Employees' Use of Work-Family Policies and the Workplace Social Context." *Social Forces* 80: 813–845.

Blau, Francine D., and Lawrence M. Kahn. 2006. "The US Gender Pay Gap in the 1990s: Slowing Convergence." *Industrial and Labor Relations Review* (October): 45–66.

Blau, Peter M., and Otis D. Duncan. 1967. *The American Occupational Structure.* New York: Wiley.

Booth, Alan, and Paul Amato. 1991. "Divorce and Psychological Stress." *Journal of Health and Social Behavior* 32: 396–407.

Boushey, Heather. 2007. "Values Begin at Home, but Who's Home?" *American Prospect* (March): A2–A4.

———. 2008. "'Opting Out'? The Effect of Children on Women's Employment in the United States." *Feminist Economics* 14(1): 1–36.

Brines, Julie. 1994. "Economic Dependency, Gender, and the Division of Labor at Home." *American Journal of Sociology* 100(3): 652–688.

Budig, Michelle, and Paula England. 2001. "The Wage Penalty for Motherhood." *American Sociological Review* 66(2): 204–225.

Budig, Michelle J., and Melissa J. Hodges. 2010. "Differences in Disadvantage." *American Sociological Review* 75: 705–728.

Cancian, Francesca M. 1987. *Love in America: Gender and Self-Development.* New York: Cambridge University Press.

Cha, Youngjoo. 2010. "Reinforcing Separate Spheres." *American Sociological Review* 75: 303–329.

Chao, Elaine, and Phillip Rhones. 2007. *Women in the Labor Force: A Databook*. Washington, DC: U.S. Department of Labor.

Charles, Maria, and David B. Grusky. 2004. *Occupational Ghettos: The Worldwide Segregation of Women and Men*. Stanford, CA: Stanford University Press.

Ciabattari, Teresa. 2001. "Changes in Men's Conservative Gender Ideologies: Cohort and Period Influences." *Gender & Society* 15: 574–591.

Cohen, Philip N., and Suzanne M. Bianchi. 1999. "Marriage, Children and Women's Employment: What Do We Know?" *Monthly Labor Review* 122: 22–31.

Collins, Patricia Hill. 1991. *Black Feminist Thought: Knowledge, Consciousness, and the Politics of Empowerment*. New York: Routledge.

Coltrane, Scott. 1996. *Family Man: Fatherhood, Housework, and Gender Equity*. New York: Oxford University Press.

Conley, Dalton. 2004. *The Pecking Order: Which Siblings Succeed and Why*. New York: Pantheon Books.

Connell, R.W. 1987. *Gender and Power: Society, the Person and Sexual Politics*. Stanford, CA: Stanford University Press.

Coontz, Stephanie. 1992. *The Way We Never Were: American Families and the Nostalgia Trap*. New York: Basic Books.

———. 1997. *The Way We Really Are: Coming to Terms with America's Changing Families*. New York: Basic Books.

Corbett, Christianne, Catherine Hill, and Andresse St. Rose. 2008. *Where the Girls Are: The Facts About Gender Equity in Education*. Washington, DC: American Association of University Women Educational Foundation.

Correll, Shelley J., Stephen Benard, and In Paik. 2007. "Getting a Job: Is There a Motherhood Penalty?" *American Journal of Sociology* 112(5): 1297–1338.

Corrigall, E. A., and A. M. Konrad. 2007. "Gender Role Attitudes and Careers: A Longitudinal Study." *Sex Roles* 56(11): 847–855.

Cotter, David, Paula England, and Joan Hermsen. 2008. *Moms and Jobs: Trends in Mothers' Employment and Which Mothers Stay Home*. Chicago: Council on Contemporary Families Fact Sheet.

Crittenden, Ann. 2001. *The Price of Motherhood: Why the Most Important Job in the World Is Still the Least Valued*. New York: Metropolitan Books/Henry Holt.

Damaske, Sarah. 2009. "Brown Suits Need Not Apply: The Intersection of Race, Gender, and Class in Institutional Network Building." *Sociological Forum* 24: 402–424.

Davis, Shannon. 2007. "Gender Ideology Construction from Adolescence to Young Adulthood." *Social Science Research* 36: 1021–1041.

Davis, Shannon N., and L. D. Pearce. 2007. "Adolescents' Work-Family Gender Ideologies and Educational Expectations." *Sociological Perspectives* 50(2): 249–271.

Deil-Amen, Regina, and James Rosenbaum. 2004. "Charter Building and Labor Market Contacts in Two Year College." *Sociology of Education* 77: 245–265.

Delphy, Christine. 1984. *Close to Home: A Materialist's Analysis of Women's Oppression*. Amherst: University of Massachusetts Press.

Deutsch, Francine. 1999. *Halving It All: How Equally Shared Parenting Works*. Cambridge, MA: Harvard University Press.

———. 2007. "Undoing Gender." *Gender & Society* 21: 106–127.

Dill, Bonnie Thorton. 1988. "Our Mothers' Grief: Racial Ethnic Women and the Maintenance of Families." *Journal of Family History* 13: 415–431.

DiPrete, Thomas, and Claudia Buchman. 2006. "Gender Specific Trends in the Value of Education and the Emerging Gender Gap in College Completion." *Demography* 43: 1–24.

DiPrete, Thomas, and Margaret L. Krecker. 1991. "Occupational Linkages and Job Mobility Within and Across Organizations." *Research in Social Stratification and Mobility* 10: 91–131.

Douglas, Susan J., and Meredith W. Michaels. 2004. *The Mommy Myth: The Idealization of Motherhood and How It Has Undermined Women*. New York: Free Press.

Douthat, Ross. 2009. "Liberated and Unhappy." *New York Times*, May 26.

Dowd, Maureen. 2005. "Men Just Want Mommy." *New York Times*, January 13.

Drentea, Patricia. 1998. "Consequences of Women's Formal and Informal Job Search Methods for Employment in Female-Dominated Jobs." *Gender & Society* 12(3): 321–338.

Dye, Jane Lawler. 2006. *Fertility of American Women: 2006*. Washington, DC: U.S. Census Bureau.

Edin, Kathryn, and Maria Kefalas. 2005. *Promises I Can Keep: Why Poor Women Put Motherhood Before Marriage*. Berkeley: University of California Press.

Ehrenreich, Barbara. 2001. *Nickel and Dimed: On (Not) Getting By in America*. New York: Metropolitan Books.

Elder, Glen H. 1995. "The Life Course Paradigm: Social Change and Individual Development." Pp. 101–140 in *Examining Lives in Context: Perspectives on the Ecology of Human Development*, edited by P. Moen, G. H. Elder Jr., and K. Luscher. Washington, DC: American Psychological Association.

———. 1998. "The Life Course as Developmental Theory." *Child Development* 69: 1–12.

Elder, Glen H., Jr., Monica Kirkpatrick Johnson, and Robert Crosnoe. 2003. "The Emergence and Development of Life Course Theory." Pp. 3–19 in *Handbook of the Life Course*, edited by J. T. Mortimer and M. J. Shanahan. New York: Lower Academic/Plenum.

England, P. 1992. *Comparable Worth: Theories and Evidence*. New York: Aldine de Gruyter.

———. 2005. "Emerging Theories of Care Work." *Annual Review of Sociology* 31(1): 381–399.

———. 2010. "The Gender Revolution: Uneven and Stalled." *Gender & Society* 24: 149–166.

England, Paula, Karen Christopher, and Lori L. Reid. 1999. "How Do Intersections of Race/Ethnicity and Gender Affect Pay Among Young Cohorts of African Americans, European Americans and Latino/as?" Pp. 139–182 in *Latinas and African Americans at Work: Race, Gender and Economic Inequality*, edited by I. Brown. New York: Russell Sage Foundation.

England, Paula, and Nancy Folbre. 1999. "The Cost of Caring." *Annals of the American Academy of Political and Social Science* 561: 39–51.

England, Paula, Carmen Garcia-Beaulieu, and Mary Ross. 2004. "Women's Employment Among Blacks, Whites and Three Groups of Latinas: Do More Privileged Women Have Higher Employment?" *Gender & Society* 18: 494–509.

Ewick, Patricia, and Susan Silbey. 2003. "Narrating Social Structure." *American Journal of Sociology* 108: 1328–1372.

Fan, Pi-Ling, and Margaret Mooney Marini. 2000. "Influences on Gender-Role Attitudes During the Transition to Adulthood." *Social Science Research* 29: 258–283.

Ferree, Myra M. 1976. "Working-Class Jobs: Housework and Paid Work as Sources of Satisfaction." *Social Problems* 23(4): 431–441.

————. 1984. "Sacrifice, Satisfaction and Social Change: Employment and the Family." Pp. 61–79 in *My Troubles Are Going to Have Trouble with Me: Everyday Trials and Triumphs of Women Workers*, edited by K. B. Sacks and D. Remy. New Brunswick, NJ: Rutgers University Press.

————. 1987. "Family and Job for Working-Class Women: Gender and Class Systems Seen from Below." Pp. 289–301 in *Families and Work*, edited by N. Gerstel and H. E. Gross. Philadelphia: Temple University Press.

Flanagan, Caitlin. 2006. *To Hell with All That: Loving and Loathing Our Inner Housewife*. New York: Little, Brown.

Folbre, Nancy. 2001. *The Invisible Heart: Economics and Family Values*. New York: New Press.

Friedan, Betty. 1963. *The Feminine Mystique*. New York: Norton.

Furstenberg, Frank F., Jr., Ruben G. Rumbaut, and Richard A. Settersten Jr. 2005. "On the Frontier of Adulthood: Emerging Themes and New Directions." Pp. 3–25 in *On the Frontier of Adulthood: Theory, Research and Public Policy*, edited by R. A. Settersten, F. F. Furstenberg, and R. G. Rumbaut. Chicago: University of Chicago Press.

Fussell, Elizabeth, and Frank F. Furstenberg. 2005. "The Transition to Adulthood During the Twentieth Century: Race, Nativity and Gender." Pp. 29–75 in *On the Frontier of Adulthood: Theory, Research and Public Policy*, edited by R. A. Settersten, F. F. Furstenberg, and R. G. Rumbaut. Chicago: University of Chicago Press.

Fussell, Elizabeth, and Anne H. Gauthier. 2005. "American Women's Transition to Adulthood in Comparative Context." Pp. 76–109 in *On the Frontier of Adulthood: Theories, Research and Public Policy*, edited by R. A. Settersten, F. F. Furstenberg, and R. G. Rumbaut. Chicago: University of Chicago Press.

Galinsky, Ellen. 1999. *Ask the Children: What America's Children Really Think About Working Parents*. New York: William Morrow.

Garey, Anita I. 1999. *Weaving Work and Motherhood*. Philadelphia: Temple University Press.

Garfinkel, Harold. 1967. *Studies in Ethnomethodology*. Englewood Cliffs, NJ: Prentice-Hall.

Gerson, Kathleen. 1985. *Hard Choices: How Women Decide About Work, Career, and Motherhood*. Berkeley: University of California Press.

————. 1993. *No Man's Land: Men's Changing Commitments to Family and Work*. New York: Basic Books.

————. 2002. "Moral Dilemmas, Moral Strategies, and the Transformation of Gender: Lessons from Two Generations of Work and Family Change." *Gender & Society* 16: 8–28.

————. 2010. *The Unfinished Revolution: How a New Generation Is Reshaping Family, Work and Gender in America*. New York: Oxford University Press.

Gerstel, Naomi. 2000. "The Third Shift: Gender, Employment, and Care Work Outside the Home." *Qualitative Sociology* 23: 467–483.

Gerstel, Naomi, and Kate McGonagle. 1999. "Job Leaves and the Limits of the Family and Medical Leave Act: The Effects of Gender, Race and Class." *Work and Occupations* 26: 510–534.

Ginsburg, Faye D. 1989. *Contested Lives: The Abortion Debate in an American Community*. Berkeley: University of California Press.

Glass, Jennifer. 1990. "The Impact of Occupational Segregation on Working Conditions." *Social Forces* 68: 779–796.

Glauber, Rebecca. 2008. "Race and Gender in Families and at Work." *Gender & Society* 22(1): 8–30.

Glenn, Evelyn N., G. Chang, and L. R. Forcey. 1994. *Mothering: Ideology, Experience and Agency.* New York: Routledge.

Goldin, Claudia. 1990. *Understanding the Gender Gap: An Economic History of American Women.* New York: Oxford University Press.

———. 2006a. "The Rising (and Then Declining) Significance of Gender." Pp. 67–101 in *The Declining Significance of Gender?*, edited by F. D. Blau, M. C. Brinton, and D. B. Grusky. New York: Russell Sage Foundation.

———. 2006b. "The Quiet Revolution That Transformed Women's Employment, Education, and Family." *American Economic Review* 96: 1–21.

Goldstein, Joshua, and Catherine Kenney. 2001. "Marriage Delayed or Marriage Forgone? New Cohort Forecasts of First Marriage for U.S. Women." *American Sociological Review* 66(4): 506–519.

Goldthorpe, John H. 1984. "Women and Class Analysis: In Defence of the Conventional View." *Sociology* 17: 465–488.

Goldthorpe, John H., David Lockwood, Frank Bechhofer, and Jennifer Platt. 1968. *The Affluent Worker: Industrial Attitudes and Behavio* r. London: Cambridge University Press.

Gornick, Janet C., and Marcia Meyers. 2003. *Families That Work: Policies for Reconciling Parenthood and Employment.* New York: Russell Sage Foundation.

Greenhouse, Steven. 2008. *The Big Squeeze: Tough Times for the American Worker.* New York: Knopf.

Greenstein, Theodore. 2000. "Economic Dependence, Gender and the Division of Labor in the Home." *Journal of Marriage and Family* 62: 332–335.

Grodsky, Eric, and Catherine Riegle-Crumb. 2010. "Those Who Choose and Those Who Don't: Social Background and College Orientation." *Annals of the American Academy of Political and Social Science* 627: 14–35.

Gupta, Sanjiv. 2007. "Autonomy, Dependence, or Display? The Relationship Between Married Women's Earnings and Housework." *Journal of Marriage and Family* 69(2): 399–417.

Hacker, Jacob. 2006. *The Great Risk Shift.* New York: Oxford University Press.

Haney, Lynne A. 2002. *Inventing the Needy: Gender and the Politics of Welfare in Hungary.* Berkeley: University of California Press.

Hansen, Karen V. 2005. *Not-So-Nuclear Families: Class, Gender, and Networks of Care.* New Brunswick, NJ: Rutgers University Press.

Harrington, Mona. 1999. *Care and Equality: Inventing a New Family Politics.* New York: Knopf.

Harris, Richard, and Juanita Firestone. 1998. "Changes in Predictors of Gender Role Ideologies Among Women: A Multivariate Analysis." *Sex Roles* 38: 239–252.

Hartmann, Heidi. 1976. "Capitalism, Patriarchy, and Job Segregation by Sex." *Signs* 1: 137–169.

Hays, Sharon. 1996. *The Cultural Contradictions of Motherhood.* New Haven, CT: Yale University Press.

———. 2003. *Flat Broke with Children: Women in the Age of Welfare Reform.* New York: Oxford University Press.

Heath, Anthony, and Nicky Britten. 1984. "Women's Jobs Do Make a Difference: A Reply to Goldthorpe." *Sociology* 18: 475–490.

Heckman, James. 1974. "Shadow Prices, Market Wages, and Labor Supply." *Econometrica* 42: 679–694.

Hertz, Rosanna. 1986. *More Equal Than Others: Women and Men in Dual-Career Marriages.* Berkeley: University of California Press.

———. 2006. *Single by Chance, Mothers by Choice: How Women Are Choosing Parenthood Without Marriage and Creating the New American Family.* New York: Oxford University Press.

Hewlett, Sylvia A. 2002. *Creating a Life: Professional Women and the Quest for Children.* New York: Talk Miramax Books.

———. 2007. *Off-ramps and On-ramps: Keeping Talented Women on the Road to Success.* Boston, MA: Harvard Business School Press.

Higginbotham, Elizabeth. 2001. *Too Much to Ask: Black Women in the Era of Integration.* Chapel Hill, NC: University of North Carolina Press.

Higginbotham, Elizabeth, and Mary Romero. 1997. *Women and Work: Exploring Race, Ethnicity, and Class.* Thousand Oaks: Sage.

Hill, Shirley. 2002. "Teaching and Doing Gender in African American Families." *Sex Roles* 47: 493–506.

Hirshman, Linda R. 2006. *Get to Work: A Manifesto for Women of the World.* New York: Viking.

Hochschild, Arlie R. 1989. *The Second Shift: Working Parents and the Revolution at Home.* New York: Viking.

———. 1997. *The Time Bind: When Work Becomes Home and Home Becomes Work.* New York: Metropolitan Books.

Hodson, Randy. 1989. "Gender Differences in Job Satisfaction: Why Aren't Women More Dissatisfied?" *Sociological Quarterly* 30: 385–399.

Hoffman, Lois, Norma Wladis, and Lise M. Youngblade. 1999. *Mothers at Work: Effects on Children's Well-Being.* New York: Cambridge University Press.

Hostetler, Andrew J., Stephen Sweet, and Phyllis Moen. 2006. "Gendered Career Paths: A Life Course Perspective on Returning to School." *Sex Roles* 56: 85–103.

Howe, Louise K. 1977. *Pink Collar Workers: Inside the World of Women's Work.* New York: Putnam.

Howell, Joseph T. 1973. *Hard Living on Clay Street: Portraits of Blue Collar Families.* Garden City, NY: Anchor Press.

Hughes, Everett C. 1958. *Men and Their Work.* Glencoe, IL: Free Press.

Jacobs, Jerry A. 1989. *Revolving Doors: Sex Segregation and Women's Careers.* Stanford, CA: Stanford University Press.

Jacobs, Jerry A., and Kathleen Gerson. 2004. *The Time Divide: Work, Family, and Gender Inequality.* Cambridge, MA: Harvard University Press.

Jacobs, Jerry A., David Karen, and Katherine McClelland. 1991. "The Dynamics of Young Men's Career Aspirations." *Sociological Forum* 6: 609–639.

Johnson, Jennifer. 2002. *Getting By on the Minimum: The Lives of Working-Class Women.* New York: Routledge.

Johnston, Deirdre D., and Debra H. Swanson. 2003. "Invisible Mothers: A Content Analysis of Motherhood Ideologies and Myths in Magazines." *Sex Roles* 49: 21–23.

Juhn, Chinhui, and Kevin Murphy. 1997. "Wage Inequality and Family Labor Supply." *Journal of Labor Economics* 15: 72–97.

Kalleberg, Arne L. 2007. *The Mismatched Worker.* New York: Norton.

Kane, Emily. 2000. "Racial and Ethnic Variations in Gender-Related Attitudes." *Annual Review of Sociology* 26: 419–439.

Kanter, Rosabeth M. 1977. *Men and Women of the Corporation.* New York: Basic Books.

Kelly, Erin L., Samantha K. Ammons, Kelly Chermack, and Phyllis Moen. 2010. "Gendered Challenge, Gendered Response: Confronting the Ideal Worker Norm in a White-Collar Organization." *Gender & Society* 24: 281–303.

Kilbourne, Barbara, Paula England, George Farkas, Kurtl Beron, and Dorothea Weir. 1994. "Returns to Skill, Compensating Differentials, and Gender Bias: Effects of Occupational Characteristics on the Wages of White Women and Men." *American Journal of Sociology* 100: 689–719.

Kimmel, Michael S. 1996. *Manhood in America: A Cultural History*. New York: Free Press.

Kingston, Paul, Ryan Hubbard, Brent Lapp, Paul Schroeder, and Julia Wilson. 2003. "Why Education Matters." *Sociology of Education* 76(1): 53–70.

Komarovsky, Mirra. 1964. *Blue-Collar Marriage*. New York: Random House.

Kornhauser, Arthur W. 1965. *Mental Health of the Industrial Worker: A Detroit Study*. New York: Wiley.

Koropeckyj-Cox, Tanya, and Gretchen Pendall. 2007. "Attitudes About Childlessness in the United States." *Journal of Family Issues* 28(8): 1054–1082.

Kuperberg, Arielle, and Pamela Stone. 2008. "The Media Depiction of Women Who Opt Out." *Gender & Society* 22: 497–519.

Landry, Bart. 2000. *Black Working Wives: Pioneers of the American Family Revolution*. Berkeley: University of California Press.

Lareau, Annette. 2003. *Unequal Childhoods: Class, Race, and Family Life*. Berkeley: University of California Press.

Levitan, Sarah A., and Clifford M. Johnson. 1982. *Second Thoughts on Work*. Kalamazoo, MI: W.E. Upjohn Institute for Employment Research.

Levy, Frank. 1995. "Incomes and Income Inequality." Pp. 1–57 in *The State of the Union: America in the 1990s*, edited by R. Farley. New York: Russell Sage Foundation.

Levy, Frank, and Richard Michel. 1991. *The Economic Futures of American Families: Income and Wealth Trends*. Washington, DC: Urban Institute Press.

Lorber, Judith. 1994. *Paradoxes of Gender*. New Haven: Yale University Press.

Loscocco, Karyn. 1990. "Reactions to Blue-Collar Work: A Comparison of Women and Men." *Work and Occupations* 17(2): 152–177.

Luker, Kristin. 1984. *Abortion and the Politics of Motherhood*. Berkeley: University of California Press.

Malat, Jennifer, Rose Clark-Hitt, Diana Jill Burgess, Greta Friedemann-Sanchez, and Michelle Van Ryn. 2010. "White Doctors and Nurses on Racial Inequality in Health Care in the USA." *Ethnic and Racial Studies* 33: 1431–1450.

Martin, Michel. 2009. "Can I Just Tell You? Palin's Exit Challenges Ideas About Powerful Women." National Public Radio, July 6. http://www.npr.org/templates/story/story.php?storyId=106293440.

Marx, Karl, and Friedrich Engels. 1978. *The Marx-Engels Reader*, 2nd ed., edited by Robert C. Tucker. New York: Norton.

May, Vanessa. 2008. "On Being a 'Good' Mother." *Sociology* 42: 470–486.

McCall, Leslie. 2001. *Complex Inequality: Gender, Class and Race in the New Economy*. New York: Routledge.

———. 2011. "Women and Men as Class and Race Actors." *Gender & Society* 25: 94–100.

McGrath, Monica, Maria Driscoll, and Mary Gross. 2005. *Back in the Game*. Philadelphia, PA: Wharton Center for Leadership and Change.

McLanahan, Sara. 2002. "Life Without Father: What Happens to the Children?" *Contexts* 1: 35–44.

Milgrom, Eva M., and Trond Petersen. 2006. "The Glass Ceiling in the United States and Sweden: Lessons from the Family-Friendly Corner of the World, 1970 to 1990." Pp. 156–211 in *The Declining Significance of Gender?*, edited by F. D. Blau, M. C. Brinton, and D. B. Grusky. New York: Russell Sage Foundation.

Milkie, Melissa, and Pia Peltola. 1999. "Playing All the Roles: Gender and the Work-Family Balancing Act." *Journal of Marriage and the Family* 61: 476–490.

Mills, C. Wright. 1940. "Situated Action and the Vocabulary of Motives." *American Sociological Review* 6: 904–913.

———. 1959. *The Sociological Imagination*. New York: Oxford University Press.

Mishel, Lawrence R., Jared Bernstein, and Sylvia A. Allegretto. 2007. *The State of Working America: 2006 – 2007*. Ithaca, NY: ILR Press.

Moen, Phyllis. 1992. *Women's Two Roles: A Contemporary Dilemma*. New York: Auburn House.

———. 2001. "The Gendered Life Course." Pp. 179–196 in *Handbook of Aging and the Social Sciences*, edited by L. George and R. Binstock. San Diego: Academic Press.

———. 2003. *It's About Time: Couples and Careers*. Ithaca, NY: ILR Press.

Moen, Phyllis, and Kelly Chermack. 2005. "Gender Disparities in Health." *Journals of Gerontology Series B: Psychological Sciences and Social Sciences* 60(2): S99–S108.

Moen, P., M. A. Erickson, and D. Dempster-McClain. 1997. "Their Mother's Daughters? The Intergenerational Transmission of Gender Attitudes in a World of Changing Roles." *Journal of Marriage and Family* 59(2): 281–293.

Moen, Phyllis, and Shin-Kap Han. 2001. "Gendered Careers: A Life-Course Perspective." Pp. 42–57 in *Working Families: The Transformation of the American Home*, edited by R. Hertz and N. Marshall. Berkeley: University of California Press.

Moen, Phyllis, and Patricia Roehling. 2005. *The Career Mystique: Cracks in the American Dream*. Lanham, MD: Rowman and Littlefield.

Murnane, Richard J., John B. Willett, and John H. Tyler. 2000. "Who Benefits from Obtaining a GED? Evidence from High School and Beyond." *Review of Economics and Statistics* 82: 23–37.

National Institute of Mental Health. 2008. "The Numbers Count: Mental Disorders in America." Washington, DC: National Institutes of Health. Accessed March 26, 2009. http://www.nimh. nih.gov/health/publications/the-numbers-count-mental-disorders-in-america/index.shtml.

Nelson, Margaret, and Joan Smith. 1999. *Working Hard and Making Do: Surviving in Small-Town America*. Berkeley: University of California Press.

Newman, Katherine S. 1999. *No Shame in My Game: The Working Poor in the Inner City*. New York: Knopf and the Russell Sage Foundation.

Orbuch, Terri L. 1997. "People's Accounts Count." *Annual Review of Sociology* 23: 455–478.

Pallas, Aaron. 2000. "The Effects of Schooling on Individual Lives." Pp. 499–525 in *The Handbook of the Sociology of Education*, edited by M. T. Hallinan. New York: Kluwer/Plenum.

Parker, Lonnae O'Neal. 2005. *I'm Every Woman: Remixed Stories of Marriage, Motherhood, and Work*. New York: Amistad.

Parsons, Talcott. 1974. "Family Structure in the Modern United States." Pp. 243–253 in *The Family: Its Structures and Functions*, edited by R. L. Coser. London: Macmillan.

Pavalko, Eliza. 1997. "Beyond Trajectories: Multiple Concepts for Analyzing Long-Term Processes." Pp. 129–147 in *Studying Aging and Social Change: Conceptual and Methodological Issues*, edited by M. Hardy. Thousand Oaks: Sage.

Pavalko, Eliza K., and Brad Smith. 1999. "The Rhythm of Work: Health Effects of Women's Work Dynamics." *Social Forces* 77(3): 1141–1162.

Pavalko, Eliza K., and Shari Woodbury. 2000. "Social Roles as Process: Caregiving Careers and Women's Health." *Journal of Health and Social Behavior* 41(1): 91–105.

Pearlin, Leonard I. 1989. "The Sociological Study of Stress." *Journal of Health and Social Behavior* 30: 241–256.

Perälä-Littunen, Satu. 2008. "Gender Equality or Primacy of the Mother? Ambivalent Descriptions of Good Parents." *Journal of Marriage and Family* 69: 341–351.

Percheski, Christine. 2008. "Opting Out? Cohort Differences in Professional Women's Employment Rates from 1960 to 2005." *American Sociological Review* 73(3): 497–517.

Peterson, Karen S. 2002. "Having It All—Except Children." *USA Today*, April 8.

Pew Research Center. 2007. "From 1997 to 2007: Fewer Mothers Prefer Full-Time Work." Accessed June 19, 2008. http://pewresearch.org/assets/social/pdf/WomenWorking.pdf.

Pierce, Jennifer L. 1995. *Gender Trials: Emotional Lives in Contemporary Law Firms.* Berkeley: University of California Press.

Porter, Eduardo. 2006. "Stretched to Limit, Women Stall March to Work." *New York Times*, March 2.

Presser, Harriet B. 2003. *Working in a 24/7 Economy: Challenges for American Families.* New York: Russell Sage Foundation.

Ratcliff, Kathryn, and Janet Bogdan. 1988. "Unemployed Women: When 'Social Support' Is Not Supportive." *Social Problems* 35(1): 54–63.

Reskin, Barbara F., and Michelle L. Maroto. 2011. "What Trends? Whose Choices? Comment on England." *Gender & Society* 25: 81–87.

Reskin, Barbara F., and Patricia A. Roos. 1990. *Job Queues, Gender Queues: Explaining Women's Inroads into Male Occupations.* Philadelphia: Temple University Press.

Ridgeway, Cecilia, and Shelley Correll. 2004. "Unpacking the Gender System: A Theoretical Perspective on Gender Beliefs and Social Relations." *Gender & Society* 18: 510–531.

Risman, Barbara J. 1998. *Gender Vertigo: American Families in Transition.* New Haven, CT: Yale University Press.

———. 2009. "From Doing to Undoing: Gender as We Know It." *Gender & Society* 23: 81–84.

Risman, Barbara J., Maxine P. Atkinson, and Stephen P. Blackwelder. 1999. "Understanding the Juggling Act: Gendered Preferences and Social Structural Constraints." *Sociological Forum* 14: 319–344.

Roksa, Josipa, Eric Grodsky, Richard Arum, and Adam Gamoran. 2007. "Changes in Higher Education and Social Stratification in the United States." Pp. 165–191 in *Stratification in Higher Education: A Comparative Study*, edited by Y. Shavit, R. Arum, and A. Gamoran. Stanford, CA: Stanford University Press.

Rose, Mike. 2004. *The Mind at Work: Valuing the Intelligence of the American Worker.* New York: Viking.

Rose, Stephen, and Heidi Hartmann. 2004. *Still a Man's Labor Market: The Long-Term Earnings Gap.* Washington, DC: Institute for Women's Policy Research.

Rosen, Ellen I. 1987. *Bitter Choices: Blue Collar Women in and out of Work.* Chicago: University of Chicago Press.

Rosenbaum, James E. 2001. *Beyond College for All: Career Paths for the Forgotten Half.* New York: Russell Sage Foundation.

Roth, Louise M. 2006. *Selling Women Short: Gender Inequality on Wall Street.* Princeton: Princeton University Press.

Rubin, Lillian B. 1976. *Worlds of Pain: Life in the Working-Class Family.* New York: Basic Books.

———. 1994. *Families on the Fault Line: America's Working Class Speaks About the Family, the Economy, Race, and Ethnicity.* New York: HarperCollins.

Rumberger, Russell W., and Stephen P. Lamb. 2003. "The Early Employment and Further Education Experiences of High School Dropouts: A Comparative Study of the United States and Australia." *Economics of Education Review* 22: 353–366.

Ryan, Mary P. 1981. *Cradle of the Middle Class: The Family in Oneida County, New York, 1790–1865.* New York: Cambridge University Press.

Sarkisian, Natalia, and Naomi Gerstel. 2006. "Marriage: The Good, the Bad, and the Greedy." *Contexts* 5: 16–21.

Schieman, Scott, Paul Glavin, and Melissa Milkie. 2009. "When Work Interferes with Life: Work-Nonwork Interference and the Influence of Work-Related Demands and Resources." *American Sociological Review* 74: 966–988.

Schor, Juliet. 1991. *The Overworked American: The Unexpected Decline of Leisure.* New York: Basic Books.

Scott, Marvin, and Stanford Lyman. 1968. "Accounts." *American Sociological Review* 33: 46–61.

Segura, Denise. 1994. "Working at Motherhood: Chicana and Mexican Immigrant Mothers and Employment." Pp. 211–233 in *Mothering: Ideology, Experience and Agency*, edited by E. N. Glenn, G. Chang, and L. R. Forcey. New York: Routledge.

Shafer, Emily Fitzgibbons. 2011. "Wives' Relative Wages, Husbands' Paid Work Hours, and Wives' Labor-Force Exit." *Journal of Marriage and Family* 73: 250–263.

Sidel, Ruth. 1990. *On Her Own: Growing Up in the Shadow of the American Dream.* New York: Viking.

Skolnick, Arlene. 1979. "Public Images, Private Realities: The American Family in Popular Culture and Social Science." Pp. 297–318 in *Changing Images of the Family*, edited by V. Tufte and B. Myerhoff. New Haven, CT: Yale University Press.

Smith, Anna M. 2001. "Mass-Market Magazine Portrayals of Working Mothers and Related Issues, 1987 and 1997." *Journal of Children and Poverty* 7: 101–119.

Sørensen, Annemette. 1994. "Women, Family and Class." *Annual Review of Sociology* 20: 27–47.

Spain, Daphne, and Suzanne M. Bianchi. 1996. *Balancing Act: Motherhood, Marriage, and Employment Among American Women.* New York: Russell Sage Foundation.

Spenner, K. I., and R. A. Rosenfeld. 1990. "Women, Work, and Identities." *Social Science Research* 19(3): 266–299.

Spivey, Christy. 2005. "Time Off at What Price? The Effects of Career Interruptions on Earnings." *Industrial and Labor Relations Review* 59: 119–140.

Stacey, Judith. 1990. *Brave New Families: Stories of Domestic Upheaval in Late Twentieth Century America.* New York: Basic Books.

Stack, Carol B. 1974. *All Our Kin: Strategies for Survival in a Black Community.* New York: Harper and Row.

Stickney, Lisa T., and Alison M. Konrad. 2007. "Gender-Role Attitudes and Earnings: A Multinational Study of Married Women and Men." *Sex Roles* 57(11): 801–811.

St. George, Donna. 2007. "Part-Time Looks Fine to Working Mothers: 60% Prefer It to Full-Time or No Job." *Washington Post*, July 12.

———. 2009. "Most Stay-at-Home Moms Start That Way, Study Finds: Many Are Younger, Less Educated, Hispanic." *Washington Post*, October 1.

Stone, Pamela. 2007. *Opting Out? Why Women Really Quit Careers and Head Home.* Berkeley: University of California Press.

Stone, Pamela, and Meg Lovejoy. 2004. "Fast-Track Women and the 'Choice' to Stay Home." *Annals of the American Academy of Political and Social Science* 596: 62–83.

Teachman, Jay D. 2002. "Stability Across Cohorts in Divorce Risk Factors." *Demography* 39: 331–351.

Thoits, Peggy A. 1995. "Stress, Coping, and Social Support Processes: Where Are We? What Next?" *Journal of Health and Social Behavior* 35: 53–79.

Townsend, Nicholas. 2002. *The Package Deal: Marriage, Work, and Fatherhood in Men's Lives.* Philadelphia, PA: Temple University Press.

Turner, R. Jay, and Donald A. Lloyd. 1999. "The Stress Process and the Social Distribution of Depression." *Journal of Health and Social Behavior* 40: 371–404.

Uchitelle, Louis. 2006. *The Disposable American: Layoffs and Their Consequences.* New York: Knopf.

U.S. Bureau of Labor Statistics. 2008. *Women in the Labor Force: A Databook, Report 1011.* Washington, DC: U.S. Department of Labor.

———. 2009. *Employment and Earnings, 2009 Annual Averages and the Monthly Labor Review.* Washington, DC: U.S. Department of Labor.

U.S. Census Bureau. 2007. "Selected Social Characteristics in the United States: 2005–2007." American Community Survey. Washington, DC: U.S. Census Bureau. Accessed April 28, 2009. http://factfinder.census.gov/servlet/ADPTable?_bm=y&-geo_id=01000US&-qr_name=ACS_2007_3YR_G00_DP3YR2&-gc_url=null&-ds_name=ACS_2007_3YR_G00_&-_lang=en&-redoLog=false.

———. 2010. "Money Income of Households—Percent Distribution by Income Level, Race and Hispanic Origin in Constant (2007) Dollars." The 2010 Statistical Abstract: Report # 674. Accessed July 21, 2010. http://www.census.gov/compendia/statab/cats/income_expenditures_poverty_wealth/household_income.html.

Vallas, Steven P. 1990. "Comments and Observations on the Nature of Work." Pp. 348–369 in *The Nature of Work: Sociological Perspectives*, edited by K. Erikson and S. P. Vallas. New Haven: Yale University Press.

Vespa, Jonathan. 2009. "Gender Ideology Construction: A Life Course and Intersectional Approach." *Gender & Society* 23: 363–387.

Waldfogel, Jane. 1997. "The Effect of Children on Women's Wages." *American Sociological Review* 62(2): 209–217.

Warren, Elizabeth, and Amelia W. Tyagi. 2003. *The Two-Income Trap: Why Middle-Class Mothers and Fathers Are Going Broke.* New York: Basic Books.

Webber, Gretchen, and Christine Williams. 2008. "Mothers in 'Good' and 'Bad' Part-Time Jobs: Different Problems, Same Results." *Gender & Society* 22: 752–777.

Weiner, Lynn Y. 1985. *From Working Girl to Working Mother: The Female Labor Force in the United States, 1820 – 1980.* Chapel Hill: University of North Carolina Press.

Wells, Barbara, and Maxine B. Zinn. 2004. "The Benefits of Marriage Reconsidered." *Journal of Sociology and Social Welfare* 31(4): 59–80.

West, Candace, and Don Zimmerman. 1987. "Doing Gender." *Gender & Society* 1(2): 125–151.

Wilcox, Bradford, and Steven Nock. 2006. "What's Love Got to Do with It? Equality, Equity, Commitment and Women's Marital Quality." *Social Forces* 84: 1321–1345.

Wilensky, Harold. 1960. "Work, Careers, and Social Integration." *International Social Science Journal* 60: 543–560.

Williams, Joan C. 1991. "Gender Wars: Selfless Women in the Republic of Choice." *New York University Law Review* 66: 1573–1574.

———. 2000. *Unbending Gender: Why Family and Work Conflict and What to Do About It*. New York: Oxford University Press.

———. 2007. "The Opt-Out Revolution Revisited." *American Prospect* (February): 12–15.

———. 2010. *Reshaping the Work-Family Debate: Why Men and Class Matter*. Cambridge, MA: Harvard University Press.

Williams, Joan C., and Heather Boushey. 2010. *The Three Faces of Work-Family Conflict: The Poor, the Professionals and the Missing Middle*. Berkeley and Washington, DC: Center for American Progress and the Center for WorkLife Law.

Williams, Sonya, and Shin-Kap Han. 2003. "Career Clocks: Forked Roads." Pp. 80–97 in *It's About Time: Couples and Careers*, edited by P. Moen. Ithaca, NY: ILR Press.

Zavella, Patricia. 1987. *Women's Work and Chicano Families: Cannery Workers of the Santa Clara Valley*. Ithaca, NY: Cornell University Press.

Zernike, Kate. 2007. "Why Are There So Many Single Americans?" *New York Times*, January 21.

Index